Rehabilitation in Psychiatric Practice

Rehabilitation in Psychiatric Practice

Edited by

R G McCreadie

BSc, MD, MRC Psych
Consultant Psychiatrist
and Director of Clinical Research
Crichton Royal Hospital, Dumfries

Pitman

PITMAN BOOKS LIMITED
39 Parker Street, London WC2B 5PB

PITMAN PUBLISHING INC.
1020 Plain Street, Marshfield, Massachusetts

Associated Companies
Pitman Publishing Pty Ltd, Melbourne
Pitman Publishing New Zealand Ltd, Wellington
Copp Clark Pitman, Toronto

First Published 1982

Library of Congress Cataloging in Publication Data
Main entry under title:
Rehabilitation in psychiatric practice.
   Includes bibliographies and index.
   1. Mentally ill—Rehabilitation. I. McCreadie,
R.G. (Robin G.) [DNLM: 1. Mental disorders—Rehabil-
itation. WM 29.1 R345]
RC439.5.R43   616.89′1   82-288
ISBN 0–272–79647–6   AACR2

British Library Cataloguing in Publication Data
Rehabilitation in psychiatric practice.
   1. Mentally ill—Rehabilitation
   I. McCreadie, R.G.
   362′.0425   RC576

ISBN 0–272–79647–6

Text set in 10/12pt Linotron 202 Times, printed and bound
in Great Britain at The Pitman Press, Bath

Contents

Contributors

N Behl, MB, BS, Registrar, Warlingham Park Hospital, Warlingham.

W I Fraser, MD, FRCPsych, DPM, Consultant Psychiatrist, Gogarburn Hospital, Edinburgh.

J Hughes, BM, BCh, BSc, MRCP, MRCPsych, Lecturer, Department of Psychiatry, University of Southampton, Southampton.

D James, MB, ChB, DipEd, DCH, DPM, MRCPsych, Consultant Psychiatrist, Royal Hospital for Sick Children, Glasgow.

P W Kershaw, MD, FRCPE, FRCPsych, DPM, DObst, RCOG, Consultant Psychiatrist, Gartnavel Royal Hospital, Glasgow.

H C H Koch, BSc, PhD, Dip Clin Psychol, Senior Clinical Psychologist, Whitchurch Hospital, Cardiff.

M Lee-Evans, BA, MSc, Top Grade Clinical Psychologist, Rampton Hospital, Retford.

R G McCreadie, BSc, MD, MRCPsych, DPM, Consultant Psychiatrist and Director of Clinical Research, Crichton Royal Hospital, Dumfries.

C McDonald, MD, MRCPsych, Consultant Psychiatrist, Warlingham Park Hospital, Warlingham.

A A McKechnie, MD, FRCPsych, DPM, Consultant Psychiatrist, Bangour Village Hospital, Broxburn.

J K W Morrice, MD, FRCPsych, DPM, Consultant Psychiatrist, The Ross Clinic, Aberdeen.

M A Plant, BSc, MA, PhD, Sociologist, Alcohol Research Group, Department of Psychiatry, University of Edinburgh, Edinburgh.

D M Shaw, PhD, FRCP, FRCPsych, Honorary Consultant Psychiatrist, Whitchurch Hospital, Cardiff.

P Sudhakar, MB, BS, Registrar, Warlingham Park Hospital, Warlingham.

A P Thorley, MA, MB, MRCPsych, Consultant Psychiatrist, St Nicholas Hospital, Newcastle upon Tyne.

P Tyrer, MD, MRCP, FRCPsych, Consultant Psychiatrist, Mapperley Hospital, Nottingham.

1 Introduction

R G McCreadie, BSc, MD, MRC Psych, DPM

What is rehabilitation? How best can it be defined in relation to psychiatric practice? Scrutiny of lay dictionaries is of some help; for example, the *Oxford English Dictionary* states:

> to rehabilitate: to restore to privileges, reputation, or proper condition; restore to effectiveness by training (especially . . . after illness).

Chambers Dictionary defines it as:

> to rehabilitate: to make fit after disablement or illness for earning a living or playing a part in the world.

These definitions therefore imply that the process brings about a return to a previous effective state. All very well; but what then is the difference between rehabilitation and treatment? The *Oxford English Dictionary* has this to say about treatment:

> to treat: to deal with or act upon (person, thing) with a view to obtaining a particular result . . . (how would you treat a sprained ankle?).

This in medical terms is perhaps not all that different from its definition of rehabilitation.

However, *Black's Medical Dictionary* takes us considerably further. It defines rehabilitation as:

> rehabilitation: the restoration to health and working capacity of a person incapacitated by disease, mental or physical, or by injury. It is a word that came into prominent use during the 1939–45 war, reflecting the growing awareness of the medical profession that the treatment of a sick or injured person does not end at the moment of recovery from the immediate effects of illness or injury.

A major difference, therefore, between the words treatment and rehabilitation which this definition highlights is a temporal one. Treatment usually implies the application of remedies to acute illness; it is something which is rather short-lived. On the other hand, rehabilitation suggests a longer, more comprehensive approach to the management of illness, an approach which also recognizes and attempts to strengthen a patient's assets. It is this, above all else, that we would like to emphasize. This book

1

is not quite a textbook on the long-term management of psychiatric illness—but it is close to it. We believe that the 'treatment' of psychiatric disorder does not stop with, say, the successful amelioration of depressive symptoms by ECT, the diminution of anxiety by benzodiazepines, or the dampening of delusions by neuroleptics. A lot more work needs to be done to 'restore to proper condition'; and this is rehabilitation.

We also think the word treatment more than rehabilitation implies that something is done *to* a patient; that the patient is passive, the therapist active. Rehabilitation on the other hand suggests to us that the patient can and must play his part in the restoration of his 'proper condition'. Throughout this book, the contributors emphasize first the alliance that needs to be forged between patient and therapist, and secondly, the patient's active participation in various programmes that is necessary if rehabilitation is to succeed.

We have suggested above that rehabilitation is a comprehensive approach to a patient's management. If this is so, then not only medical staff but other professionals will be involved in the process. This approach, clumsily named multi-disciplinary, is obvious throughout this book. At different times during any given individual's rehabilitation, psychiatrist, psychologist, nurse, social worker or occupational therapist may have specialized skills, specialized knowledge which will aid the patient's recovery to an effective level. Other groups not usually thought of as contributing to 'treatment' but who certainly can contribute to rehabilitation may be involved: employers and voluntary organizations are two such groups. A team approach therefore is essential. The question of who should lead the team and how it should be constituted is discussed in a number of different ways by different contributors.

There is another 'group' that gets caught up in the process of rehabilitation: the patient's family. As the current wisdom is that patients should be managed wherever possible outside hospital, the patient's family will inevitably have to share the brunt of the patient's illness. For a proper return to effectiveness the family must be engaged in the process of rehabilitation. Each contributor to this book is aware of the crucial part the family has to play; again active participation is usually necessary.

When we say that a 'return to effectiveness' is an important aim in rehabilitation, we do not necessarily mean a return to full effectiveness. Psychiatric disorder often brings with it permanent handicaps; the best that may be achieved is a partial amelioration of the patient's difficulties. Realistic goals have to be set in rehabilitation.

In summary, rehabilitation aims at a comprehensive, usually long-term approach to the management of psychiatric illness, an approach which will involve not only the members of different disciplines but also the active participation of the patient and usually his family.

We feel that it is timely that a book on rehabilitation should be published.

In recent years much interest in psychiatry has been directed towards the care of the acutely ill patient and much less towards the management of long-term problems. However, the majority of beds in psychiatric hospitals are occupied by long-stay patients, the majority of admissions to short-stay wards are readmissions, day-hospitals are catering increasingly for a long-stay population, and out-patient clinics have many reattenders. In short, much psychiatric illness tends to run a chronic course, a fact which perhaps does not receive sufficient emphasis in psychiatric textbooks.

This book is aimed primarily at psychiatrists in training, although we hope that trainees in the other disciplines which play such an important part in rehabilitation might also find much that is relevant. For junior doctors, the rotational system of training in psychiatry often means that they spend only brief periods in different sub-specialities; thus they have little practical experience of managing patients over lengthy periods of time. Rehabilitation as we have suggested can be a lengthy process; results, good or bad, may take a long time to appear. It is therefore not surprising that trainees often find it difficult to understand what rehabilitation is 'about'. They see little in the way of change in the patient's mental state, behaviour, or social effectiveness; they are not impressed by the techniques used. In short, many trainees find patients with long-standing psychiatric problems unattractive (the same of course can be said of trainees in general medicine when they observe chronic physical illness). However, most trainees who remain in psychiatry will be appointed to consultant posts within the National Health Service. A major part of any consultant's workload is the management of chronic illness and therefore a knowledge of rehabilitative techniques is essential.

This book does not come from an ivory tower; almost all the contributors are clinicians with many years' practical experience of the subject about which they write. Not only do they describe the various techniques in rehabilitation; more importantly they are aware of the pitfalls and everyday obstacles which prevent the proper implementation of these techniques. Such difficulties are not avoided; indeed, they are highlighted as consideration of them may make the difference between clinical success or failure.

One possible pitfall in a multi-author book is unnecessary repetition. Although each contributor was asked to write about a discrete area in psychiatric practice, we were somewhat apprehensive in case the same rehabilitative procedures would crop up again and again. Happily this proved not to be so. Indeed, what we hope might be one of the strengths of this book is the description of an extremely wide variety of techniques that have been used to combat different problems. Although one technique may be used mainly in a given problem, might there be a case for using it in another field? We hope therefore that the book will be read as a whole and that clinicians may take rehabilitative procedures from one area and transfer them to their own field of practice.

Part 1 **The Psychoses**

2 Affective Disorders

D M Shaw, PhD, FRCP, FRC Psych
H C H Koch, BSc, PhD, Dip Clin Psychol

Classical definitions of affective disorders often are of 'recurrent phasic illnesses with complete normality between them', a description which could be taken to imply both lack of all symptoms in the remission phases, and the return to the original premorbid personality without any damage to or change in the level of psychological functioning by the episode. Many but not all patients return to completely normal mood in remission. The second assumption of a return to the premorbid personality may be valid, although it may apply mainly to non-recurrent mild or moderate illness, and after severe illness to only some individuals with particularly resilient personalities. For the remainder, the condition may leave the patient in need of various forms of rehabilitation. Rehabilitation in this disorder merits further studies with a careful comparison of the merits and demerits of all the various forms of therapy available. The methods described here for rehabilitation are based on practice, theory and research currently available and should be regarded as only tentative models in a developing field.

There are problems in defining sub-groups of depressed patients in that there is considerable overlap between depressions which have been subdivided according to the convention of 'normal', 'reactive', 'neurotic', 'secondary' and biological disorders, primary or secondary, according to Winokur (1979), or according to one of the other conventions. The whole area of classification of depression remains a problem. This area of contention has been introduced here only because the group under discussion fulfils the 'biological' or endogenous/psychotic criteria (about which most systems agree). However, other forms of depression can accompany or follow 'classical affective' illness, and the types of affective illness as defined to date tend to be associated with different previous personalities. These may modify responses to illness and rehabilitation.

The aim of this chapter is to describe the nature of the experience of affective disorder, its natural history, premorbid personality and other factors which have a bearing on whether or not and the degree to which an individual will develop psychological and social damage from his illness, and how he will react to the offer of rehabilitation. From then on the main interest is on cognitive, psychotherapeutic and social means of amelioration of the secondary problems arising from affective illness.

Details of occupational therapy, day hospital care and the superficial supportive care given to most patients on follow up have not been described and have been 'taken as read'.

As a working hypothesis, the unipolar/bipolar dichotomy has been accepted.

Affective Disorders: the Background

The Nature of the Experience of Affective Illness
(*a*) *Depression*. Even mild depressive illness is an unpleasant experience which the patient can distinguish from 'normal depression'. In its more severe form, the individual lives through what is perhaps the worst form of suffering known to man, an extreme 'emotional pain'. The syndrome is accompanied by cognitive, emotional and somatic symptoms, but the emphasis here is on the effect of the illness in evoking changes in cognitive, emotional and behavioural life *de novo* as a result of the experience of the disorder. For those who develop these secondary phenomena they are important for the ultimate well-being of the individuals, as is the illness itself.
(*b*) *Mania*. The experience of mania or hypomania may be that of anything from mild inexplicable happiness to an exalted state of euphoria, with feelings of boundless energy, drive and libido. Sometimes when mania is bound up with feelings of hostility or irritability it can be unpleasant. Patients also find 'mixed states' of 'driven overactivity' resembling mania/hypomania, but with a depressive affective tone, particularly distressing.

The Natural History of Affective Disorders
The main contributions to our knowledge of the natural history of affective illness have been those of Angst and Perris and the current position has been summarized by Angst *et al* (1979). The median age of onset was 34·7 in bipolar patients and 45·3 in unipolar individuals (Angst *et al* 1979). Those bipolar patients having mania in early episodes tended to start earlier than those with later onset of mania. In the long-term observations of Angst *et al* (1979), of those in their sample who remained and who could be assessed for quality of remission, only two thirds of the unipolar and just over a half of the bipolar patients had had full remissions from the previous episode, a finding which cannot be overstressed. On the other hand 44 per cent of the unipolar group but only 16 per cent of the bipolar group had had a relapse-free period of at least five years. Fifty per cent of episodes lay between 3·2 and 11·5 months in unipolar and between 2·5 and 7·6 months in bipolar illness with a trend for cycles (the time between the onset of illness and the next) to shorten with age and with increase in their number.

Mitchell-Heggs (1971) demonstrated a peak age of onset of first affective illness in females in the 20 to 30 age group and a very minor peak in the 40 to 50 age group. Males had a more uniform spread of age of onset. Their sample could have been atypical, but many had had long periods of prodromal symptoms before seeking psychiatric advice—a mean of one year four months in those who had the best response to treatment. Thus, the experiences before and during the illness are different for the two forms of illness, but apart from the patients with unipolar illness who have only one or two attacks, the expectation is that of a recurrent and usually worsening illness. A proportion—about 15 per cent—will die by suicide (Guze and Robins 1970), in some the illness remits incompletely, and a few become chronically ill.

Thus, although the outlook is not uniformly bad for some patients, particularly those with unipolar illness who are fortunate enough to have substantial periods of remission, and a limited number of episodes, there remains a substantial number of individuals whose recovery from illness is either recurrent or incomplete.

Acceptance or Denial of Susceptibility to Affective Illness

Whatever the age of the patient, the first episode of depression or mania is a shattering experience. For those in late teenage or early twenties the condition arises during the processes of maturation which sometimes seem to be arrested until after the illness has passed (discussed in more detail below). It is as though the awareness of this particular form of vulnerability—an inability to rely on the limits of one's changes in mood at a time when mood is not too stable anyway—can be very destructive of confidence.

An older person having the initial illness will be disturbed by the experience—for them it is peculiar when a lifetime of stability is so abruptly terminated. There is a loss of emotional supports and the security of their familiar world disappears. They have the advantage over the younger patient of a more crystallized personality and experience of other traumatic events in their lives.

One of the first questions often asked towards the end of the illness is if the illness will return. Others deny illness, attribute it to circumstances and consider it a chance occurrence unlikely to happen again.

Time proves them right or wrong. If the latter, they may come to partial or complete acceptance of their susceptibility to what may be becoming a lifelong disability.

Preventative or Prophylactic Treatment

The acceptance or rejection of the problem of affective illness is particularly important when the illness has become so frequent that it is worth starting on some form of preventative treatment. Prophylactic therapy requires acceptance, a high degree of long-term motivation and the discipline to continue it over long periods, often while experiencing failure, especially during the early stages. Patients may have to live with side-effects.

A patient who cannot tolerate prophylactic drugs, or who fails to benefit, will feel particularly hopeless. Those in whom illness is prevented may continue to attend for treatment. Unexpectedly perhaps, some whose illness is only attenuated may be content to manage with something which is less severe even if the symptoms are not cleared entirely. With a proportion of patients, however, success breeds failure. A year or more in normal mood may lead to unwarranted confidence and the belief that prophylaxis can be abandoned with impunity.

Mania and hypomania provide their own very special problems. Understandably patients like their hypomanic phases and some may reject lithium where their energy, enthusiasm, zest, ebullience, high drive and libido help them in their work and/or make them particularly attractive to their spouses (Schou 1968). A conflict of interests arises when the depressive phases are severe, or the mania is severe with a loss of insight and a pattern of behaviour leading to marital, financial and legal complications.

Some patients still refuse to 'part' with their 'good' phases, or discontinue lithium therapy to experience what Van Putten (1975) called a 'manic reprieve', and some young people think that mild hypomania is the normal state.

To help such individuals both as regards their regular illnesses and to achieve their earlier functioning is sometimes impossible. It becomes a long struggle to minimize the effect of traumas and secondary psychosocial effects to themselves and their families.

Resistant Illness

Some patients have severe and/or rapidly recurring illness. Recurrence rates of four episodes per year usually mean resistance to lithium and other drug therapies, but other patients pass into treatment-resistance at any time. Many have a gradual increase in the number of recurrences until illness is continuous or remissions are brief (Angst *et al* 1979). These are a particularly challenging group as regards management. Although we have not collected a series, a proportion of patients with rapidly recurrent affective illness appear to improve if their psychosocial milieu can be bettered (but it must be admitted that it is not possible to do this for many patients at this stage).

The special problems of rehabilitation of the very rare situation where a patient has had stereotactic surgery for intractable illness will not be discussed here.

The patients mentioned above whose illness does not respond to all current therapies are in a near hopeless position in that their condition may have destroyed their family and social lives, has lost them their jobs and has not been modified by attempts to alter their psychosocial circumstances. This is the apparent end of the road as far as hope for recovery is concerned, apart from the few who recover spontaneously, sometimes after many years, or who come to stereotactic tractotomy.

Previous Personality in Affective Disorder as Assessed Retrospectively

The previous personality in affective illness is underemphasized in many clinical assessments. It may be considered in the light of how the mental disturbance will be tolerated, how the patient will adapt to the onslaught of this traumatic experience and how he will cope or fail with the return to a well-adjusted existence. In some conditions, previous personality could be a predisposing factor (e.g. the ulcer- or coronary-prone individual). It is thought by some that any differences in premorbid personality between patients with affective illness and normal control subjects are more likely to reflect basic genetic factors which are the determinants of both the premorbid personality and the susceptibility to affective illness (Glatzel 1974), i.e. the premorbid personality is a subclinical manifestation of the illness. Leonhard (1972) for instance described hypomanic, hypomelancholic and cyclothymic temperaments in the families of individuals containing patients with mania, depression and manic-depression.

It must be remembered that the study of premorbid personality is fraught with difficulties, and by necessity most studies are based on personality questionnaires completed retrospectively. Perris and d'Elia (1969), Perris (1966), Angst (1966) and Perris (1971) suggested that unipolar patients were low in cyclothymia, but tended to be asthenic and to have a melancholic type of personality. This consisted of trends towards orderliness, conscientiousness, meticulousness, high achievement drives and conventional thinking. Von Zerssen (1977) thought the 'melancholic type' was a fairly constant finding in unipolar patients and occurred in their families, but a proportion of bipolar individuals also shared these traits.

As a general rule the findings in bipolar patients were of personalities nearer to those in normal controls. Cyclothymia was a premorbid trait however in some patients. Akiskal et al (1977) found that cyclothymic individuals merged imperceptibly into bipolar illness (where cyclothymia is defined as incomplete short cycles of bipolar mood change). The relatives of bipolar and cyclothymic patients had similar distributions of cyclothymic and bipolar relatives, and they concluded that cyclothymia was an attenuated form of bipolar illness. About one third of patients with cyclothymia went on to full manifestation of illness. The importance of this to rehabilitation is that cyclothymic individuals have a high incidence of marital problems, unstable work records, episodic drug and alcohol abuse but 'uneven creativity', suggesting to the authors a form of social defiance. A proportion of bipolar patients will be culled from individuals of this type of premorbid personality.

Tellenbach (1976) spoke of people with melancholic traits as being unable to bear the feeling of not fulfilling their high standards, and often of working in a situation whch made the achievement of their standards impossible. Potential melancholics were unable to change their rigid attitude towards work achievement and were almost prisoners of their principles of orderliness which they could not abandon even if it was urgently required by the actual situation. Von Zersson (1977) found that unipolar patients who had recovered worried about difficulties long before they occurred, found it difficult to change their work habits and did not like jobs which needed rapid decisions. They could not undertake responsibility without feeling under pressure and could not concentrate in disturbing surroundings. Metcalfe *et al* (1975) observed that these patients did not rehash and dramatize small incidents that had occurred to make a more amusing story, and they were deeply moved by other people's misfortunes. Metcalfe (1968) said that an asthenic worrying personality with no tendency to mood swings, and absence of day-dreaming was common in unipolar individuals. Losses were difficult to handle and there was some dependency on accustomed surroundings and on persons to whom they had developed a close intimate relationship.

It would be predicted that melancholic types might be more accepting of long-term therapy than some bipolar patients, particularly those with a predominantly manic type of previous personality.

Unipolar patients may have other characteristics which have a bearing on past, present and future functioning and adjustment. Lewinsohn (1974) suggested that depressed individuals had not developed certain social skills, such as the ability to 'emit behaviour' which was positively reinforced by others. In other words, their behaviour was such as not to evoke in the people around them responses which helped the patients to develop and maintain self-esteem. They tended to be repressed, introverted individuals lacking in confidence and assertiveness, dependent, pessimistic and with a low self-image.

Bipolar patients in contrast in remission had less need of approval, less dependency, fewer guilt feelings and inner conflicts and a more strongly developed need to dominate and lead (Strandman 1978). In some ways during normal mood unipolar patients had many of the characteristics of patients with neurotic depression and unclassified depressive conditions. There must be many more factors in the premorbid personality of patients with affective illness yet to be revealed. One question to be answered is that of sub-groups, and indeed Kupfer *et al* (1978) have proposed two populations of unipolar individuals. One responded to tricyclic antidepressants and has a premorbid personality similar to that of the bipolar group, and the other tended not to respond to tricyclics and to have chronically anxious and obsessional type of previous personality.

Three alternative ways of assessing the relevance of previous personality have been proposed: first, that personality will determine in part how well an individual will tolerate the mental disturbance experienced during affective disorder; secondly, that previous personality may be one of the predisposing factors which make an individual vulnerable to the development of affective disorder; thirdly, the previous personality may be a sub-clinical manifestation of a genetically determined disorder which includes the appearance of affective episodes. Current research has not provided the clinician with an answer to this problem either with regard to his concept of the disorder or to his practical management of the condition. Faced with three such rational and plausible possibilities, the clinician can only try to come to some partial understanding of the part played by the premorbid personality by considering an individual patient as belonging to one or more of the following categories:

(1) Affective disorder with good premorbid personality adjustment.
(2) Affective disorder with poorly adjusted premorbid personality; both of which are genetically determined.
(3) Affective disorder with a poor premorbid personality which has contributed to the onset, development and consequences of the illness.
(4) Affective disorder with a poor premorbid personality which will determine how well the individual tolerates and overcomes the deleterious effects of his illness.

No prospective research has been carried out as to the type of premorbid personality preceding affective illness.

Relationship of Age to Aftermath of Affective Illness
The median age of first onset of affective illness is discussed above but these ages are not normally distributed (Hamilton 1979, Mitchell-Heggs 1971), being skewed towards the younger-aged group. This is more obvious in females where there is a marked peak of first attacks in the 20 to 30 decade. A significant number started earlier than this.

There are few data in the literature about the impact on the patient on onset at different ages, so any comments in this area only reflect the clinical impressions of the authors. As mentioned above, onset of affective illness in the maturing individual in our patients seems to have had specific undesirable effects which need to be considered in rehabilitation. No doubt, for a person in late teenage or early 20s, the impact of affective illness must be particularly overwhelming. They are without either the maturity or the experience of other traumatic events in their lives with which to compare the degree of suffering and the awareness of their vulnerability.

The reaction of a young person to illness may be like that of an adult, but very occasionally the result is temporarily delinquency. These 'young starters' require special care in rehabilitation. Alternatively, there may be neurotic behaviour sometimes aimed, in their view, at preventing the feared condition from returning. They have youth and adaptability on their side however, and if they stay well, then response to rehabilitation is good.

However, young people emerging from affective illness of any duration are conspicuous by the arrest in their maturity. Towards the other end of the age scale, one of the groups most difficult to manage in recovery are those with anxious, premorbid personalities whose adaptation to stress has been marginal. Some men in this group put in for early retirement while still recovering and similarly both sexes can slip into invalidism at this stage. The 'pipe and slippers' response of a man in premature retirement works for some, for others it becomes a bitterly regretted mistake, often followed by the development of anxiety, reactive depression and hopelessness. It is very difficult to rehabilitate such individuals.

Presence of Other Physical/Psychiatric Conditions in Affective Disorders
Rehabilitation of patients disturbed in some way following affective illness is going to be influenced by the concurrent presence of physical disability and/or other primary or secondary psychiatric illness.

Physical illness often precipitates an episode of affective illness and the need to treat cancer, endocrine disease, an operation, etc., may override the immediate demands of the psychiatric condition. It goes without saying that, in many instances, the presence of mental and physical disease (often a chronic disability) is going to complicate readjustment after recovery from the affective condition.

There may be associations between obsessional states and depressive illness, and phobias and hypochondriasis may develop during episodes of depression. These do not necessarily recede with the successful treatment of the affective episode, but may remain as abnormal entities in their own right.

Psychological and Social Consequences of Affective Illness

By 'psychological' is meant behavioural, cognitive and emotional components, and by 'social' the interpersonal factors including marital, familial and other interactions with larger groups with whom the patient associates.

When first meeting a person with affective illness who is experiencing a significant change in mood, particularly of depression, all the endogenous or biological features (e.g. appetite loss, sleep disturbance and motor retardation) may or may not be present, but a proportion should be present in the group under discussion. Such people also describe disturbances of behaviour, thinking and emotion. These may have occurred before, at the time or following the biological features.

Cognitive Effects

The cognitive or thinking components of depressed mood in general were described by Beck (1967) and later by Rush and Beck (1978), and these provide a theoretical basis for cognitive therapy. There is substantial empirical support for the cognitive theory of depression (Beck 1976, Neuringer 1961, Velten 1968, Teasdale and Bancroft 1977). It is based on three postulates advanced to account for depressive thinking: 'the cognitive triad', 'schemas' and 'cognitive errors'. By the 'cognitive triad' is meant the three main cognitive patterns in which

(*a*) the patient construes himself;
(*b*) his experiences; and
(*c*) his future, in a negative manner.

As regards himself, his view is of an inadequate and unworthy individual tending to under-estimate and criticize himself, and lacking in those 'essential attributes' for being happy. Paradoxically at times the depressed person may revert to the mirror image of this denigrating state by developing a short-lived feeling of positive self-worth. If this is so, it may indicate a very unstable and changeable concept of self. Similarly his day-to-day experiences tend to be interpreted in a negative way. Demands made on him are considered to be insuperable and unfulfillable, and he misinterprets the interactions in his world as evidence of defeat or his inadequacies. Most importantly, the patient perceives alternatives negatively even when there are more positive and more plausible interpretations. With such a negative view of himself and his world, it is understandable that he will anticipate that his current difficulties will continue indefinitely. When he thinks of undertaking a task, he will anticipate failure. Beck (1976) considered that some of the other psychological and somatic accompaniments of the 'depressive syndrome' were consequences of negative cognitive patterns, a view which is certainly one explanation for some of the features of affective illness. In addition, in part, cognitive disturbances could explain loss of motivation and drive, the urge to escape and/or avoid some circumstances and tasks, as well as the development of dependency. The patient's negative view of ordinary tasks may be unrealistic and convince the individual that things will turn out badly. This leads to the seeking of help, reassurance and support from others who appear to the patient to be more competent and capable. Cognitive schemes refer to the irrational attitudes which a depressed patient may develop despite contrary objective evidence of good/achieving parts of their lives. Two typical depressive views are:

'One must be competent and achieving in every way in order to have any personal value'
'It is intolerably painful and unacceptable for things not to be the way one would like them to be'.

Cognitive errors include arbitrary inference (drawing conclusions without adequate evidence), selective abstraction (focusing on detail out of context), over-generalization (deductions based on single incidents), magnification and rumination (views resulting from errors in evaluation) and personalization (a baseless tendency to relate outside occurrences to one's self). Some cognitive schemas seem to be based on early experiences, and one tentative view is that latent patterns are reactivated when there have been similar events to those which embedded the negative attitude initially. For instance, marital difficulties may bring back to life a loss. This may have associations with the part played by life events in contributing to the precipitation of affective disorder (Brown *et al* 1977, Paykel *et al* 1969).

Such life events have been found to be 'exits' from the social setting (e.g. deaths, separation, divorce) and undesirable events in the areas of health, finance and employment. Both types of events may be considered by the depressed patient as a loss, or more importantly they mirror or repeat a more or equally traumatic loss earlier in life. The role of early bereavements is controversial, however.

Emotional Effects

One of the emotional changes found in affective disorder is a change in the experiencing of normal feelings. This is often described by patients as a lack of feeling, of 'deadness inside' and an inability to feel. When there is a severe loss such as that of a spouse, or parent, the severely depressed patient may not go through the normal processes of sadness, grief and bereavement. Beck *et al* (1963) suggested that severity of depression correlated with losses in childhood. Hill (1969) found that such individuals have a higher frequency of suicide attempts than others in the depressive population. In individuals with 'losses' in childhood the mean onset of the first unipolar psychotic depression was found to be ten years earlier than in those without this experience (Perris 1969). One possible mechanism by which loss in childhood affects this depressive illness is via traits of hostile dependency (i.e. a need to rely on others while resenting doing so). In theory friction with others created by hostile dependency could create unfavourable circumstances which could bring forward the occurrence of depressive illness.

On another level the trauma of a depressive illness can evoke reactive or neurotic depression, and anxiety disorders, and in the young the process of maturation may be delayed until the illness passes. At all ages even when the illness has passed neurotic patterns induced by affective illness may become autonomous of the initial depressed mood.

Behavioural Effects

Patients with depressive affective disorder lose their drive and initiative and withdraw from meeting and interacting with others. Seligman (1974) postulated that this was due to 'learned helplessness' which was a conviction that an individual was incapable of ameliorating his or her painful situation and as a result withdrew emotionally and behaviourally. Depressed people often say that they are apathetic, and that 'there is no point in trying to overcome a particular problem' at the time when they are extended to the limit, coping with their depression, and their apparent lack of control over the chronic, unpredictable mood changes. Again, as in the cognitive and emotional effects of depression, this feeling of helplessness can outlast and become autonomous of the illness so that when the affective illness has passed, withdrawal and lack of drive for solving even simple problems may persist.

Social Effects

In addition to generalized social withdrawal, a long-standing depression may lead to profound disturbances in relationships within the marriage and family. This will include the 'power pattern' established early in marriage—a usually stable feature of the relationship (Hooper *et al* 1978). However, roles may be drastically modified so that for instance the more dependent member becomes much more independent and vice versa. This was illustrated by Weissman and Paykel (1974) who showed that in depressed women the role of the acutely depressed patient changed to one of 'submissive dependency' with a new balance of power within the marriage at the expense of the emotional sharing which existed previously. The well spouse will have to cope with an inadequate 'other half', financial problems, additional work, the care of the children and the general holding together of the family. There may also be secondary gain from this disturbed relationship if it becomes a substitute for the emotional fulfilments of a more normal couple. This phenomenon of secondary gain is one of the most resistant psychological effects of depressive illness and it prevents the relinquishing of the otherwise transient, immature and maladaptive manifestations accompanying a period of severe suffering. The degree of tolerance and understanding shown by the non-depressed partner is variable with some opting out early, and others showing an amazing depth of understanding, tolerance, compassion and willingness to persevere. Later, marital stability can be threatened when a patient with long-standing depression becomes 'well'.

The feelings of inadequacy in other members of the family may be projected on to the depressed person often to the detriment of the depressed person's attempts to overcome the psychological effects of his illness. Excuses, allowances, blame and ridicule may be used by others in the family in their covert and often unconscious attempts to keep the depressed person as a 'patient'. Effects on the younger members (children) will often be profound in terms of modelling, learning of depressive behaviour and absence of adequate parental nurturing of adult emotional development (i.e. parental abdication (Framo 1974)).

Bipolar manic-depressive patients manufacture their own very special kind of marital and occupational chaos, which can result in all sorts of disasters both during and after recovery. The manic patient may be promiscuous, develop grandiose schemes, spend money he does not have, become bankrupt, indulge in behaviour which loses him friends and jobs, gets into trouble with the police in bizarre ways, and sometimes frightens his family by his irritable, overbearing, overactive and inconsiderate ways. On the other hand some hypomanic individuals have some extra attractiveness for their spouses aided by their high sexual drive.

The problems of the depressed patient are compounded by his many absences from work and social groups and by his or her own quite understandable loss of confidence in ability to do a job and relate to his colleagues and friends. Other people find it difficult to cope with the patient's erratic, inadequate, inefficient, dependent or demanding behaviour; the outcome is loss of promotion, demotion or redundancy and exclusion from various groups, leading to further psychological trauma. Cassidy *et al* (1957) estimated that about a quarter of depressives experience a major degree of social and personal disruption as a result of their illness, but this may be an under-estimate.

Rehabilitation

Adequate rehabilitation of patients who have had affective disorder requires that the many psychological and social factors described above be assessed in detail by the team caring for the patient. If rehabilitation is to be undertaken this needs sufficient time and clinical resources to begin the process of modification which may then be continued by the patient and his family for some time following one episode or for a longer period after multiple episodes. All too often the rehabilitation or psychosocial aftercare involves only part of the treatment needed because of lack of time and resources, pressure from work where a job is in jeopardy, or rejection of treatment by patient and family.

Psychological treatment approaches to neurotic or psychological depression have been well documented and the available empirical evidence has been reviewed (e.g. Whitehead 1979). There are fewer descriptions of these treatments as they apply to the psychological and social costs of affective disorder even though these may be more profound than in other forms of depression. In the following section the various psychological and social treatments are described together with their appropriateness to the rehabilitation of affective disorder and the present state of knowledge.

Psychological Therapies: General Discussion

Broadly speaking psychological therapies as applied to affective disorder can be divided into:

(a) cognitive-behavioural; and
(b) psychodynamic/emotive therapies.

These have been discussed by Whitehead (1979) and Koch (1980). The cognitive-behavioural therapies derive from four main premises. These are that:

(1) Depressive behaviour can be modified by changing the external or environmental rewards and punishments (reinforcement).
(2) Depressive behaviour is maintained by a lack of reward (positive reinforcement) which can be reinstated.
(3) It can be demonstrated that the view that an individual lacks control over his environment can be altered.
(4) Depression is maintained by the individual's negative thoughts of himself, his world and his future which can be reversed.

Psychodynamic or emotional psychotherapies derive from three main premises. These are that:

(1) Depression is maintained by the habit of avoiding the expression of intense anger and loss and by the directing of these feelings internally. The aim is to facilitate the awareness and expression of these feelings.
(2) Such avoidance of intense and painful feelings is built up, is repeated compulsively or becomes 'overlearnt'. This avoidance comes from past relationships with parental figures and is repeated in current mirror-like relationships. Treatment consists of increasing awareness, both emotionally and intellectually, of the nature of this compulsive repetition.
(3) Depression is maintained by unsatisfactory social and interpersonal relationships and treatment is aimed at the discussion and amelioration of these problems.

Although theoretically the cognitive-behavioural and psychodynamic/emotional schools of psychopathology have been at odds with each other concerning the direction of interaction in the maintenance of depressed mood, it has been pointed out in a preceding section that cognitive, behavioural and emotional disturbances are *all* displayed during affective disorder and when in some cases they continue into the 'recovery phase' have particular relevance to rehabilitation.

The two forms of psychological therapy mentioned will now be discussed in greater detail.

Cognitive-behavioural Therapy
During regular meetings with the patient the focus is on thoughts and behaviour, present experiences and planning events for the near future. The patient is encouraged to clarify and describe his beliefs, attitudes and

ideas and to test their validity. For instance, although accepting a patient's thoughts as truthful the therapist invites the patient to test them for their accuracy as reflecting reality, e.g. 'Nobody likes me' and 'I never see anything good', may be truthful but inaccurate. The patient is helped to identify the assumptions underlying his current 'automatic' thoughts using logic, persuasion and evidence from present behaviour to help the patient to regard the statement 'I am unable to learn', for example, as an idea requiring validation, rather than a belief. In general, a session begins with a discussion of previously set homework focused on recording or altering the patient's thinking and ends with the setting of further homework. Early therapy aims at increasing activity and decreasing withdrawal.

During the set 'exercises', the patient learns to monitor and recognize his patterns of thinking as they relate to his behaviour patterns. The specific homework consists of a set task (graded task assignment (GTA)). GTA consists of subdividing major tasks into 'mini-tasks' which are within his capability. Thus, the technique not only increases activity by inducing the patient to undertake more complex tasks but also helps him to recognize and correct unrealistic thoughts which might otherwise maintain the degenerating view of himself.

In addition, a diary is kept of events and thoughts which are construed as negative or positive. This encourages the view that some experiences are positive, and the patient is sensitized to his negative thoughts and given evidence with which to test the validity and logic of each thought. The latter stages of cognitive therapy involve identification of some of the assumptions he had which are so often associated with depression, e.g. 'I must be successful in whatever I undertake'.

Initially, the patient may see little point in undertaking such a programme but is persuaded to take part and assess any results as it progresses. After initial reluctance, the patient starts with cognitive and behavioural 'role-playing' and finds that this has beneficial effects. It makes him feel more positive and puts him into a more rewarding milieu since everybody responds more positively to the new behaviour. In addition, he can begin to generalize these new attitudes into his relationships with his family.

Psychodynamic/emotive Therapy

The first part of such therapy consists of establishing a good rapport with the patient in which trust and good will are built up. Having done this the next aim is discovery and understanding of the compulsive re-enactment. It is often initially suggested that depressed mood covers an underlying anxiety or fear about other more difficult feelings. Even if this is readily accepted it is often the case that the patient is unaware of what these other feelings are. During subsequent interviews the possibility that these other feelings alluded to earlier consist of feelings of anger and of loss are discussed with the therapist basically interpreting or clarifying one type of basic psychodynamic 'triangle', namely the triangle of conflict described by Malan (1979). Figure 2.1 below indicates how people may use defensive or avoidance manoeuvres, which may be the experience of depression to deal with anxiety or conflict over hidden feelings of anger, loss and helplessness.

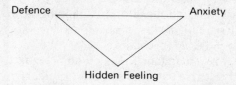

Figure 2.1   Psychodynamic triangle of conflict

The clarifications and interpretations made are repeatedly discussed during subsequent psychotherapeutic interviews. Following this, the aim is to explore the fundamental experience which threatened the patient so much and led to the development of his current ways of responding to others. Usually a specific precipitating event might alert the therapist to the kind of conflict most likely to be operating. In such instances it is not possible to pinpoint the time of onset of the disorder clearly or the specific psychological processes present at the initiation of illness. However, during the interviews it often becomes clearer that the pattern of relating to the therapist or to important figures outside the therapeutic relationship, e.g. spouse, is a mirror of the pattern played by the patient with parental figures in the distant past. For example, it might become clear that the way of relating to the therapist was a reflection of the relationship the patient experiences with his wife. The growing awareness of his emotional make-up may prompt him to ask more and more 'Why am I like this?'. When invited to look for links with his past family life he may begin to describe clear feelings of hostile dependency as a young child towards his parents. We now begin to see the second psychodynamic triangle of person and the idea of compulsive re-enactment. Figure 2.2 indicates how people 'transfer' or 'generalize' feelings from fundamental relationships to current marital and therapeutic relations.

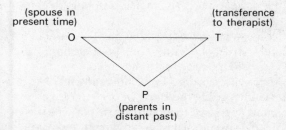

Figure 2.2   Psychodynamic triangle of person

The patient often resists this type of therapy by searching for current simple reasons for being depressed, e.g. a simple life event, and nearly always succeeds in finding seemingly plausible ones. The psychodynamic therapist must take care not to be unwittingly sidetracked by these. They are usually part of a superficial layer of depression over a deeper-rooted disposition to becoming depressed. At an advanced stage of therapy this consists of going over life patterns again and again and explaining how present dealing with the life situations and the concomitant feelings are often in accordance with the old psychogenic mechanisms.

Gradually, the patient begins to understand the emotional and psychodynamic side of his life history, learns to avoid old ways of dealing with his feelings and transforms these conflicts to more creative expression of feelings.

The matching of either of these therapeutic approaches to a particular patient's need is a complex problem. It is often found, unfortunately, that the use of a particular form of psychotherapy in general is decided more in terms of the personality and preference of a particular therapist than by reference to a particular patient's needs. Although the personality and style of interaction of the therapist can never be feasibly ignored, it would seem to be more appropriate to base the form of therapy *primarily* on the specific needs of the patient at the time of this assessment. We have tended to find that, when a patient has suffered psychological damage from his affective illness, instead of there being two distinct groups of patients who have had affective disorder and have either cognitive-behavioural effects or emotional effects, in most patients there is a mixture of the two. The choice of either of these two types of therapy therefore depends on the predominant problem presented by a particular patient at any one point in time. For example, a particular patient may impress the therapist with his continual and overriding negative expression of his actions and his environment rather than a characteristic avoidance of difficult feelings, and vice versa. Situations in which these forms of psychotherapy do not seem appropriate are those in which the therapist is unable to focus and clarify specific psychological effects on which to base a therapeutic approach. This has two implications. First, it may be that with these particular patients there are no specific psychological effects of note, or secondly, that at this present time the patient or the patient–therapist match is unable to clarify such effects.

When reviewing the outcome studies of psychological treatment of depression, one is immediately struck by either the poor definition of depressive population studies or the paucity of studies involving patients with accurately diagnosed affective disorder. In Whitehead's (1979) review, only one of the thirteen studies using the Beck Depression Inventory as the main measuring instrument appeared to include those patients with a well-established diagnosis of affective disorder. Wadsworth and Barker (1979) described treatment involving a somewhat strange combination of meaningless activity resulting in expression of anger plus group therapy. No significant change in mood was found. Rush *et al* (1977) reported on cognitive therapy with chronic relapsing depression. These patients, although previously not helped by drug therapy showed prompt and sustained improvement with therapy according to clinical and self-report measures. Weissman (1979) found that amitriptyline, once weekly psychodynamic therapy and combined treatment were significantly superior in producing symptom remissions in increasing order of effectiveness.

Marital/Family Therapy
Individual psychological treatments should include cognizance of marital, family and social effects to some extent. However, it is nearly always necessary to step out of the one-to-one relationship with the patient on recovery from affective illness. This alternative to individual patient contact may vary from simple social manipulations with straightforward letter-writing recommending rehousing to meeting the spouse and probably the whole family to assess carefully the presence or absence of the possible social effects of one member of the family unit having a traumatic depressive illness. When profound disruption has occurred and the relative family members are still physically present, family therapy is usually always indicated. For practical reasons, brief marital therapy is usually preferred to whole family therapy. This involves a regular meeting over a small number of weeks with patient and spouse to explore the effects of the patient's illness on the marital relationship, especially in relation to power and control and the transient development of inappropriate communication and behaviour, e.g. non-patient taking over all responsibility; sexual dysfunction, etc. This often leads to a sensitive discussion or uncovering of the couple's emotional resources built (or not, as the case may be) over the years prior to the illness.

Having described and discussed the common psychological and social treatments which should be considered in each case of affective disorder, it is relevant to digress slightly to consider relapse. One conclusion from the discussion of cognitive therapy is that, if it is established that dysfunctional attitudes contribute to maintaining a depressed mood, then patients treated with cognitive therapy may be afforded some prophylaxis against relapse compared to other treatments or no treatment. In terms of life-event research, Paykel and Tanner (1976) found that depressed women who relapse experience significantly more life events in the three months before relapse and especially in the month immediately preceding it. This study described major life events (including deaths and other exit social events) in mainly neurotic depressions and only in a small number of patients experiencing affective disorder. Surtees and Ingham (1980) in their study of unipolar depressive illness confirmed this finding. Surtees (1980) also found that social support in terms of confiding relationships with reciprocity between confidant and patient concerning personal matters has some immunizing effect following recovery from depressive illness. To the best of our knowledge there has been no investigation of the relationship between relapse in the early stages of recovery from affective disorder and what we would like to call 'soft' life events. By 'soft' life events is meant repetitive, difficult or emotionally stressing events occurring at home, at work or on a psychiatric ward, e.g., in the latter, aggression (threatened or accomplished), attempted or actual suicide, i.e. patient-related events. Soft life events in this situation would also include staff-related events, e.g. symptoms being accepted at face value by staff members, illness-related events, e.g. appearance of new symptom, lack of progress, change of drugs, or family-related events, e.g. family not visiting, expressing conflicting attitudes or apparently preferring to be without the patient. For the inpatient, soft life events will also include events during leave from hospital or after discharge from hospital in which the patient has to fit into the family on returning home and work, e.g. temporary demotion or lateral promotion. The most important soft life events however would be in the patient's day-to-day life. Until this aspect of a patient's life has been investigated the role of soft life events cannot be under-estimated.

We have attempted to set out clearly the many factors which each contribute to the experience, effects and rehabilitation of affective illness. At times it may have appeared that we have been viewing the many components as mutually exclusive. This was certainly not intended. The manner in which the psychological and social processes interact has been described. This interaction and perhaps the more complex one involving mood changes which have psychosocial as well as biological effects is a large area for further definition.

Conclusion

Many patients pass through an affective illness or illnesses without any obvious deterioration. However, if the illness is moderate to severe, prolonged, recurrent or treatment resistant, then as a result of this experience some develop secondary cognitive, psychological and behavioural deterioration requiring rehabilitation.

The main characteristics of affective illness relevant to the development of these changes, and the acceptance and response to rehabilitation are discussed. It is assumed that ordinary outpatient, day patient, occupational facilities are available and the subject matter therefore concentrates on the more intensive rehabilitative programmes involving psychotherapy, cognitive therapy and social care.

References

Akiskal, H S, Djenderedjian, A H, Rosenthal, R H and Khani, M K (1977). Cyclothymic disorder. Validating criteria for inclusion in the bipolar affective group. *American Journal of Psychiatry* **134**, 1227–33

Andreasen, N C and Winokur, G (1979). Newer experimental methods for classifying depression. *Archives of General Psychiatry* **36**, 447–52

Angst, J (1966). *Zur Aetiologie und Nosologie endogener depressiver Psychosen.* Springer, Heidelberg

Angst, J and Weiss, P (1968). Aetiologie und Verlauf endogener Depressionen. In *Aetiologie, Symptomatologie und Verlauf depressiver Erkrankungen.* Fortbildungskurse

Angst, J, Felder, W and Frey, R (1979). The course of unipolar and bipolar affective disorders. In *Origin, Prevention and Treatment of Affective Disorders* (eds M Schou and E Strömgren). Academic Press, London, pp 215–26

Beck, A T (1967). *Depression: Clinical, Experimental and Theoretical Aspects.* Harper and Row Inc., New York

Beck, A T (1976). *Cognitive Therapy and the Emotional Disorders.* International University Press, New York

Beck, A T, Sethi, B B and Tuthill, R W (1963). Childhood bereavement and adult depression. *Archives of General Psychiatry* **9**, 295–302

Brown, G W, Harris, T and Copeland, J R (1977). Depression and loss. *British Journal of Psychiatry*, **130**, 1–18

Cassidy, W L, Flanagan, M B, Spellman, M and Coker, M E (1957). Clinical observations in manic-depressive disease. *Journal of American Medical Association*, **164**, 1535–46

Framo, J L (1974). Symptoms from a family transactional viewpoint. In *Progress in Group and Family Therapy* (C J Sager and H S Kaplan). Butterworth

Gershon, E S, Dunner, D L, Sturt, L and Goodwin, F K (1973). Assortative mating in the affective disorders. *Biological Psychiatry* **7**, 63–74

Glatzel, J (1974). Kritische Anmerkungen zum 'Types Melancholicus'. Tellenbach. *Arch. Psychiat. Nervenkr.* **219**, 197–206

Guze, S B and Robins, E (1970). Suicide and primary affective disorders. *British Journal of Psychiatry* **117**, 437–8

Hamilton, M (1979). Mania and depression, classification, description and course. *Psychopharmacology of Affective Disorders* (eds E S Paykel and A Coppen). A British Association for Psychopharmacology Monograph. Oxford University Press, Oxford, pp 1–13

Hill, O (1969). The association of childhood bereavement with suicidal attempt in depressive illness. *British Journal of Psychiatry* **115**, 301–4

Hooper, D, Vaughan, P W, Hinchliffe, M K and Roberts, F (1978). The melancholy marriage. *British Journal of Medical Psychology* **51**, 387–98

Koch, H C H (1980). Psychological aspects of depression in general practice. *The Practitioner* **225**, 65–73

Kupfer, D J, Pickar, D, Himmelhoch, J M and Detre, T P (1978). Are there two types of unipolar depressions? *Archives of General Psychiatry* **22**, 866–71

Leonhard, K (1972). In *Psychiatrie der Gegenwart.* Vol. II, part 1 (eds Kisker, K P, Meyer, J E, Müller, M and Strömgren, E.) Springer, Berlin, 183–212

Lewinsohn, P (1974). A behavioural approach to depression. In *The Psychology of*

Depression: Contemporary theory and research (eds R J Friedman and M M Katz). John Wiley & Sons, New York

Malan, D H (1979). *Individual Psychotherapy and the Science of Psychodynamics*. Butterworth

Metcalfe, M (1968). The personality of depressive patients. In *Recent Developments in Affective Disorders* (eds A Coppen and A Walk). RMPA special publication No. 2. Headley Bros, Ashford, Kent

Metcalfe, M, Johnson, A L and Coppen, A (1975). The Marke–Byman temperament scale in depression. *British Journal of Psychiatry* **126,** 41–8

Mitchell-Heggs, N (1971). Aspects of the natural history and clinical presentation of depression. *Proceedings of the Royal Society of Medicine* **64,** 1171–4

Neuringer, C (1961). Dichotomous evaluations in suicidal individuals. *Journal of Consulting and Clinical Psychology* **25,** 445–60

Overall, J E, Hollisker, C E, Johnson, M and Pennington, V (1966). Neurology of depression and differential response to drugs. *Journal of the American Medical Association* **195,** 946–8

Paykel, E S (1974). Recent life events and clinical depression. In *Life Stress and Illness* (eds E K Gunderson and R H Rakes). Thomas Springfield, Illinois, pp 134–63

Paykel, E S and Tanner, J (1976). Life events, depressive relapse and maintenance treatment. *Psychological Medicine 6,* 481–5

Paykel, E S, Myers, J K, Dienelt, J K, Kleman, G L, Lindethal, J J and Peppier, M P (1969). Life events and depression. *Archives of General Psychiatry* **21,** 753–60

Perris, C (1966). A study of bipolar (manic-depressive) and unipolar recurrent psychoses. *Acta Psychiatrica Scandinavica,* Supplement 194

Perris, C (1969). Separation of bipolar from unipolar recurrent depressive psychoses. *Behavioural Neuropsychiatry* **1,** 17–25

Perris, C (1971). Personality patterns in patients with affective disorders. *Acta Psychiatrica Scandinavica,* Supplement 194

Perris, C and d'Elia, G (1969). Pathoplastic significance of the premorbid situation in depressive psychoses. *Acta Psychiatrica Scandinavica* **40,** Suppl 180, 87–100

van Putten, T (1975). Why do patients with manic-depressive illness stop their lithium? *Comprehensive Psychiatry* **16,** 179–83

Rush, A J and Beck, A T (1978). Cognitive therapy of depression and suicide. *American Journal of Psychotherapy,* 201–18

Rush, A J, Beck, A T, Kovacs, M and Hollor, S (1977). Comparative efficacy of cognitive therapy and pharmacology in the treatment of depressed outpatients. *Cognitive Therapeutic Research* **1,** 17–37

Schou, M (1968). Lithium and psychiatric therapy and prophylaxis. *Journal of Psychiatric Research* **6,** 67–95

Seligman, M E P (1974). Depression and learned helplessness. In *The Psychology of Depression* (eds H S Friedman and M M Katz). Washington DC, Winston.

Strandman, E (1978). Psychogenic needs in patients with affective disorders. *Acta Psychiatrica Scandinavica* **58,** 16–29

Surtees P G (1980). Social support, residual adversity and depressive outcome. *Social Psychology* **15,** 71–80

Surtees, P G and Ingham, J G (1980). Life stress and depressive outcome: application of a dissipation model to life events. *Social Psychology* **15,** 21–31

Teasdale, J D and Bancroft, J (1977). Manipulation of thought content as a determinant of mood and corugator EMG in depressed patients. *Journal of Abnormal Psychology* **86**, 235–41

Tellenbach, H (1976). *Melancholie* (1st edn 1961) 3rd edn. Springer, Berlin

Velten, E (1968). A laboratory task for induction of mood states. *Behavioural Research and Therapy* **6**, 473–82

Wadsworth, A P and Barker, H R (1979). A comparison of two treatments for depression. *Journal of Clinical Psychology* **32**, 443–9

Weissman, M (1979). The psychological treatments of depression. *Archives of General Psychiatry* **36**, 1261–9

Weisman, M M and Paykel, E S (1974). *The Depressed Woman: A Study of Social Relationships*. Chicago University Press, p. 23

Whitehead, A (1979). Psychological treatments of depression: a review. *Behavioural Research and Therapy* **17**, 459–509

Winokur, G (1979). Unipolar depression. Is it divisible into autonomous subtypes? *Archives of General Psychiatry* **36**, 47–52

Zerssen, D von (1977). Premorbid personality and affective disorder. In *Handbook of Studies on Depression* (ed. G D Burrows). *Excerpta Medica*, pp. 79–103

3 Schizophrenia

R G McCreadie, BSc, MD, MRCPsych, DPM

The length of an illness can be determined by comparing prevalence and incidence rates. When schizophrenia is examined in this way the mean duration of the illness is found to be approximately fifteen years (Cooper 1978). Thus schizophrenia for most sufferers is a chronic illness which will be characterized by acute exacerbations of positive psychotic symptoms such as delusions and hallucinations set against a background of persistent negative symptoms such as loss of drive, withdrawal, blunting of affect and poverty of thought. The illness will cause great distress to relatives who may have to support an almost intolerable burden for many years (Creer and Wing 1974).

The main aims in the rehabilitation of such individuals must be first to maintain and reinforce the non-psychotic aspects of the patient's personality by allowing and encouraging him to lead as normal and ordinary a life as possible throughout the course of his illness; and secondly to prevent further deterioration in his mental state and behaviour. Although much of what is written below applies especially to chronically ill patients, rehabilitative measures should be considered after the first episode of a schizophrenic illness.

General Principles

Three of the most important aspects of a normal, ordinary life are work, leisure activities and accommodation. Rehabilitation should aim to help the schizophrenic in all three areas.

Work

The schizophrenic through his illness may well have lost his job and be unemployed for some considerable time. Finding a suitable job in the community will be a difficult task. Where unemployment in the general population is high in a catchment area served by a psychiatric hospital, the placing of schizophrenics in open employment is well nigh impossible. Other alternatives must be considered.

Sheltered workshops for the mentally ill, the responsibility of local authorities, are few and far between. Thus the burden of employment of many schizophrenics, both inpatients and outpatients, falls on the mental hospital industrial therapy unit. Such units often have difficulty attracting a variety of jobs and rely heavily on simple repetitive tasks; but of course for many schizophrenics this may be the limit of their abilities. Non-manual work is especially hard to attract; some sympathetic hospital administrators may be willing to farm out clerical work but problems of confidentiality can arise.

Wages at industrial therapy units are low, the upper limit usually being that above which there is a reduction in social security benefits. The complaints of attenders at such units about low wages are especially hard to counter when the patients compare themselves to non-attenders who are not asked to pay for their board and lodging in hospital.

None the less the hospital industrial therapy unit can give valuable work experience and plays an important part in the rehabilitation of the chronic schizophrenic. It has been shown that the ability to work there and to develop satisfactory social relationships is a useful pointer to his ability to hold down a job in open employment (Watts 1978).

The expansion of industrial therapy units has overshadowed to some extent occupational therapy departments. There have been few studies comparing their efficacy and acceptability; one such study (Miles 1971) suggested that the industrial unit is more successful in improving the patient's willingness and ability to work, although there were improvements in the patients attending the occupational therapy department as well. In occupational therapy female middle-class patients improved most.

In the rehabilitation process the next stage for a schizophrenic if he is working well in the hospital therapy unit is often the government-sponsored Employment Rehabilitation Centre. Unfortunately these centres which assess in detail a person's ability to work seem more geared to the needs of the physically disabled. Many schizophrenics feel their attendance at such centres is a waste of time.

The Disabled Persons Act 1944 stipulates that in companies employing more than twenty people three per cent of the workforce should be registered as disabled. This might seem a useful entry for schizophrenics into open employment. Unfortunately few employers fill their quota and prosecutions under the Act are rare. Also, many schizophrenics resent being labelled 'disabled'. Some employers are sympathetic to schizophrenics' needs. The 'enclave' system whereby groups of patients work together in open employment with probably lower productivity targets than their workmates has been successfully implemented for the mentally handicapped and occasionally for groups of schizophrenics. The co-operation of the relevant trade union is necessary but is usually obtained if they are involved in the project from the beginning.

In theory therefore, in the rehabilitation of the schizophrenic, there should be steady progress from one type of work experience to another, the end result being a return to ordinary employment. The current economic climate however militates against success.

Leisure Activities

Leisure activities are important in an ordinary person's life. Loss of drive, frequently found in chronic schizophrenics, may have brought about his retreat from such activities. He should be encouraged to regain his interest.

Two important activities for many people are watching television and visiting the pub. There is no reason therefore to be dismayed if many schizophrenics inside and outside hospital spend many hours each week watching television; a recent BBC survey suggests the average in the general population is 18 hours weekly (personal communication, BBC Broadcasting Research Department). Unfortunately many patients in the TV lounge in the long-stay ward will not be watching in any real sense; they will have little idea as to the content of the programme. The television will be merely 'moving wallpaper'.

Men prefer to do their drinking in pubs with other people (Dight 1976). If a schizophrenic wants to drink he should therefore be encouraged to go to the pub with relatives, friends, or with one or two other patients; if an inpatient he might also be accompanied by a member of the nursing staff. Taking home a 'carry-out' is a common practice and should not inevitably be frowned upon by nursing staff. Excessive drinking among chronic schizophrenics is not usually a serious problem.

A number of social activities are often organized by hospitals for inpatients. Bus runs are all very well for the physically frail as this may be the only way for them to get out of hospital. For ambulant schizophrenics however it would be preferable if they could travel independently in small groups to visit places of interest. Formal dances, another aspect of hospital life, may not mirror life outside. Discos may be more appropriate for younger patients. Film shows within the hospital should be for the more severely handicapped; others should go to the local cinema.

Holidays are an important leisure activity. Inpatients should be encouraged to go on holiday with relatives. When this is not possible small groups of patients should make their own independent holiday arrangements. Hospital exchanges whereby patients spend a week or two in another psychiatric hospital should be reserved only for those who need considerable nursing care. Larger escorted groups may go on holiday. Although some hospitals take over completely a boarding house or hotel in a resort, it would be better if patients could share hotels with other guests.

Chronic schizophrenics, inpatients and outpatients, should be encouraged to join organizations outside the hospital. Women's guilds and other church organizations are usually very sympathetic to psychiatric patients. Voluntary organizations such as the local association for mental health should be contacted with a view to befriending patients, but the befriending should be clearly linked to a purposeful activity.

Accommodation

Many chronic schizophrenics have accommodation problems. Most inpatients of long standing will have little or no contact with relatives. For them the ward is home. Others may have spent less time as inpatients but none the less have drifted both socially and geographically and thus found themselves homeless.

In the process of rehabilitation the schizophrenic may experience several types of living arrangement. He may progress from the ward to a hostel, group home, digs or single-person accommodation. Wherever he stays privacy is important. For inpatients nurse-supervised dormitories should be reserved for the disturbed and probably contain no more than four patients. Others should have single rooms. This may be difficult to achieve for structural reasons, and 'cubicalization' of large dormitories is a part answer. Patients discharged to hostels and group homes should have their own room. Wherever patients go when they leave hospital, care must be taken to ensure that the new living conditions are not less attractive than the hospital environment they leave. Group homes and hostels can too readily become neglected 'back wards' (Lamb and Goertzel 1971). Daytime activities must be arranged, e.g. attendance at the local hospital industrial therapy unit (see above). Having somewhere that he can call his own will encourage the schizophrenic to gather personal possessions which is an important aspect of everyone's life.

Wards and hostels, and perhaps group homes, should contain patients of both sexes to allow normal exchanges between the sexes to take place.

If patients are to lead independent lives in accommodation outside hospital then they must be able to fend for themselves. Shopping, cooking, budgeting and laundering are only a few of the activities of daily living which many schizophrenics, both inpatients and outpatients, may find difficult. Help with such activities should be provided by nurses and occupational therapists; programmes for each individual patient should be drawn up.

In practice there are still many chronic schizophrenics in the community with inadequate accommodation, especially in cities. The rootless schizophrenic is well recognized and often is cared for by the penal system rather than the health service. Prison sentences for minor crimes are usually inappropriate for chronic schizophrenics, but there is an unfortunate tendency nowadays for staff in some psychiatric hospitals to refuse to accept responsibility for such patients. Also, some schizophrenics refuse all forms of custodial care. Basic provisions such as soup kitchens and night shelters may prove acceptable; if they are, some destitute men may eventually accept more permanent accommodation (Leach and Wing 1978).

In conclusion, the approximation of the chronic schizophrenic's life to that of an ordinary person is an important part of the rehabilitation process but is not easily obtained. It is usually simpler to impose a routine on groups of patients than to develop individual programmes. Lack of staff, lack of resources and lack of enthusiasm militate against success.

Specific Measures

The principles outlined above encourage the schizophrenic to lead an ordinary life. There are however more specific measures which aim to prevent further deterioration in the patient's mental state and behaviour; the three most important are medication, social forms of treatment and psychological therapies.

Drug Treatment

The effectiveness of antipsychotic drugs in the treatment of acute schizophrenia has long been known (Cawley 1967) but the use of such drugs in chronic schizophrenia remains somewhat controversial, especially in inpatients.

Inpatients
Important life events and family tensions are factors which can precipitate relapse in schizophrenia (see below). Such factors are less likely to act in long-stay inpatients and the need for antipsychotic drugs in patients who show few symptoms may well be less than in outpatients. However double-blind discontinuation studies of neuroleptics in inpatients (Davis 1975) show that when the drugs are withdrawn a significant number of such patients do relapse with a deterioration in mental state and behaviour. The discontinuation studies show though that many inpatients switched to placebo do not relapse. There is probably a place therefore for cautiously lowering the dose and if this is successful stopping the drug in many patients. Therapy can be quickly restarted if there is an increase in symptoms.

Inpatient populations also contain significant numbers of chronically very disturbed schizophrenics. Neuroleptics in high doses have been given to these patients. Drugs such as fluphenazine decanoate (McLelland *et al* 1976) and haloperidol (McCreadie and McDonald 1977) in very high doses may bring modest improvements in the patient's mental state but side-effects such as sedation and impairment of liver function can occur. It is probably unwise to use high doses of such drugs for lengthy periods of time.

Outpatients

The role of drugs in the rehabilitation of the outpatient is more clear. In a study of patients recently recovered from an acute schizophrenic breakdown (Leff and Wing 1971) it was found that oral medication such as chlorpromazine and trifluoperazine was significantly more effective than placebo in preventing relapse over a 12-month period. It was also suggested that the group of patients who benefited most from maintenance therapy were those with an 'intermediate prognosis' (Leff 1973); those with a good prognosis probably do not need medication while those with a bad prognosis will relapse no matter what is given to them. Patients with a good prognosis include those who are suffering from a first episode of illness, have symptoms of 'endogenous' depression, have a good pre-morbid personality and whose illness is of acute onset.

In recent years long-acting intramuscular antipsychotic drugs have been more favoured than oral medication as maintenance therapy. A double-blind discontinuation study of fluphenazine decanoate in outpatient chronic schizophrenics previously well maintained on this drug (Hirsch *et al* 1973) clearly showed its effectiveness; 66 per cent switched to placebo injections relapsed over nine months, while only eight per cent on active medication did so. However, oral medication such as pimozide given to patients well supervised in the community can be as effective as intramuscular drugs (Falloon *et al* 1978).

In the rehabilitation of schizophrenics compliance with any form of treatment is a major problem. Drug compliance is no exception. Probably 20 per cent of a general inpatient population (Hare and Willcox 1967) and almost 50 per cent of outpatient schizophrenics (Renton *et al* 1963) do not take their oral medication. Intramuscular medication is not the complete answer as a small but steadily increasing number of patients resent regular injections over a lengthy period of time and refuse further treatment (Johnson and Freeman 1973). Regular and continuous treatment however may not be necessary. Intermittent oral therapy has obvious economic and practical advantages and may be as effective as the same medication given continuously (reviewed by Prien and Klett 1972). Intermittent oral therapy may also be as effective as intramuscular therapy in compliant patients (McCreadie *et al* 1980). Such 'drug holidays' may be several days each week or several weeks every few months. One possible danger of drug holidays is that they might bring with them a higher incidence of irreversible tardive dyskinesia (see below, Jeste *et al* 1979).

It is not yet clear for how long maintenance drug treatment should be continued. The answer is probably indefinitely, as recent studies have shown that relapse rates are high following drug withdrawal in schizophrenics who successfully completed two years (Hogarty *et al* 1976) or up to four years (Johnson 1979) of maintenance therapy.

Antipsychotic medication can not only bring advantages but also hinder progress. Side-effects can be troublesome. The well-recognized effects of neuroleptics on the autononomic nervous system, such as a dry mouth and postural hypotension, may be irritating to the patient but do not usually interfere with rehabilitation. The same cannot be said of extra-pyramidal side-effects. Probably 20 to 40 per cent of patients prescribed oral neuroleptics and possibly a higher percentage given intramuscular drugs experience such effects (Johnson 1977). Not only the tremor and rigidity of parkinsonism, but also akathisia and, increasingly recognized, akinesia or slowness (Rifkin *et al* 1975) may interfere with manual skills necessary for proper functioning at work and in the home. They may indeed lead the patient to poor drug compliance with possibility of relapse (Van Putten 1974).

Tardive dyskinesia is now recognized as an important side-effect of neuroleptics. Its prevalence is hard to estimate partly because of the plethora of ways in which it can be assessed (Gardos *et al* 1977) and partly because different populations have been studied but probably up to 40 per cent of patients on long-term medication experience this disorder (Crane 1973) the most easily recognizable form of which is the bucco-lingual masticatory syndrome. In a mild form the disorder usually shows itself as infrequent champing movements with occasional protrusion of the tongue; at the other extreme movements of tongue, lips and jaw may be so frequent and gross as to interfere with eating, swallowing and breathing. Patients do not usually complain of this condition but the unsightly nature of the abnormal movements can lead relatives and friends to complain bitterly; thus an impediment to rehabilitation may exist.

Antiparkinson drugs are frequently used to counteract the side-effects of neuroleptics. Their efficacy is doubtful (Mindham *et al* 1972) except probably to relieve acute symptoms such as a dystonic reaction. There is some evidence that if given for long periods they increase the likelihood of tardive dyskinesia (Crane 1973). There is as yet no generally satisfactory drug treatment for tardive dyskinesia (Mackay and Sheppard 1979). Stopping the neuroleptic may be effective in some cases but in others the condition may worsen.

In conclusion, neuroleptics play an important part in the amelioration of the positive psychotic symptoms of schizophrenia and can prevent their reappearance. Their role in negative symptoms is less clear. Their use must be carefully monitored; side-effects may lead to loss of treatment adherence, poor social functioning and on occasion rejection by relatives.

Social Forms of Treatment

The management of the chronic schizophrenic in hospital, his resettlement in the community, and the importance of the family and of life events have been studied intensively over two decades in the United Kingdom by the Medical Research Council Social Psychiatry Unit. The results have been published in detail, both the original studies in inpatients (Wing and Brown

1970) and outpatients (Brown *et al* 1966); there have also been important replication and followup studies (Brown *et al* 1972, Vaughn and Leff 1976).

Within the psychiatric hospital it was found that there was a clear relationship between the type of environment in which the chronic schizophrenic lived and the severity of symptoms. If the environment was impoverished, that is the patient had few personal possessions, was largely inactive throughout the day, had little contact with the outside world and lived in a ward with many restrictions, then the negative symptoms of schizophrenia such as apathy, loss of volition, blunting of affect and poverty of thought were more severe. Where the environment was more stimulating the symptoms were less obvious. There was also a relationship between an impoverished environment and institutionalism, defined as a lack of desire to leave hospital.

The first series of studies showed only a relationship between the 'social poverty' and 'clinical poverty' syndromes; they could not demonstrate which was causal. After the initial survey however considerable changes were introduced into the hospitals studied with the result that the environment for many of the patients became more stimulating; the poverty of the social milieu decreased. Where this happened, it was found that the negative symptoms of schizophrenia lessened; where the environment remained the same the patients did not improve; thus it was suggested that the environment could influence the course of the schizophrenic illness. The effect of the environmental changes on institutionalism was less marked; it seemed that the length of time a patient had been in hospital was the crucial factor.

The importance of this large study, carried out in three hospitals, and other more modest surveys, especially the elegant description of 'institutional neurosis' (Barton 1976) in the rehabilitation of the chronic schizophrenic is considerable. They suggest that deterioration in the patient's mental state and behaviour can be modified by manipulation of the hospital environment. Encouraging the patient to have personal possessions, providing him with useful and interesting activities, welcoming his contact with the outside world through visits, letters and excursions, and lessening ward restrictions are likely to diminish the negative symptoms of schizophrenia.

It was found however that the single most important factor which contributed to the clinical poverty syndrome was the amount of time spent doing nothing. This finding was an added spur to the further development of industrial therapy departments. Not only were these units valuable in the resettlement of patients in the community (see above); not only were they morally justifiable in their attempt to increase the patient's dignity by providing him with what could be useful employment; but also there were now sound clinical reasons for developing them in so far as they might help prevent further deterioration in long-stay inpatients who had little prospect of ever leaving hospital.

A course must be steered however between understimulating and overstimulating a chronic schizophrenic inpatient. Too busy a unit, too much pressure can precipitate an exacerbation of schizophrenic symptoms (Wing *et al* 1964).

Some schizophrenics resettled in the community and many who have never been long-stay inpatients live with relatives. The Medical Research Council Social Psychiatry Unit has demonstrated the importance of family life in the course of a schizophrenic illness and thus how it can affect the patient's rehabilitation. Through detailed interviews a measure of the emotion expressed by relatives towards the patient has been devised. When a relative shows high 'expressed emotion' (high E E)—and this largely means that the relative is critical and hostile when discussing the patient—the chances of that patient relapsing with a reappearance or exacerbation of schizophrenic symptoms when he returns home are greatly increased. Conversely, if he returns to a warm, supportive or neutral environment, relapse is less likely. It was also found that the time a patient spent in 'face-to-face contact' with a high E E relative is important; more than 35 hours a week of such contact is likely to lead to relapse.

In theory these findings should help in the rehabilitation of the schizophrenic. In everyday clinical practice however, without the benefit of a training in interview techniques, and with time in short supply, it might be difficult to decide which relatives fall into the high E E category. Gross examples are obvious but others may not be so clear. Devising a simple scale which would correlate well with the more detailed interview would be a valuable research project. If such relatives can be identified it may be best to advise the patient not to return home when discharged from hospital but to live elsewhere. Such advice is easy to give but more difficult to implement. There may not be other relatives sufficiently interested in the patient to want him in their home or the high E E relative may express his objection to the patient living with someone else. Alternative accommodation such as digs, a group home or hostel may not be readily available—especially the last.

If the patient has to live with a high E E relative then face-to-face contact should be reduced. If the patient is not working he should attend a day centre, probably the local psychiatric hospital's industrial rehabilitation unit, or the relative if he does not work should be encouraged to seek employment. They should develop separate leisure activities. Another approach presently under investigation by the Medical Research Council Social Psychiatry Unit is to counsel relatives through group discussions (Kuipers *et al* 1981). Low and high E E relatives meet together regularly over a period of months; can the low E E relatives modify the attitudes of the high and thus be a useful tool in rehabilitation? The results are awaited with interest.

It has been suggested (Vaughn and Leff 1976) that if patients return to low E E relatives then maintenance antipsychotic drugs are not necessary.

Such therapy should be given only to protect patients from hostile, critical relatives. The numbers in the study however were small and the finding needs to be replicated in a larger sample. It is certainly the experience of most clinical psychiatrists that patients living with supportive relatives or in more 'neutral' environments such as group homes or digs can relapse. Such relapse may be due to 'life events' (see below; Leff and Vaughn 1980).

Schizophrenics, both inside and outside hospital, experience 'life events'. Such events are usually classified according to their apparent independence of the patient's control as 'independent', or 'possibly independent'. Examples of the former are discovering a burglary and hearing of a relative's illness; examples of the latter are the patient changing his job or his friends. It has been shown (Brown and Birley 1968, Birley and Brown 1970) that a significant concentration of independent events occurs in the three weeks before the onset or relapse of schizophrenia. In the rehabilitation of the schizophrenic it is clearly impossible to predict or prevent the majority of independent life events. When they do occur however the mental state and behaviour of the patient should be closely scrutinized. More frequent contact with the community nurse or psychiatrist and alteration of dose or introduction of antipsychotic medication may prevent relapse. This is speculative as one study (Leff *et al* 1973) has in fact suggested that outpatient schizophrenics on drugs are only likely to relapse if exposed to life events; that is drugs may not protect the patient against such events.

In conclusion, social factors both within and outwith the hospital can have a marked effect on the course of a schizophrenic illness. Rehabilitative measures should take these factors into account. At present more success has probably been achieved through manipulation of the hospital environment; it is more difficult to alter a family's attitudes towards a schizophrenic patient.

Psychological Therapies

Before the introduction of physical methods of treatment custodial care and psychotherapy were the main approaches in the management of chronic schizophrenics. Psychological techniques are still used and now include individual and group therapy, social therapy, and behaviour modification.

Individual and Group Therapy

In an authoritative review of psychosocial treatments of schizophrenia (Mosher and Keith 1979) the authors found that controlled studies of individual psychotherapy in schizophrenics, many of whom were chronic, had largely negative results and that there was no clear evidence of any benefits to be gained in chronic patients receiving this form of treatment. Likewise, with group therapy, most controlled studies failed to show any impressive change in chronic schizophrenics. However, the authors believe that the case against psychotherapy in schizophrenia is still 'not proven'. They suggest that such factors as insufficient exposure to psychotherapy, failure to define adequately the characteristics of the therapy and the therapists, and use of inappropriate outcome measures bedevil research in this area. They believe that what is needed are comparative studies in which treatment should be started after the patient's psychosis has subsided but while he is still an inpatient and it should be continued after discharge from hospital. Control groups would include patients maintained on and withdrawn from drugs. Therapy should continue for at least six months and measures of outcome should focus mainly on social and interpersonal variables rather than readmission rates.

It must be said however that other forms of treatment of schizophrenia, both physical and psychological, have been shown to be effective; lack of obvious success with individual and group psychotherapy would suggest to many critics that these treatments are indeed ineffective.

Social Therapy
A recent series of papers has examined among other things the effect of social therapy in the aftercare of schizophrenics (Hogarty *et al* 1974 a and b, Goldberg *et al* 1977, Hogarty *et al* 1979). In these studies social therapy, or major role therapy, consisted of intensive individual and family social casework provided by an experienced social worker. The therapy was seen as a way to respond to interpersonal, personal, and social needs in patients discharged to live in the community. Practical problems including situational crises were tackled. The main aim was to improve the patient's performance at home and at work by, for example, improving the quality of interpersonal relationships, teaching self-care and giving advice about finance.

It was found that on average social therapy was no more effective than placebo in preventing relapse. In patients with few symptoms however relapse rates were less over a two-year period when compared with patients who did not receive social therapy. Conversely, patients who still had symptoms such as disorganized overactivity, depression, and loss of insight had a greater chance of relapse if given social therapy. It is probable that such patients who were precariously adjusted were overstimulated and thus relapsed (see above, Wing *et al* 1964). It was also found that, when social therapy was given along with fluphenazine decanoate, relapse rates tended to be less than when patients received fluphenazine alone. It seems that social therapy alone is not all that helpful in preventing relapse but it may be of some value when combined with drugs.

When the effects of social therapy on the adjustment of *non-relapsed* patients were studied (Hogarty *et al* 1974 b) it was found that during a two-year period following hospital discharge those treated with combined drug and social therapy adjust better than those taking the drug alone.

Maximum benefits required both maintenance drug and social treatments to continue for more than a year.

Behaviour Modification

In recent years clinical psychologists and others have attempted to modify the behaviour of chronic schizophrenics, especially inpatients; the results have recently been comprehensively reviewed (Gomes-Schwartz 1979). The two main techniques are operant conditioning and social skills training. A third technique, systematic desensitization, is not usually helpful in the anxious, unassertive schizophrenic (Weinman *et al* 1972) and has fallen into disuse; probably chronic schizophrenics lack the necessary cognitive skills for successful desensitization.

Operant Conditioning. Put simply, the theory behind operant conditioning suggests that, if a particular piece of behaviour results in 'good consequences' for a patient, then that behaviour will be more likely to occur again; it has become strengthened by 'reinforcement'. Behaviour therapists can therefore teach and maintain appropriate behaviour through positive reinforcement and reduce inappropriate behaviour through negative reinforcement. Positive reinforcers are usually rewards or privileges, negative reinforcers punishments, usually withdrawal of privileges.

In the rehabilitation of the schizophrenic the effectiveness of these procedures usually depends on which behaviours are selected for modification; basic self-care, social interaction, positive psychotic symptoms and aggressive behaviour are the four main groups. Positive psychotic symptoms such as delusions and hallucinations may diminish if rational conversation is increased through social and token reinforcement. Alternatively negative reinforcement such as aversion therapy or 'time-out' may diminish the positive symptoms. Such improvements are usually transitory (Davis *et al* 1976) and possibly spurious; it may be that the patient simply chooses not to report his still-occurring symptoms. In the case of aggression such negative reinforcers as fines and time-out may actually increase rather than decrease the unwanted behaviour (reviewed by Gomes-Schwartz 1979).

Most attention in operant conditioning in chronic schizophrenia has been directed to lack of self-care and withdrawn behaviour. The fact that many patients in the same long-stay ward have similar handicaps led to the development of the '*token economy*'. All patients who participate in such an economy purchase privileges with tokens which are contingent upon appropriate behaviour. For the chronic schizophrenic common privileges are cigarettes, watching television, and visits outside the ward (especially to the pub). Behaviour which is rewarded usually includes satisfactory personal hygiene, dress, eating habits, and verbal communication.

There is no doubt that the introduction of a token economy into a long-stay ward for deteriorated schizophrenics can produce improvement (reviewed by Gomes-Schwartz 1979). What is less clear however is what ingredients are necessary in the programme to produce beneficial effects. In a recent controlled study lasting one year (Hall *et al* 1977) both patients who received contingent and non-contingent tokens improved in the areas of social withdrawal, appearance and routine behaviour when compared with a control group who received no special treatment. The improvement therefore could not be due to contingent tokens; it was concluded that social reinforcement, the feedback of information, and suggestions and instructions to nurses were important factors.

Paradoxically, although contingent tokens may not be a necessary part of the token economy it seems that ward staff want to carry on using them. They help to structure the response to patients and allow nurses to give a tangible reward for appropriate behaviour. None the less token economies frequently break down. Reasons for breakdown appear to fall into five categories (Hall and Baker 1973). Patient selection may be poor; catatonic and paranoid patients are said to do badly. Nursing and other ward staff may be inadequately trained and either unintentionally or deliberately sabotage programmes. The supervising psychologist may spend too little time with ward staff with a subsequent fall-off in morale. Hospital administrators may not co-operate. Finally the outside community may be antagonistic.

For successful rehabilitation the gains obtained in a token economy ward should be maintained when the chronic schizophrenic is either discharged from hospital or transferred to another unit. Unfortunately, what few follow-up studies have been carried out do not provide much evidence for this (reviewed by Hersen 1976). It may be that token economy programmes teach patients how to earn tokens rather than how to interact with the community. Gains might be maintained if relatives and staff in other units were also taught simple behavioural techniques.

Social Skills Training. Chronic schizophrenics are often deficient in social skills such as starting, continuing and finishing a conversation, complaining, asking for help, dealing with aggression and self-control. Training in such skills involves a range of techniques including modelling, role-play and feedback on performance through the playback of video tapes. Social reinforcement in the form of praise is given as the role-playing approaches that which is required for successful social interaction. The hope is that when the patient is able to role-play successfully in an artificial situation he will be able to cope with the same real-life situations. Controlled studies on social skills training in chronic schizophrenics are few and far between and rarely are only schizophrenics included (reviewed by Hersen and Bellack 1976). One recent controlled study which examined mainly schizophrenics (Shephard 1978) suggested a clear improvement in social functioning for the treated group, an improvement which generalized from the immediate treatment situation to the rest of the patients' activities in a day hospital. There is still little evidence that learned social skills generalize to a wider range of naturally occurring situations or that they are maintained over lengthy periods of time. Much more research needs to be carried out in this area.

In conclusion psychological techniques are probably of little value in altering the primary symptoms of schizophrenia. Their main role in the rehabilitation of the schizophrenic is the prevention, or amelioration of the secondary handicaps.

This review has suggested that in the rehabilitation of the schizophrenic a wide variety of techniques can be used and can be of help. The proper implementation of such techniques will need the co-operation of people from several disciplines: psychiatrists, nurses, psychologists, social workers, and occupational therapists. It is rare to find in the same psychiatric hospital at least one senior member of each discipline interested in the problems of the chronic schizophrenic. It is better however to have a small nucleus of enthusiasts rather than a larger group containing people paying only lip-service to rehabilitation. Also, changes in schizophrenics brought about by rehabilitative measures take place over many months, if not years. If people want to witness for themselves the beneficial effects of rehabilitation they must be prepared to spend lengthy periods of time working with this group of patients.

Enthusiasm must be tempered with realism. It must be recognized that not all patients will benefit from rehabilitation. There will inevitably be a hard core of chronically disturbed schizophrenics who fail to respond to any extent to all forms of treatment. Such patients will remain in hospital indefinitely. A fuller description of such patients is given in Chapter 5.

Finally, the burden on the community of resettled chronic schizophrenics must again be stressed (Creer and Wing 1974). It may be financially cheaper for schizophrenics to live with relatives but the cost measured by distress to relatives unable to cope satisfactorily with the patient may be great. Only a detailed assessment of the strengths and weaknesses of both patients and relatives will determine accurately what rehabilitative measures are appropriate.

References

Barton, R (1976). *Institutional Neurosis*. John Wright, Bristol

Birley, J L T and Brown, G W (1970). Crises and life changes preceding the onset or relapse of acute schizophrenia: clinical aspects. *British Journal of Psychiatry* **116**, 327–34

Brown, G W and Birley J L T (1968). Crises and life changes and the onset of schizophrenia. *Journal of Health and Social Behaviour* **9**, 203–14

Brown, G W, Bone, M, Davison, B and Wing, J K (1966). *Schizophrenia and Social Care*. Oxford University Press, London

Brown, G W, Birley, J L T and Wing, J K (1972). Influence of family life on the course of schizophrenic disorders: a replication. *British Journal of Psychiatry* **121**, 241–58

Cawley, R H (1967). The present status of physical methods of treatment of schizophrenia. In *Recent Developments in Schizophrenia* (eds A Coppen and A Walk). Special Publication No 1, Headley Brothers, Ashford, Kent

Cooper, B (1978). Epidemiology. In *Schizophrenia: Towards a New Synthesis* (ed. J K Wing). Academic Press, London

Crane, G E (1973). Persistent dyskinesia. *British Journal of Psychiatry* **122**, 395–406

Creer, C and Wing, J K (1974) *Schizophrenia at Home*. National Schizophrenia Fellowship, 78 Victoria Road, Surbiton, Surrey

Davis, J M (1975). Overview: Maintenance therapy in psychiatry: I. Schizophrenia. *American Journal of Psychiatry* **132**, 1237–45

Davis, J R, Wallace, C J, Liberman, R P and Finch, B E (1976). The use of brief isolation to suppress delusional and hallucinatory speech. *Journal of Behaviour Therapy and Experimental Psychiatry* **7**, 267–75

Dight, S E (1976). *Scottish Drinking Habits*. HMSO, London.

Falloon, I, Watt, D C and Shepherd, M (1978). A comparative controlled trial of pimozide and fluphenazine decanoate in the continuation therapy of schizophrenia. *Psychological Medicine* **8**, 59–70

Gardos, G, Cole, J and Labrie, R (1977). The assessment of tardive dyskinesia. *Archives of General Psychiatry* **34**, 1206–12

Goldberg, S C, Schooler, N R, Hogarty, G E and Roper, M (1977). Prediction of relapse in schizophrenic outpatients treated by drug and sociotherapy. *Archives of General Psychiatry* **34**, 171–84

Gomes-Schwartz, B (1979). The modification of schizophrenic behaviour. *Behaviour Modification* **3**, 439–68

Hall, J and Baker, R (1973). Token economy systems: breakdown and control. *Behaviour Research and Therapy* **11**, 253–63

Hall, J N, Baker, R D and Hutchison, K (1977). A controlled evaluation of token economy procedures with chronic schizophrenic patients. *Behaviour Research and Therapy* **15**, 261–83

Hare, E H and Willcox, D R C (1967). Do psychiatric in-patients take their pills? *British Journal of Psychiatry* **113**, 1435–40.

Hersen, M (1976). Token economies in institutional settings. *Journal of Nervous and Mental Disease,* **162**, 205–11

Hersen, M and Bellack, A S (1976). Social skills training for chronic psychiatric patients: rationale, research findings, and future directions. *Comprehensive Psychiatry* **17**, 559–80

Hirsch, S R, Gaind, R, Rohde, P D, Stevens, B C and Wing, J K (1973). Out-patient maintenance of chronic schizophrenic patients with long-acting fluphenazine: double-blind placebo trial. *British Medical Journal* **1**, 633–7

Hogarty, G E, Goldberg, S C, Schooler, N R and Ulrich, R F (1974a). Drug and sociotherapy in the aftercare of schizophrenic patients. II Two-year relapse rates. *Archives of General Psychiatry* **31**, 603–8

Hogarty, G E, Goldberg, S C and Schooler, N R (1974b). Drug and sociotherapy in the aftercare of schizophrenic patients. *Archives of General Psychiatry* **31**, 609–18

Hogarty, G E, Ulrich, R F, Mussare, F and Aristigueta, N (1976). Drug discontinuation among long-term successfully maintained schizophrenic outpatients. *Diseases of the Nervous System* **37**, 494–500

Hogarty, G E, Schooler, N R, Ulrich, R, Mussare, F, Ferro, P and Herron, E (1979). Fluphenazine and social therapy in the aftercare of schizophrenic patients. *Archives of General Psychiatry* **36**, 1283–94

Jeste, D V, Potkin, S G, Sinha, S, Feder, S and Wyatt, R J (1979). Tardive dyskinesia—reversible and persistent. *Archives of General Psychiatry* **36**, 585–90

Johnson, D A W (1977). Practical considerations in the use of depot neuroleptics for the treatment of schizophrenia. *British Journal of Hospital Medicine* **17**, 546–58

Johnson, D A W (1979). Further observations on the duration of depot neuroleptic maintenance therapy in schizophrenia. *British Journal of Psychiatry* **135**, 524–30

Johnson, D A W and Freeman, H (1973). Drug defaulting by patients on long-acting phenothiazines. *Psychological Medicine* **3**, 115–19

Kuipers, L, Berkowitz, R and Leff, J P (1981). Interaction between drug effects and social phenomena: their effects on the schizophrenic patient. *Clinical Research Reviews* **1**, 69–74

Lamb, R H and Goertzel, V (1971). Discharged mental patients—are they really in the community? *Archives of General Psychiatry* **24**, 29–34

Leach, J and Wing, J K (1978). The effectiveness of a service for helping destitute men. *British Journal of Psychiatry* **133**, 481–92

Leff, J P (1973). Influence of selection of patients on results of clinical trials. *British Medical Journal* **4**, 156–8

Leff, J P and Vaughn, C (1980). The interaction of life events and relatives expressed emotion in schizophrenia and depressive neurosis. *British Journal of Psychiatry* **136**, 146–53

Leff, J P and Wing, J K (1971). Trial of maintenance therapy in schizophrenia. *British Medical Journal* **3**, 559–604

Leff, J P, Hirsch, S R, Gaind, R, Rohde, P D and Stevens, B C (1973). Life events and maintenance therapy in schizophrenic relapse. *British Journal of Psychiatry* **123**, 659–60

McCreadie, R G and McDonald, I M (1977). High dosage haloperidol in chronic schizophrenia. *British Journal of Psychiatry* **131**, 310–16

McCreadie, R G, Dingwall, J M, Wiles, D H and Heykants, J J P (1980). Intermittent pimozide versus fluphenazine decanoate as maintenance therapy in chronic schizophrenia. *British Journal of Psychiatry* **137**, 510–17

Mackay, A V P and Sheppard, G P (1979). Pharmacotherapeutic trials in tardive dyskinesia. *British Journal of Psychiatry* **135**, 489–99

McLelland, H A, Farquharson, R G, Leyburn, P, Furness, J A and Schiff, A A (1976). Very high dose fluphenazine decanoate. *Archives of General Psychiatry* **33**, 1435–9

Miles, A (1971). Long-stay schizophrenic patients in hospital workshops: a comparative study of an industrial unit and an occupational therapy department. *British Journal of Psychiatry* **119**, 611–20

Mindham, R H J, Gaind, R, Anstee, B H and Rimmer, L (1972). Comparison of amantadine, orphenadrine and placebo in the control of phenothiazine-induced parkinsonism. *Psychological Medicine* **2**, 406–13

Mosher, L R and Keith S J (1979). Research on the psychosocial treatment of schizophrenia: a summary report. *American Journal of Psychiatry* **136,** 623–31

Prien, R F and Klett, C J (1972). An appraisal of the long-term use of tranquillizing medication with hospitalized chronic schizophrenics: a review of the drug discontinuation literature. *Schizophrenia Bulletin* **5,** 64–73

Renton, C A, Affleck, J W, Carstairs, G M and Forrest, A D (1963). A follow up of schizophrenic patients in Edinburgh. *Acta Psychiatrica Scandinavica* **39,** 548–81

Rifkin, A, Quitkin, F and Klein, D F (1975). Akinesia. *Archives of General Psychiatry* **32,** 672–4

Shephard, G (1978). Social skills training: the generalization problem—some further data. *Behaviour Research and Therapy* **16,** 287–8

van Putten, T (1974). Why do schizophrenic patients refuse to take their drugs? *Archives of General Psychiatry* **31,** 67–72

Vaughn, C E and Leff, J P (1976). The influence of family and social factors on the course of psychiatric illness. *British Journal of Psychiatry* **129,** 125–37

Watts, F N (1978). A study of work behaviour in a psychiatric rehabilitation unit. *British Journal of Social and Clinical Psychology* **17,** 85–92

Weinman, B, Gelbart, P, Wallace, M and Post, M (1972). Inducing assertive behaviour in chronic schizophrenics: a comparison of socio-environmental, desensitization, and relaxation therapies. *Journal of Consulting and Clinical Psychology* **39,** 246–52

Wing, J K and Brown, G W (1970). *Institutionalism and Schizophrenia.* University Press, Cambridge.

Wing, J K, Bennet, D H and Denham, J (1964). *The Industrial Rehabilitation of long-stay schizophrenic patients.* Medical Research Council Memo No. 42. HMSO, London.

4 A Psychogeriatric Rehabilitation Programme

C McDonald, MD, MRC Psych

The elderly mentally ill have emerged in the general thrust for medical services for Britain's increasingly aged population (HMSO Statistical Report Series No. 12 1969). It was demonstrated that from 1954 to 1969 the number of over-75 year olds in mental hospitals had increased considerably—22 per cent increase for men and 12 per cent for women. In addition, the demand for such beds was expected to continue rising. At the last available census (HMSO Statistical Report Series No. 12 1973) the figures for in-patients in mental hospitals in England showed that in 1970 there were 34 970 patients over 65 while in 1973 the figure had risen to 35 695.

In response to this demand new consultancies in psychogeriatrics have been created, or 'special responsibility for psychogeriatrics' on a part-time basis has been written into some contracts. The Royal College of Psychiatrists has formed a section to monitor the standards of professional care in this area. As a result of these appointments, consultants—perhaps without formal senior registrar training in the field—have found themselves in jobs which involve very large workloads. Not surprisingly in these circumstances the creation of a psychogeriatric service for new and acute cases is given priority. However, when this first step has been achieved it is usually possible for the psychiatrist to turn to the problem of rehabilitation from within the mental hospital population which he has inherited. To guide him in this task there is little available knowledge in the literature and this chapter is offered more in the hope of encouraging activity and stimulating further ideas than as a model of services to follow. In the main I have described our experiences in initiating rehabilitation programmes in Warlingham Park Hospital, Croydon, a hospital which has reduced beddage from an apogee of 1150 in 1953 to approximately 480 (1980). This reduction which is somewhat in advance of the national rate has been facilitated by joint planning of services with the Social Services Department of the London Borough of Croydon since 1964. In addition, Croydon is a densely urban population, so rehabilitation services would almost certainly have to be planned for local conditions and programmed within a feasible expansion of local facilities.

Our experience in Croydon is offered as a guide, not as a model. Furthermore, it will emerge clearly that certainly in the initial stages the creation of rehabilitative and resettlement facilities for this age group is a managerial rather than a clinical task. The clinical challenge emerges after dealing with a backlog of accumulated social problems.

While adopting a flexible approach to many local variables, it is still helpful to create an average model of the task facing the psychogeriatrician in his long-stay in-patient population. If we assume a mental hospital serving a catchment area of 200 000 people with 30 000 over the age of 65—the 'standard' Health District—then the case distribution would be very roughly: 200 in-patient beds occupied by over 65's; 15 acute beds allocated to functional illness of the elderly; 60 to severe dements (doubly incontinent); 85 to mild dements (occasional incontinence in spite of regular toileting); and 40 to the 'graduate' class. There will also be 70 long-stay patients aged 55–64—the 'undergraduate' class.

These terms may need a word of explanation. The terms come from DHSS Guidelines issued in 1972 (HM(72)71):

'Graduates' has come to be the term used for 'those patients who entered mental hospitals many years ago before modern methods of treatment were available, a high proportion of whom have become institutionalized. In many cases links with their relatives have been severed and the hospital has become their home.'

'Mild dementia'—'mildly confused and may have a tendency to wander but, though occasionally restless, overactive, noisy or aggressive, do not need continuous nursing care. Their condition may be associated with certain physical disorders such as some degree of incontinence.'

'Severe dementia'—'requiring group observation with individual nursing attention as occasion arises throughout the 24 hours. Persistent incontinence without treatable cause may be a principal factor determining this requirement.'

One category not mentioned in HM(72)71 has been added: the chronic hospital population aged 54–65. This population contains the majority of the graduates who will be created over the next ten years—hence the label 'undergraduates'. It makes administrative sense to deal with this group here to try to prevent the future overloading of psychogeriatric beds. Fortunately this also makes clinical sense in that the rehabilitation problems posed by this group more nearly resemble those of the elderly graduates than those of the young patient in the 'new chronic sick' category.

This 'model' service is not the 'target service' implied by published government norms for bed allocation. 'Model' is used in the sense of typical of the type of workload which the psychogeriatrician may encounter.

It would be well to consider why we have inherited a 'graduate' population. It is not simply a matter of 'modern methods of treatment' not being available as implied above. Mental illnesses in middle age are recurrent but also self-limiting in the vast majority of cases, so sufferers should have been dischargeable after variable lengths of time. The social stigma attached to mental illness must have been a potent factor. Goffman (1968) describes three facets of stigma with which we must reckon in rehabilitation. First, the relatives of the mental patient were stigmatized to such an extent that the family not only withdrew from the patient but also often went to considerable lengths to conceal from their society the truth as to what had really befallen him. Secondly, the patient feels stigmatized, that is he feels his personal identity to have been undermined or spoiled to a greater or lesser extent. Lastly, after discharge the ex-patient must look out for the stigmata in his behaviour revealing to those in his new social nexus his secret past. If this happens, then he must deal with their reactions to him, a stigmatized person. Ignoring the subtleties of interpersonal relationships here involved, it is clear that care must be taken to rehabilitate the patient into an accepting environment.

With a few exceptions, of which more will be said later, the caring and accepting nexus at which discharges will be aimed will be residential places provided by the Social Services Department of the Local Authority. These range in type from boarding-out places, through group homes, residential hostels to Part III provision for the elderly including specialized homes for the elderly, mentally infirm (HEMI's). Clearly a rehabilitation programme which does not establish facilities to which ex-patients can be discharged is not only doomed to failure but runs the risk of causing antagonism in patients and staff because expectations are dashed.

Preparing the Way

Adjustment of social services provisions cannot be achieved overnight. It may be that a local authority is already providing places up to, or in excess of, the recommended national index. It does not follow that this accommodation will be suitable to accept rehabilitated psychogeriatric patients or that staff attitudes will be accepting. The psychogeriatrician needs to be involved both in social services planning and in the work and working of the homes. By dealing with psychiatric crises in the homes the doctor educates lay staff and also alleviates their often irrational fears of mildly disturbed behaviour. This kind of involvement is best served by the formal allocation, by contract, of one session of the consultant's week to liaison with the local authority. In Croydon we have run a repeating series of lectures which deal with the types of medical and behavioural problems which lay staff are likely to encounter in handling their increasingly aged residents. Before a long-stay graduate is discharged, the prospective Matron comes to the hospital, meets the patient and talks to the charge nurse, social worker and ward doctor about the patient's background and present handicaps. Any idiosyncrasies with their special management demands are dealt with at that time. Of course when the Matron accepts her new resident she knows that, if she or the new resident finds the placement unsuitable after a one-month settling-in period, the patient will be accepted back into hospital while alternative plans are made. A most important supportive service for Matrons is provided by a team of psychogeriatric community nurses. Each patient discharged from hospital to Part III accommodation is allocated to such a nurse. After checking directly that the general practitioner does not object, the nurse will visit the Home regularly to discuss with the Matron the ex-patient's settling-in and progress. Minor upsets can be dealt with then and potential breakdowns can often be spotted and averted by the nurse who can advise appropriate action such as change in medication, an out-patient appointment or specialist home visit. For its part, the hospital team should sympathize with lay people's difficulties and uncertainties in handling even mild psychiatric upset, and early readmission, virtually on Matron's demand, helps to generate a climate of confidence which will allow of the maximum number of placements in the long run.

The First Screening

Faced with an average mental hospital psychiatric population, as approximately proportioned above, a quick screening test is needed in order to find those patients who have the minimum intellectual capacity to be at least potentially rehabilitable. Our own occupational therapists applied three tests. First, the patient was asked to count beads differentiating shapes and colours—a test reminiscent of the Goldstein Scheerer Colour Form Sorting Test (Goldstein and Scheerer 1941). Secondly, she was asked to draw around wooden shapes and lastly to wind a wool ball. These tasks have the advantage of being within the occupational therapists' experience and can be readily and quickly administered. Patients who managed these activities with minimal or no supervision, or who managed with encouragement from the staff, joined the pool of potential rehabilitees (see Table 4.1). The next stage was a screening by medical staff. A survey of physical and behavioural handicaps led to the identification of a further group of patients for whom placement was clearly impossible. The emphasis at this stage should be on eliminating the impossible rather than finding people with a clear high success probability.

The Financial Screening

At this stage we have prepared the main discharge channel and identified the potential discharges—or those patients for whom discharge does not seem totally impossible. Although Warlingham Park Hospital had become famous for its community care programme and had taken care to survey its patient population with a view to finding patients who could survive in the community, a number of elderly patients were found for whom there seemed no obstacle to immediate discharge. The next move was a financial

Table 4.1   Occupational therapy grading tests and their changing patterns

Tests:	1. Counting and differentiating shapes and colours of beads
	2. Drawing around wooden shapes
	3. Winding wool ball/sanding and polishing

Grading:	A	Managed activity with minimal or no supervision
	B	Managed activity with encouragement
	C	Managed activity with much encouragement, help and physical assistance
	D1	Unable to co-operate
	D2	Unwilling to co-operate (regraded according to general performance in OT)

Results of Assessment (in Grades)

January	A		B		C		D1		Total
	No. of Pts	%	No. of Pts	%	No. of Pts	%	No. of Pts	%	
1973	119	46	32	12·5	35	13	74	28·5	260
1974	113	48·5	28	12	24	10·5	68	29	233
1975	98	47	19	9	18	9	74	35	209
1976	105	48	29	13	13	6	71	33	218
1977	98	45	17	8	21	10	80	37	216

screening performed by the psychiatric social worker to identify those patients with sufficient private means to allow them even a few years in the flexibility and comfort offered by fee-paying residential care. It may have been that the attitudes of surveying doctors had been pessimistic in the area of 'old age' but there is no doubt that even in an active hospital patients in this age range had been overlooked. Patients were found who were 'ward workers' and who 'enjoyed working' in the hospital laundry, hospital stores, etc. When examined, such patients were almost always found to have no impediment to immediate discharge.

Tackling Institutionalization in the Elderly

After this easily obtained bonus in quick and successful discharges (the patients who 'liked working' in the various departments adjusted remarkably well to retirement and expressed no desire to return to the hospital), there remained a body of patients clearly institutionalized. Barton (1966) has defined institutionalization as

a disease characterized by apathy, lack of initiative, loss of interest in things and events not immediately personal or present, submissiveness and sometimes no expression of feelings of resentment at harsh or unfair orders. There is also a lack of interest in the future and an apparent inability to make practical plans for it, a deterioration in personal habits, toilet and standards generally, a loss of individuality and a resigned acceptance that things will go on as they are—unchangingly, inevitably and indefinitely.

In our case, to these deficits must be added the inflexibility and cognitive insecurity that comes with increasing age.

We then set about devising a programme to be run by the occupational therapists which would have the effect of countering institutionalization, bringing the patient up to date in the greatly changed world outside hospital and motivating him to want to find a place in that outside world (see Table 4.2). The programme was staffed initially by a senior grade occupational therapist employed for five mornings per week, supervising a group of eight selected patients. In the afternoons the group joined the routine occupational therapy programme which was of course continued

Table 4.2   Rehabilitation programme for elderly mental hospital patients

Monday	Tuesday	Wednesday	Thursday	Friday
(9–11.45) Personal care Craft activities	(9–11.45) Personal care Craft activities	(9–11.45) Personal care Craft activities	(9–11.45) Personal care Craft activities	(9–11.45) Personal care Craft activities
(10–12.30) Outing	(9–10.30) Shoe cleaning groups	(9.30–10.30) Small group coffee	(9–10.30) Shoe cleaning groups	(9–10.30) Small group coffee
	(9.30–10.30) Small group coffee	(10.30–11.45) Table games with volunteers	(9.30–10.30) Small group coffee	(9–1.00) Small group coffee and eat lunch in Domestic Science Room
	(10.30–11.30) Community singing		(10–11.00) Shopping at hospital shop	
			(11–12) Art department	
			(10–12.30) Alternate weeks outings	
11.45–12.00 Clearing up on ward for lunch				
(2.15–3.15) Diversional OT	(2.15–3.15) Beauty care for small group	(2.15–3.15) Diversional OT	(2.15–3.15) Beauty care for small group	(2.15–3.15) Diversional OT

throughout for the main body of psychogeriatric patients. Soon the care was intensified and individualized by the addition of supervised volunteer participation.

A ward was allocated to house those selected for the project. Its large dormitory space was cubicalized in single units or groups of four beds, these being the conditions most typical of the accommodation to which it was hoped to discharge the patients.

Patients accepted for work in the groups were assessed by the occupational therapists in the areas of reading, writing, arithmetic, money, orientation in space and time, individual activities, group activities, exercises, outings, cooking, industrial type jobs, co-ordination, speed, verbalization, comprehension, memory (short-term and long-term), awareness, initiative, responsibility, sociability and confidence.

The variety of handicaps was enormous and ranged far beyond the description of institutionalization already given, although each of the handicaps listed was found in abundance. For example, we found a patient who always wrote his name in a different way each time he signed his signature, a patient who took ten minutes to walk out of a room, a patient who only wrote in capital letters, a patient who would only communicate in sign language, a patient who refused to do anything if he judged that physical activity was involved in the task, a patient preoccupied by looking at light through his moving fingers, a patient who didn't associate his name with himself, a patient who refused to focus her eyes on anything except food, etc.

The list of such behaviour could be extended but the examples given are probably sufficient to indicate that the behavioural anomalies do not fit into psychiatric textbook categories, nor do they relate to the clinical diagnoses attached to the patients.

One advantage of this profile obtained in each individual patient was that the occupational therapist was alerted to target symptoms and another was that it provided a baseline against which the effects of the rehabilitation programme could be judged. While no attempt was made at a 'blind' evaluation, the occupational therapists' second analysis of the patients' behaviour one year later showed that they believed that their patients had improved in almost all spheres. This is perhaps more impressive when one remembers that the programme ran for only eight weeks; thereafter, if the patient was judged to have reached a level suitable for discharge, she was placed on the waiting list for Local Authority Part III accommodation. They were then 'maintained' as a group on this experimental ward receiving an alternative programme similar to but less intensive than the initial eight week course.

As experience accumulated it was suspected that males were more difficult to rehabilitate than females, and in order to test this, eight males considered suitable for the programme were compared on several criteria with eight females also considered suitable. The eight females were selected as being outstandingly difficult in their behaviour. The men were found on clinical testing to be more deteriorated in their cognitive functions although the average ages of the sexes were similar as was their mean duration of stay in hospital. We speculated that men admitted prior to the 1950s were involved in extremely paternalistic if not regimented environments—walking groups, farm groups, locked wards, etc. Women on the other hand tended to be placed in occupations which were then associated with the female role, laundry and needleroom work, domestic care, etc., and which required some initiative as well as maintaining self-respect. In addition, it seems likely that male charge nurses created ward environments clearly different from those found on female wards. There was on the male wards little evidence of written stimulation, television was watched passively while discussion took place on the female wards, and men had few personal possessions (because of theft, which was virtually absent on the female wards). Certainly, less privacy was provided on the male wards and, while women were encouraged to remain independent in their toilet, only one man shaved himself and soap had been put out of their reach because one man had made himself ill by eating it! It seemed clear that men in hospital had been subjected to a less stimulating and challenging environment than women.

A Complementary Problem Group

My own belief is that a rehabilitation scheme for the over 65s in our mental hospitals should be linked to a complementary scheme for the chronic patients aged 55–65. If someone joins the 'graduate' group on celebrating his 65th birthday in hospital, dare we designate this younger group the 'undergraduates'? The undergraduates have similar behavioural problems to be solved and as with the graduates it would be unrealistic to attempt to prepare the majority of them for gainful employment. If the undergraduate group is not managed vigorously, it will become the graduate group of the future while conversely every discharge from this group has an enhanced multiplier effect on the hospital beddage because, of course, if ignored the patient could live in hospital for the next forty years!

Experience with a special occupational therapy programme to meet the needs of the undergraduates and prepare them for life outside hospital, again in Part III and HEMI accommodation, has proved most encouraging. This group presents special clinical challenges and discussion of these is beyond the scope of this chapter; however, it is suggested that the rehabilitation of the 'undergraduate' group is complementary to that of the graduate groups and that since the discharge targets of both groups are largely identical, the administration and clinical direction of both groups should be integrated.

Reaction

Rehabilitation programmes which have an obvious and profound effect on the hospital must expect to meet with opposition. There is still a loose link between the beddage of a mental hospital and the grading of both its Sector Administrator and its Divisional Nursing Officer. At one stage in our programme, when a bed was declared redundant by the medical staff, it would be dismantled and placed in a corner of the dormitory so that it might still appear in the regional statistics. Ward closures do not mean nursing redundancies but nurses fear that the removal of charge nurse positions will affect their career prospects. As beds reduce, the cost per bed tends to rise because the overheads remain largely unchanged. As the better patients are discharged the nursing needs on each ward increase while the nurses have less or no patient help with which to cope with the increased load. Fears were expressed that patients were being discharged from a hospital which had devised a sophisticated social environment (Occupational Therapy, Patients' Services Officer, Entertainments Officer, Co-ordinator of Volunteers, volunteer projects and participation, etc.) into Part III accommodation which was perhaps less stimulating, certainly which contained less structured diversion. It was said that the patients had lived in hospital for so long that it had become their home and it would therefore be cruel to uproot them. Staff who have gone to endless trouble to ensure that patients are optimally adjusted to mental hospital life are apt to mistake good adjustment for contentment and satisfaction. All the patients were discharged on one month's 'approval', that is, either the patient or the patient's new Matron could opt for readmission at the end of the first month after discharge. No patient expressed a desire to return 'home' in this way except one, and when she learned that she could not expect a single room in the hospital, it transpired that she too preferred life in the community!

The Remainder

The next development was the realization that we were entering an area of diminishing returns. Table 4.1 shows that the percentage of patients in the more deteriorated categories was increasing. This would be expected when the better patients had been discharged and when the admission policy was such that severe dements took precedence for admission while attempts were made to support mild dements in the community whenever possible.

Both the programme for graduates and the programme for undergraduates led to a series of successful discharges. However, there inevitably remained a rump of patients who displayed behaviour resistant to such omnibus approaches. Clearly there will be the severe dements and those patients with classical symptoms of chronic schizophrenia and even affective disorder (in a few cases) in whom the symptoms remain too severe even after treatment to allow of their discharge from hospital. In addition, we have found a range of recalcitrant behaviour alluded to vaguely in the literature under the heading of 'institutionalization' or 'stereotypies' (see Chapter 5).

We would predict that the final phase of a rehabilitation programme for the elderly will involve intensive study of these obdurate behaviours and the development of treatments designed specifically for individual patients, perhaps using behavioural techniques. Our own experience in this field is limited and has identified more problems than solutions, so it would be premature to report at this stage save to emphasize that group solutions must by their nature run into areas of diminishing returns and be replaced by individual treatment programmes of greater complexity and difficulty but perhaps, because of this, of greater interest and satisfaction.

Stress and Support

The rehabilitation procedure leads to resettlement if it has been successful. Moral issues are implicit in resettlement judgements. Is one aiming to place an ex-patient in the community in a congenial environment in which he will feel at home and which he will master with the minimum of stress, or is one aiming to settle the ex-patient in an environment which he is only marginally able to master, achieving this with the aid of intensive support systems? Our own view has been that the individual's dignity is enhanced by a life style which moves as far as possible towards the independent and self-sufficient mode which is the norm for our society. It follows that the stress experienced is justified in achieving freedom from the virtual total dependence of life in the mental hospital, provided that that stress is not so high as to produce its own psychological or psychosomatic symptoms.

There is still great room for improvement in the development and deployment of such support systems. We have already mentioned the attachment of a psychogeriatric community nurse to each patient discharged to any form of Part III accommodation. This service is greatly appreciated by the matrons concerned and functions only if the patient's new general practitioner has no objections. The nurse is able not only to advise non-trained staff on how to cope with minor difficulties, for example temper displays, paranoid ideas, but also to alert medical staff when the patient's psychiatric or physical condition changes significantly. In addition, we can use the vast and bewildering array of voluntary agencies which have mushroomed throughout the country. These are so diversified in what they have to offer and so irregular in their availability that detailed knowledge of their local availability has become the job of a highly specialized person, paid or unpaid. Work should be done on the assessment of the specific needs of the individual rehabilitee in terms of interests, sociability, areas of psychological need and satisfaction, finances, physical limitations and vulnerability to physical or psychological crises so that the best locally available package of voluntary and statutory support can be assembled and monitored in its application. We suggest the term 'Peripatetic Settlement Officer' for such a new breed of professional. Tentative steps towards this concept are already being made with the establishment of voluntary agency registers or indexes and the recognition by workers responsible for resettlement that every care should be taken in purveying support for their clients. However, the notion is that the job should be tackled geographically in the hope that specialization will lead to greater expertise in matching individual needs to available supports.

Strategic Considerations

Earlier the point was made that suitable planning and preparation in conjunction with the local Social Services Department was necessary for any rehabilitation scheme. The need for planning goes much wider than this because blockage in any one channel of patient flow, for example rehabilitation into Part III accommodation or acute geriatric admissions, has the effect of distorting the service. Some other resource has to be used to accommodate the patients who have encountered the blockage. This in turn overloads the back-up resources which leads to further inappropriate disposal decisions. The end result is a series of wrong placements, i.e. placements which are potentially harmful to the patient concerned (Kidd 1962). The best way to prevent this and keep the channels for patient placement open is to agree criteria for placement in Part III beds, beds in homes for the elderly mentally infirm, and in geriatric and psychogeriatric beds. Fortunately there already exists the basis for such criteria in a Government publication *Services for Mental Illness Related to Old Age* (DHSS 1972). In Croydon we have been engaged in a multi-disciplinary exercise over a two-year period to date, in which a panel assesses a cohort of referrals to Part III accommodation, from whatever source, and establishes which person should go where and with what priority. This has essentially involved elaborating the criteria of the above publication but once all parties agree on the type of case they should handle, realistic planning of resources on the basis of numbers, rates of referral, longevity, and sex distribution becomes possible.

The result of pre-planning a coherent admission policy and careful rehabilitation and resettlement programmes has been a 45 per cent reduction in the number of beds needed for the over 65s in the hospital without any reduction in the admission rate of acute cases. More importantly the cases remaining are being treated more intensively and more individually than was remotely possible in the past and the way has been cleared for the identification of clinical problems as opposed to management problems—a situation which affords greater job satisfaction in this unglamorous and still seriously neglected area of psychiatry.

References

Barton, R (1966). *Institutional Neurosis*. John Wright & Sons, Bristol

DHSS (1969). Statistical Report Series No. 12. *Psychiatric Hospitals in England and Wales 1969*. HMSO, London

DHSS (1972). *Services for mental illness related to old age*. HM(72)71. HMSO, London.

DHSS (1973). Statistical Report Series No. 12. *Psychiatric Hospitals in England and Wales 1973*. HMSO, London.

Goffman, E (1968). *Stigma. Notes on the Management of Spoiled Identity*. Pelican

Goldstein, K and Scheerer, M (1941). Abstract and concrete behaviour: an experimental study with special tests. *Psychological Monographs* **53,** No. 2, 151

Kidd, C B (1962). Misplacement of the elderly in hospital. A study of patients admitted to geriatric and mental hospitals. *British Medical Journal* **2,** 1491–5

5 Recalcitrant Behaviour Problems

C McDonald, MD, MRC Psych, N Behl, MB, BS, P Sudhakar, MB, BS

Nurse and Gleisner (1975) have reviewed the literature on social aspects of chronic mental illness and point out the general neglect in the literature of the 'old' long-stay population group. In Chapter 4 we suggested that treatment of the behavioural problems of the chronic mental hospital population in the age group 55–65 should be considered as a complementary part of a psychogeriatric rehabilitation programme. Search precedes research and this chapter draws attention to the clinical problems which exist in a chronic ageing mental hospital population.

Interest has been expressed in the problems raised in the rehabilitation of the elderly chronic mental hospital patient (McDonald 1979), but scant attention has been paid to the categorization and study of those behavioural problems which do not respond to what might be thought of as first-line rehabilitative de-institutionalization, education in activities of daily living and graduated re-introduction into a sheltered position in the community. Indeed it is difficult to find any descriptions of behavioural problems in the chronic elderly mental hospital patient beyond Barton's general descriptions of the picture of 'institutional neurosis' (1966) in which he includes withdrawal and uncommunicativeness. Pitt (1974) mentions personality and behaviour problems in the elderly. Among them he identifies incontinence as a means of 'hitting back', disinhibited behaviour, hoarding and 'set habits' (including whining). The nursing of these patients requires special dedication and all the support that theory and treatment practices can give. However, a search of nursing textbooks revealed only one reference (Anderson 1971) to hoarding, which it is claimed responds to 'stimulus and activity programmes'.

This chapter aims to describe such difficult cases, to essay an early classification and to set out treatment experiences to date.

It is proposed to abandon the psychiatric categories used in the Ninth Revision of the International Classification of Diseases, not because such diagnoses should not be made but because by themselves they give no clue as to the behaviour which prevents the placement of the patient in the community. However, the problems in presenting even a tentative classification are formidable since most classifications imply causality; and although theories exist as to the causal factors in shaping the symptoms of the institutionalized mental hospital patient, it may be found that the facts do not support the adoption of such theories without important reservations. Goffman (1957 and 1961) characterized the patients' reaction to total institutionalization as (1) social situational withdrawal; (2) rebellion; (3) colonization; (4) conversion; (5) immunization. He identified 'the social breakdown syndrome' as 'offering an explanation of the changing picture of the psychoses in recent decades and of the reported success of the varied forms of social therapy which have recently become popular'. This approach is continued by Zusman (1966) who reviewed the history of institutional care with its varying emphasis on the independence of the patients. These workers have analysed the mechanisms or dynamics at work in institutions but have not looked at the behavioural patterns independently. A similar stance was adopted by Wing (1962) who stated that 'a short stay in an institution is likely to affect only the most susceptible persons, while most people would probably be affected by a long stay in such a place'. Wing therefore attributed the development of the institutionalization syndrome or the social breakdown syndrome to (1) social pressures; (2) patterns of susceptibility; (3) length of time of exposure in the institution. As to the symptoms themselves, Miller (1961) listed chronic paranoid response, depressive reaction, chronic catatonic response, psychopathic response and passive neurotic response. The kinds of behaviour which we are studying are sometimes subsumed in the class of 'stereotypies'.

Bumke (1924) describes stereotypies in detail in schizophrenic patients but, while he mentions an association between stereotypic behaviour and dementia, he gives no details of the phenomena observed. Jasper (1962) explained stereotypies as 'after effects of previous experience'. He stressed their repetitive nature and their link with sensory input (touching repeatedly, etc.). Robertson *et al* (1958) described stereotypy in a study of the symptoms of three cases of Pick's Disease, while Mayer-Gross *et al* (1969) link stereotypies to schizophrenia:

> Some of the most striking symptoms of chronic schizophrenia, grotesque stereotypies of speech and behaviour, negativisms and many difficulties in institutional life, have almost disappeared since the tendency to habit formation (Adolf Meyer) has been acknowledged as a typical defect of the patient of this type and has been given appropriate treatment.

These workers had attempted to explain the phenomena of the range of symptoms by adducing causal theories; Mann and Cree (1976) approached the problem by examining the patient's symptoms and grouping the patients accordingly. They surveyed 'new' long-stay patients under the age of 65 and established the following groups:

(1) Those requiring continual in-patient care, including all sectioned cases (this, of course, is a debatable absolute because extended trial leave while on a treatment order can be a useful procedure in the rehabilitation of the non-compliant patient).

(2) Those likely to respond to rehabilitation training (therefore non-dementing).

(3) Those needing supervised accommodation in the community, e.g. mental after care hostels.

(4) Those needing unsupervised or semi-supervised places, e.g. Group Homes.

(5) Those able to live alone or with relatives.

(6) 'Asylum seekers'—those who expressed a preference for life in hospital over any offer of community accommodation.

(7) Those who required continuous nursing care—usually for dementia.

(8) The frail demented.

(9) Those requiring special supervision for specific handicaps, e.g. epilepsy.

It is remarkable that these groupings so closely reflect those for the over-65 age range even to the asylum seekers (30 per cent of their sample) who will be discussed later. Their sample was unprepared patients—they do not speculate on the effect of a rehabilitation programme on groups (1) or (2). When they looked at reasons why group (3) needed continuous supervision they found that they tended to be unmarried, to possess few occupational skills, showed a tendency to self-neglect, were slovenly at dressing and eating and, possibly because of institutionalization in the past, needed help with forms and bills and tended to lapse into apathetic anergic behaviour. In this way they indicated that grouping patients by behaviour patterns was more helpful in rehabilitation programmes than grouping by diagnoses.

Arising from these theoretical approaches we then asked whether recalcitrant behaviour problems are related to:

(1) Duration of institutionalization (Wing 1962);

(2) Presence of a dementing disease (Bumke's stereotypies);

(3) Habit formation (Jasper's emphasis on repetition);

(4) Diagnosis (link between stereotypies and schizophrenia);

(5) Motivelessness.

Our approach however was not to work from a causality theory which might explain the symptom range but, like Mann and Cree, to examine groups of patients who displayed specific symptoms and search for clues as to what the causal factors might be, in particular whether the evidence for the existing causal theories fitted the facts. For this purpose we identified from the wards of a typical mental hospital groups of patients with a symptom which had precluded or defeated attempts at rehabilitation, 'recalcitrant behaviour problems'.

In collecting these groups we identified behaviour patterns which are clinically important in small numbers of patients but which we think have not been described in the literature, and we also added possible aetiological factors to the above list, namely,

(6) Previous personality;
(7) Sex differences;
(8) Differential responses to therapy;
(9) Differing natural histories;
(8 and 9 would have indirect implications as to causality.)

It must be emphasized that the patients described below are those in whom vigorous rehabilitative programmes had failed. The symptoms associated with the common reasons for long-term hospitalization, e.g. delusions, hallucinations, aggression, etc., can be tolerated in the community only if present in sufficiently mild form. A patient can have 'well encapsulated' delusions of quite bizarre type but, if under no pressure to talk about these ideas or to act upon them, such a patient is quite socially acceptable in, for example, an old people's home. Conversely, hallucinations which for example compel the patient to stand and talk back to his voices, or worse still, to shout back at them, are of a severity which precludes acceptance even in a home for the elderly mentally infirm.

At this stage, rather than simply present a random list of the recalcitrant behavioural patterns which we found, we will present groupings which represent our rough initial hypotheses regarding causality to which our training and the existing literature had led us (Table 5.1).

Table 5.1

A. Severity failures: most psychiatric symptoms if present in a sufficiently severe form preclude discharge from hospital.
B. Tension habits: screaming and banging (Pitt's 'whining'), immobilizing hesitations, rending (clothes, etc.), wandering, rocking, pelvic thrusts.
C. Protest behaviour: smearing (with dirt and faeces), negativism, temper tantrums, stiffening, anti-motivation ('asylum seekers'), self-mutilation.
D. Asocial behaviour: aggression, arson and careless smoking, oral stuffing, violence substitutes—scratching, clutching, spitting, tripping, etc. Sexually toned behaviour.
E. Eccentric behaviour (Pitt's disinhibited behaviour): collecting, hoarding and stealing, sartorial bizarreries, personal degradation.

Most of these terms are self-explanatory and will evoke familiar case pictures for anyone experienced in the management of long-stay mental hospital wards. However, a few of the terms might be amplified to avoid misunderstanding. 'Immobilizing hesitations' refer to those patients with repetitive movements such as feet shuffling which effectively prevent the achievement of concerted action. 'Stiffening' is a reaction to attempts to get a patient to co-operate with suggested actions while 'immobilizing hesitations' interfere with the patient's attempts at spontaneous actions.

Table 5.2   Hoarders and stealers

Case	Sex	Age	Duration of stay in hospital	Diagnosis	Kew cognitive map	Additional information
1	M	78	6 months	Senescence	2,0,2	Obsessional pre-morbid personality. Past history of violence and bestiality.
2	M	62	1 month	Agitated depression	0,0,0	Obsessional pre-morbid personality.
3	M	75	2 years	Personality disorder	0,1,0	Past history of major fits and indecent exposure. Wanderer.
4	M	79	3 years	Agitated depression	2,2,0	Diabetic.
5	M	65	44 years	Chronic schizophrenia	0,0,0	Obsessive compulsive pre-morbid personality.
6	M	56	39 years	Chronic schizophrenia	0,3,0	Leucotomized 1947. Past history of indecent exposure.
7	F	86	56 years	Chronic schizophrenia	—	Wanderer.
8	M	73	43 years	Chronic schizophrenia	0,1,0	—
9	F	73	3 years	Senile dementia	5,6,6	—
10	M	65	9 years	Atypical dementia	1,1,1	Spina bifida occulta.
11	M	56	13 years	Chronic schizophrenia	1,0,0	Past history of car theft. Once set fire to himself. Wanderer.
12	F	75	44 years	Chronic schizophrenia	3,4,2	No stealing.
13	F	86	47 years	Chronic schizophrenia	3,3,0	Deaf. Wanderer.
14	M	80	53 years	Chronic schizophrenia	2,1,0	Wanderer.
$\bar{x}$		72·0	25·5			
SD		9·9	22·5			

'Anti-motivation' has been equated with 'asylum seekers' and refers to those patients who are grimly determined to remain in the mental hospital and resist all attempts to entice them from it. 'Oral stuffing' is the thrusting of non-masticated food into the mouth and upper pharynx to the point of dangerous choking. 'Sartorial bizarreries' refers to a whole range of eccentric dressing from towels wrapped round the head to the rather prevalent mid-calf trouser length seen in mental hospitals. 'Personal degradation' amounts to the abandonment of the social conventions in sexual or eliminative functions.

Of these behaviours, four occurred with sufficient frequency to allow us to collect groups of cases for study. These were hoarders and stealers, oral stuffers, screamers and wanderers. The case histories of these patients were searched and the relevant findings are presented in Tables 5.2, 5.3, 5.4 and 5.5 respectively. (The Kew Cognitive Map is a scale revealing *serious* cognitive failure in memory, languages and parietal function. The number presented represents a failure score with 0 being no error and 6 being maximum error, the numbers being presented in the order of memory, language, and parietal function (McDonald 1969). It could, therefore, be regarded as an indicator of the presence of significant global or patchy dementia.)

Findings

Institutionalization may become evident in certain dependency-prone personalities earlier than in other more independent personalities, but

Table 5.3   Oral stuffers

Case	Sex	Age	Duration of stay in hospital	Diagnosis	Abnormal movements	Additional information
15	F	57	22 years	Post-encephalitic hemiplegia	Tremors of right leg and right arm	Verbal and physical aggression.
16	F	61	33 years	Chronic schizophrenia	Oral dyskinesia	Dysarthria. Verbal and physical aggression.
17	F	62	2 months	Pre-senile dementia		Receptive and expressive dysphasia.
18	F	60	2 years	Pre-senile dementia	Ataxic gait	Touches and provokes other patients.
19	F	75	52 years	Catatonic schizophrenia	Tremors of arms and legs	Verbal and physical aggression. Incomprehensible speech.
20	F	68	5 years	Endogenous depression		Verbal and physical aggression.
21	M	79	59 years	Chronic schizophrenia		Incomprehensible speech. Steals food and cigarettes.
22	M	39	10 years	Huntington's chorea	Choreiform movements	Dysarthria.
23	F	86	2 years	Paranoid schizophrenia		Senescent. Cognitive failure.
24	F	80	38 years	Catatonic schizophrenia		Mute. Physically aggressive until leucotomized in 1951.
25	F	75	38 years	Chronic schizophrenia		Now shows senile dementia. Eats faeces.
26	M	48	23 years	Chronic schizophrenia		Incomprehensible speech. Steals.
27	M	66	45 years	Chronic schizophrenia		Mutters incomprehensibly under his breath. Eats lit cigarettes and cigarette packets.
$\bar{x}$		65·8	25·3			
SD		13·4	20·4			

since we were unable to identify such types with confidence we looked at duration of stay as a force towards institutionalization. There was clearly a great difference in average duration of stay in the groups studied. While the hoarders and the stuffers had average durations of stay of 25 years, there was such a spread that it was difficult to conclude that this related to the behaviour formation. However, in the cases of screamers and of wanderers, the duration of stay was startlingly short for a mental hospital population and we feel confident that institutionalization cannot be implicated as a cause of these behaviours.

In the group of wanderers, all save one were suffering from a dementing disease and the exceptional paraphrenic showed cognitive deficit in memory and language functions consistent with her age of 88. We also obtained information about the previous personalities of these patients by interviewing a relative. Only two cases did not show evidence of high-drive restless personalities. The first was our previous exception, a senescent paraphrenic who might have been driven to restlesssness by her delusions,

Table 5.4 Screamers

Case	Sex	Age	Duration of stay in hospital	Diagnosis	Kew cognitive map	Additional information
28	M	81	4 months	Senescence	3,4,4	—
29	F	69	3 months	Depression	0,0,0	Attacked visitors. Hysterectomy.
30	F	79	40 years	Chronic schizophrenia	3,3,0	Aggressive outbursts. Hoarder. Eczema.
31	F	71	7 years	Depression	4,3,4	Oral stuffer. Pernicious anaemia.
32	F	75	3 years	Depression	0,0,0	Leucotomized. Puts fingers repeatedly into rectum.
33	M	68	20 years	Chronic schizophrenia	—	Leucotomized 1947. Haemangioblastoma removed left cerebellum 1956. Abusive to fellow patients.
34	F	92	2 years	Senescence	5,3,1	Uses Zimmer frame following fracture of left femur.
35	F	101	4 years	Senescence	5,3,1	1976 stroke and fractured femur. 1976 fractured clavicle.
36	F	84	1 year	Senescence	1,0,0	—
37	F	98	5 years	Senescence	5,5,5	Carcinoma of breast removed by operation.
38	F	91	2 years	Senescence	5,6,4	Stroke. Epilepsy of recent origin.
$\bar{x}$		82·6	7·7			
SD		11·6	12·1			

and the second was a timid lady whose restlessness subsequently reversed to an inability to walk owing to 'shuffling hesitations'. We conclude, therefore, that persistent wandering behaviour is caused by a dementing process disinhibiting an existing personality trait.

The screamers were mainly women, some of whom were severely demented and some of whom were cognitively intact. All save two showed either concurrent aggression or gave a history of significant physical illness or trauma. (There was no clinical suggestion that these patients were in pain.)

Stuffing food had no relationship to diagnosis or to duration of stay in hospital. There was, however, in all save three cases evidence of neurological pathology and/or a speech defect. If dementing disease is seen as neurological pathology then only one case was exceptional. This evidence clearly places it in quite a different category of behaviour from wandering and screaming.

Hoarding and stealing seem to fall into two groups. The chronic schizophrenics accounted for all the long-stay cases. The short-stay cases were of mixed diagnoses. Four cases had a history of law breaking, three had been obsessive–compulsive in the past, and five were wanderers. These wanderers were not dementing, unlike the patients who showed only persistent wandering behaviour. If therefore hoarding and stealing relates to previous personality traits, we can conclude that the behaviour is not released by the disinhibition of dementia. It may be that the source of this common behaviour is different in the group of chronic schizophrenics as opposed to the group of mixed diagnoses.

Table 5.5 Wanderers

Case	Sex	Age	Duration of stay in hospital	Diagnosis	Kew cognitive map	Pre-morbid personality	Additional information
39	F	80	1 year	Senile dementia	5,5,3	'Always on the go'.	Behaviour progressed to immobilizing hesitations.
40	F	79	1 year	Senile dementia	5,5,5	'Meek and inoffensive'.	
41	F	64	3 years	Presenile dementia	5,5,5	'Restless housekeeper'. 'Particularly fond of walking'.	
42	F	89	1 year	Senile dementia	—	'Could not sit still at home'.	
43	F	74	2 years	Senile dementia	—	'Always on the go. Fond of walking'.	
44	F	76	2 years	Senile dementia	—	'Nervous person. Scared of aggressive people.'	
45	F	82	2 years	Senile dementia	—	'Did not relax easily. Very active'.	
46	F	85	1 year	Senile dementia	—	'Kind and friendly' (No restless traits).	
47	F	88	2 years	Paraphrenia	3,3,2		
$\bar{x}$		79.7	1.7				
SD		7.8	0.7				

Before leaving the results of our inquiry, mention should be made of our clinical experience in this area. First, we should emphasize that it is unclear why 'severity failures' exist. There seems to be a differential response to chemotherapy—patients with apparently identical symptomatology will not all respond to the same tranquillizer or antidepressant and in some cases the whole gamut of treatments for their given diagnosis is run through without effect. They tend then to be labelled 'chronic' rather than 'yet to be successfully treated'. Wandering is a behaviour which disturbs nurses greatly—they fear for the patient's safety if he wanders unnoticed from the ward. We have found the major tranquillizers only sporadically successful in this group and where they were unsuccessful we had some success with alcohol. This was given in the form of commercial brandy, or 'Labiton' (thiamine, kola nut, alcohol and caffeine), or a 40 per cent alcohol mixture prepared in the hospital pharmacy. Alcohol was also used with varying success for the screamers and bangers and, where it was successful in the wanderers or the screamers, we found that it could be withdrawn without the recurrence of the behaviour—at least for a period of some months. Perhaps this observation supports a habituative element in the causality of these behaviours.

Mention should be made of a walking programme which gave regular exercise to the wanderers but which did not stop this behaviour.

The 'asylum seekers', those with no motivation to leave hospital, proved more amenable to treatment, albeit on a protracted time scale. We found that financial sanctions were strong motivators. If the patient refused to co-operate with the occupational therapy programme, his source of pocket money—personal allowance, O.T. reward money, relatives' contributions, etc.—was cut off by medical direction. Patients who had been presumed to suffer from damage to their personalities found the drive to start attending O.T. and were then led through a programme designed to reintroduce them to the world outside hospital, to teach them the skills necessary to survive outside hospital and to re-introduce them to the satisfactions available by leading a less circumscribed life.

'Shuffling hesitations' invites an analogy with the 'yipps'—a phenomenon well recognized in golfers where a player finds that his inhibitions against making a putting stroke become so strong that the stroke, instead of being a smooth swing, becomes a staccato movement which is sometimes so severe that no contact with the ball can be made at all. The patient with the 'yipps' similarly develops a staccato inability to perform some movement which should be smooth and easy. This is not an incoordination because the thrust or pattern of the movement is still clearly discernible while the back and forward movements make the completion of the movement inefficient or impossible. For example, the 'yipps' in walking results in tiny back and forward steps with little forward and sometimes resultant backward progression. Anxiolytics like diazepam and lorazepam have proved helpful when used in conjunction with a Zimmer frame.

'Rending' refers to clothes or fabric tearing behaviour. Our impression is that this is not as common as it was in the past, and if this is so, it may be that non-restrictive ward regimes have made this outlet less necessary. Again the behaviour has a repetitive, monotonous, persistent quality which borders on compulsion and does not bear interruption. Patient trial of each major tranquillizer in turn is necessary to find the drug which allows each specific patient to abandon this behaviour. That is to say, a given patient will respond to one tranquillizer and not to another, be it chemically similar or dissimilar.

Discussion

The groups studied were not gathered in a random manner since any chronic mental hospital population is strongly skewed already by forces such as admission and discharge practices. Therefore no conclusions can be drawn which assume that the populations are proportionately representative of their disorder. However, it has been possible to test clinically whether the actual phenomena observed fit the current presumptive theories of causality, i.e. stereotypy as a chronic symptom of schizophrenia and perhaps of organic disease, tension habit formation, or disinhibition due either to a dementing process or the socially degrading effects of institutionalization.

It was found that no single causal theory was sufficient to account for the phenomena, so a revised classification is essayed in Table 5.6 which most 'meets the appearances'.

Table 5.6   Amended classification of recalcitrant behaviour problems in the elderly chronic mental hospital population

Motivated
   By *Self Gain:* asylum seeking, stealing and hoarding.
   By *Aggression:* ? screaming and banging. ? violence substitutes.
   Before Habituation: wandering, rending.
Non-Motivated
   Due to 'illness': severity failures, shuffling hesitations.
   Due to dementing process: wandering.
Unclassified as yet
   Rocking and pelvic thrusts, smearing, negativism, temper tantrums, stiffening, self-mutilation, arson and careless smoking, sexually tarred behaviour, sartorial bizarrerie, personal degradation.

If illness did not by itself account for the symptom formation or if dementia had not been found to account for disinhibited behaviour, the symptom was placed in the motivated category. This has important implications for the potential of corrective programmes. Habituated behaviour was presumed to have had an initial self-rewarding component which led to its repetition and, therefore, was classified as motivated.

Finally, no attempt was made to classify those behaviours in which clinical evidence for classification was still lacking. It is hoped that what has been said above will stimulate the search for such evidence. In the 'aggression' category the classification is felt to be inherent in the descriptive terms used, but even this should not be assumed and must eventually be tested.

References

Anderson, H C (1971). *Newton's Geriatric Nursing*. C V Mosby, St. Louis, USA

Barton R (1966). *Institutional Neurosis*. John Wright & Sons Ltd, Bristol

Bumke, O (1924). *Textbook of Mental Diseases*. Springer, Berlin

Goffman, E (1957). Characteristics of Total Institutions. In Walter Reed Army Institute of Research, *Symposium on Preventive and Social Psychiatry*. April 15–17 Washington D.C.

Goffman, E (1961). *Asylums*. Doubleday, New York

Jasper, K (1962). *General Psychopathology* (tr. J Hoeing and M W Hamilton). Manchester University Press

McDonald, C (1969). Clinical heterogeneity in senile dementia. *British Journal of Psychiatry*, **115**, 267–71

McDonald, C (1979). How we rehabilitated 42 long-stay psychiatric patients. *Geriatric Medicine*, June 1979, 53–7

Mann, S and Cree, W (1976). 'New' long-stay psychiatric patients: a national survey of fifteen mental hospitals in England and Wales, 1972/73. *Psychological Medicine* **6**, 603–16

Mayer-Gross, W, Slater, E, Roth, M (1969). *Clinical Psychiatry* (eds E Slater and M Roth). Third edition. Baillière Tindall, London

Miller, D H (1961). Psycho-social factors in the aetiology of disturbed behaviour. *British Journal of Medical Psychology* **34**, 43–52

Nurse, J and Gleisner, J (1975). Social aspects of chronic mental illness: a review of the literature. In *Aspects of the Social Care of the Mentally Ill*. British Association of Social Workers

Pitt, B (1974). *Psychogeriatrics. An Introduction to the Psychiatry of Old Age*. Churchill Livingstone, Edinburgh and London

Robertson, E E, le Roux, A and Brown, J H (1958). The clinical differentiation of Pick's disease. *Journal of Mental Science* **104**, 1000–24

Wing, J K (1962). Institutionalism in mental hospitals. *British Journal of Social and Clinical Psychology* **1**, 38–51

Zusman, J (1966). Some Explanations of the Changing Appearance of Psychotic Patients. Antecedents of the Social Breakdown Syndrome Concept. From *Evaluation of the Effectiveness of Community Mental Health Services* (ed. E M Gruenberg). Millbank Memorial Fund, New York

Part 2 **The Neuroses**

6 Psychotherapeutic Approaches

J K W Morrice, MD, FRC Psych, DPM

Rehabilitation is a familiar concept when applied to the physically disabled or to long-stay patients in psychiatric hospitals, particularly those diagnosed as chronic psychotics. When the term is applied to so-called neurotics, however, it needs to be reviewed in the light of contemporary practice.

Rehabilitation or Treatment?

In his study of Henderson Hospital, Rapoport (1960) suggested that a clear distinction should be made between rehabilitation and treatment, at least when one is dealing with personality disorders of a sociopathic kind. This challenges the assertion of Maxwell Jones (1952) that all psychiatric treatment is rehabilitation. *Chambers's Encyclopaedia* considers rehabilitation not so much a method of treatment but rather 'a concept in treatment', an idea which appeals to the present writer. The suggestion is made therefore that, as far as neurosis is concerned, treatment and rehabilitation go hand-in-hand. Certainly they are best conceptualized and practised together. It has been said that treatment focuses on the person's shortcomings, while rehabilitation recognizes and develops his assets; but in our dealings with neurotic patients this is too simple to be true.

The particular concept in treatment offered in this chapter is the psychosocial one. The aim in this approach is to understand the individual's difficulties in terms of his relationships in the social system in which he lives, most importantly family and work-place. Treatment is not simply concerned with the relief of symptoms, but more with helping a person to change his attitude and behaviour towards the important people in his life. There is thus a demand upon the patient for active participation in a learning process, a struggle towards personal growth, social competence and personal satisfaction. Clearly rehabilitation is part and parcel of such a scheme of treatment. Moreover the concept inevitably extends beyond the individual and beyond his family to outside society. It must take account of society's norms, values and economic circumstances—the things that determine very largely what we expect from one another and how we live and work together.

At the same time it would be unwise to dismiss as irrelevant Rapoport's plea for a keener awareness of the processes, aims and techniques of what we call treatment, on the one hand, and rehabilitation on the other. As he states, 'Clearly, activities that we would conceptualize as treatment may empirically serve rehabilitation ends and vice versa. But this conceptual distinction and our arbitrary cutting points may help to sort out some of the current confusions that perplex a good many contemporary practitioners in the mental health field.' He goes on from this and seeks to identify which measures, in the therapeutic regime he was studying, served treatment aims, which served rehabilitation aims within the unit itself, and which the ultimate aims of the world outside the unit. Indeed he criticizes the unit for blurring this whole area and suggests that the therapeutic activities which serve each of these aims may sometimes be 'congruent and mutually reinforcing' and sometimes 'independent and even conflicting'.

This argument has some validity. It is true that the artificial device of a psychotherapeutic group, where the participants are encouraged to share and examine their feelings together, is unlikely to be reproduced in the world outside. And it is unlikely that a work group in an outside industrial concern will interrupt its task to consider, in a constructive and insightful way, the difficulties of relationships which are hindering its successful completion. In very few homes or factories are such opportunities presented (and more's the pity, some of us believe). Therefore such occasions, taking place in a therapeutic community, represent treatment rather than rehabilitation. It is possible then to make some distinction between the 'artificial' treatment experience and the 'real' rehabilitative one. In the latter (so the argument goes) emphasis is put on the world as it is, where time and money are primary considerations and the instructions of foremen and managers are not to be lightly questioned. The distinction is there; but it may be overemphasized to the detriment of opportunities for new learning. There is much to be said in practice for seizing learning opportunities as they occur, whether this is called treatment or rehabilitation. Certainly in the past a great deal of so-called work therapy has been much more work than therapy, and the psychotherapeutic opportunities offered, in terms of new learning for the patients concerned, have not been well understood and utilized. As a patient learns from his experiences, whether it be in individual psychotherapy or in a therapeutic milieu, he will begin to practise his new behaviour with people around him. In the treatment unit, staff and fellow-patients notice and react to the change and, it is hoped, in a way which reinforces the positive elements of the new behaviour. At home, wife and family may welcome or be startled by the patient's altered attitude or style. Change in the patient has given rise to an imbalance in the marital or family system. This, however constructive it may seem to the therapist, is likely to cause some anxiety and require marital or family counselling or therapy. It might be said that treatment has started a process of social learning and change which has moved into the arena of the outside world. Where then does treatment end and rehabilitation begin? In such circumstances they are best accepted as closely interlocked, even if sometimes recognizable as separate elements.

Staff who work with a psychodynamic approach must be constantly alert to the mismatch of methods and goals. In therapeutic groups or communities it is possible to lose sight of the individual in the mass. A patient's desires or defences demand respect, even if in psychotherapy it is sometimes necessary to frustrate or question them. But in most groups and communities there are in-built checks and balances, as well as clear occasions for the emergence of individual needs. In fact the matching of needs with reality is something a therapeutic community does relatively well. But some calculated risks may have to be taken in the case of well-entrenched personality disorders or chronic neuroses, otherwise positive change may never occur. Experienced staff should not be inhibited in accepting the rich therapeutic opportunities presented by informal and spontaneous interaction with patients, by work or encounter groups, or by contact with families, because of cautions properly uttered with other therapeutic situations in view. In a therapeutic community which has clear principles and practices, the confusions emphasized by Rapoport are often more apparent than real. Indeed any close relationship, certainly a psychotherapeutic one, involves ambiguities and conflicts. It is an acceptance of these which helps the patient to draw limits and set boundaries. Whether they are seen as treatment or rehabilitation, they represent the contradictions of real life which we must all learn to tolerate.

What is Neurosis?

These comments do emphasize nevertheless the necessity for clear aims in psychotherapy. Whatever the school or technique, whether psychoanalytical psychotherapy or behaviour therapy is being employed, the therapist needs an adequate understanding of the nature of the disturbance, and this he tries to match with his therapeutic aims. Of course this may not be an easy matter. People who seek help for psychological difficulties come with a bewildering range of symptoms and complaints. These are generally classified under the headings of neurosis, personality disorder, psychosis and borderline state. But labelling can be an unrewarding activity and most patients refuse to fit neatly into pigeon-holes. Psychiatry's state of knowledge is so uncertain in some respects that classification remains a matter of debate. At one time a clear distinction was made between 'neurotic' and 'psychotic' syndromes, but changing attitudes have blurred the boundaries. Patients' signs and symptoms fluctuate in intensity and also change in their pattern. Illnesses may become more severe in relation to critical life events, or remit for no reason that is readily apparent. Some psychiatric disabilities are long-term and intractable and others have a marked tendency to recur. It follows that a rigid system of classification has little practical point. But some sort of definition of neurosis is required. The term neurosis is now generally used to signify arrest in personality development, which is usually made evident by symptom formation. The neurotic may be thought of as interrupted in his progress towards mature and adult functioning. He is threatened in his possession of a true sense of self and has lost his ability to live without undue conflict. This definition can be reframed in terms of the psychosocial approach, which seems particularly appropriate when considering rehabilitation measures.

The Psychosocial Approach

From this viewpoint the patient is seen as an individual living in a field of conflicting forces, both inside and outside himself, amid which he strives to find a balance. The fact of his patienthood indicates his failure to do so. The behaviour he has adopted to achieve balance has proved faulty, maladaptive, caused personal distress, or has brought him into conflict with those around him. The goal of therapy and rehabilitation therefore is modification of such socially inept behaviour. This does not imply that society's norms and expectations have the force of law and cannot be challenged; nor is it suggested that life should be conflict-free. Rather one is postulating that the individual, as a system within a system, is constantly involved in conflict, change, and growth. Therapy then is not concerned with achieving homeostasis (in the narrow sense of protecting what exists) but with morphogenesis, that is, mechanisms of growth and development which allow the individual to differentiate and yet remain in good functional relationship with society.

An individual's personality and his functioning are born out of two closely interacting systems—his personal needs and the sociocultural milieu. As a person in relationship to other persons, he seeks satisfaction in his role within family, work and wider society. The community and its institutions impose constraints to ensure their own survival; and in our present society, with its turbulence and economic crises, social conflicts seem to threaten to tear the whole fabric apart. Values have changed. Although working for a living is still seen as a normal activity which determines a person's income and status, it is no longer viewed as an end in itself. Nor is it even true nowadays that work is at the centre of the striving and attention of the majority of the population. So we must ask, 'Rehabilitation for what?' There must be recognition of the transitional state of our society and how it has moved from the old ethics which set high value on individual excellence, independence and hard work. New values emphasize self-expression, mass opinion and reliance on governmental action. Psychotherapy has had to abandon its long and almost exclusive preoccupation with the individual and accept the importance of the social system and milieu, finding new techniques to meet this challenge. Hence the growth of group methods, marital and family therapy, the multidisciplinary treatment team, consultation to outside agencies, and so on.

It is clear that the patient population which presents at psychiatric hospital or clinic has also changed in recent years. More and more, psychiatrists and their colleagues are being asked to help the unhappy and the alienated, those who have failed to develop a capacity for mature relationships, and those who have lost their self-esteem and sense of purpose. They present in many ways, for example as anxiety states, depressions, parasuicides, alcoholics, marital dissatisfactions or delinquents. It proves difficult and sometimes impossible to form a working therapeutic alliance with some of these patients and certainly a large proportion of them will not comply with the traditional expectations of a psychotherapeutic approach. Whatever the conventional diagnostic label that may be attached, the broad term 'chronic neurotic' will fit many; others are enveloped in some kind of social crisis (see, for example, Morrice 1976); and still others reveal deep-seated personality problems. As a group they offer a considerable challenge and, in some ways, prove more thwarting to rehabilitative efforts than the frankly psychotic. The task therefore is not so much to reach for an ideal of full functional maturity, but rather to encourage the patient to escape from his repeated excursions down dead-ends and from his maze of false solutions and failures. In so far as this is possible, a psychosocial or 'open system' approach, such as the therapeutic community, has many advantages. It combines psychotherapy and sociotherapy within a clear framework of theory and practice and thus offers treatment and rehabilitation together to the sort of patients described. Indeed the present writer finds it difficult to imagine a rehabilitative approach to neurotic illness which ignores the conscious use of some kind of therapeutic milieu.

This approach is also very much in tune with the views and findings of investigators like Brown *et al* (1975) and Henderson *et al* (1978, 1980). They suggest that neurotic breakdown is likely to occur only where the stress of life events exceeds the support offered by the individual's social network. In no way does this deny the importance of internal conflict, the relevance of a psychodynamic image of man, or the need for individual psychotherapy and personal care. But it does emphasize how the procedures we call rehabilitation must take account of the social context in which the individual exists. The way in which the external forces around him are recognized and responded to may be crucial in returning the patient to a competent role in family, work and neighbourhood.

Therapeutic Communities

Stanton (1964) in his foreword to *Ego and Milieu*, by J and E Cumming, affirms that there is no patient 'untreated' by his environment, only patients 'treated' well or ill. This is the challenge taken up by the Cummings, whose book seeks to build a theory of how the ego functions, or fails to function, in its environment. Identifying the relevant work of previous writers on the topics of ego function and therapeutic milieux, they put forward a set of articulated concepts and practices. This work and that of other contributors in the field (for example, Clark 1964; Jones 1968, 1976; and Kreeger 1975) are surprisingly unfamiliar to young practitioners in mental health. A recent and important survey of therapeutic communities, edited by Hinshelwood and Manning (1979), considers both basic ideas and their application in the light of past experience and current needs. These writings help in the understanding of the individual in his social context. They also offer a way of intervening constructively using the model we have called psycho-social. It is important therefore to examine in this chapter some of the basic ideas of therapeutic communities, their applications and limitations, and how they may link up with newer techniques in treatment and rehabilitation.

The four fundamental themes introduced by Rapoport (1960) as characteristic of the therapeutic community style still invite general acceptance. He named them: democratization, permissiveness, reality confrontation, and communalism. The words do not slip easily from tongue or pen, nor are the concepts they represent easily implemented. But they are of central importance and, while not all of the same status, lock together in a meaningful way which leads to logical practices. These practices are the hallmarks of any therapeutic community and demonstrate its concern with social structure and function. In the main they are concerned with the creation of open and face-to-face communication, the sharing of responsibility, decision-making by consensus, and the provision of living–learning opportunities. To put these ideas into play requires the wide use of group methods of various kinds. In forming all this activity there is a need for trust and honesty, as well as an atmosphere of caring.

The theme of *democratization* suggests a movement away from rigid authority towards control which is more flexible and participatory. Hospitals and clinics cannot isolate themselves, even if they wished, from the fundamental changes being experienced in Western society. Open communication and the promotion of constructive criticism are therefore not simply elements of a therapeutic community, but acceptable (if often by intent more than in practice) by all society's institutions. In a therapeutic community the unit or ward meeting gives an opportunity for face-to-face communication and discussion. The individual becomes aware that he has some importance and responsibility as a member of the whole organization. He has a say in the daily conduct of the unit in his own treatment and that of others. Such a democratic organization is not to be confused with a shapeless structure, imbued with spurious ideas of equality, and where professional skill is devalued. Rather the aim is to locate decision-making at the level where it can effectively promote the therapeutic task. This is an example of the much misunderstood and misrepresented multidisciplinary team in action. Here the team includes patients as well as staff; and it may well have to take account of the views of spouse and family as well as of the patient himself. Without the construction of clear goals and the practice of skilful leadership, all this can become an unwieldy exercise. But, if well managed, there are few arenas better than a therapeutic community in aiding the patient to recognize his maladaptive behaviour, take responsibility for changing it, and so gain a sense of mastery and satisfaction.

The word *permissiveness* is in common use nowadays and is generally applied to a lax attitude towards deviant behaviour. This is not what the term implies in the culture of a therapeutic community, particularly when attention is given (as it should be) to linking the concept to reality confrontation. The intention is to render behaviour available for scrutiny. The difficulties which patients experience in their life together and the disturbances which result are discussed (rather than simply forbidden) in the expectation that causes can be uncovered and understood. Habitual unhelpful attitudes or repetitive behaviour of a self-defeating kind are the real-life problems which come to light. The successful working through of such problems is likely to involve the handling of transference and requires staff to be possessed of psychodynamic awareness. But this method of managing disturbed behaviour gives the opportunity for all to share new social learning.

A permissive orientation is not always easy to maintain since some patients—particularly adolescents and sociopaths—are quick to test out limits. What needs to be contrived is a nice balance between the needs of the individual and the needs of the total group. At times staff authority may require clear expression. Moreover, if the unit contains a wide range of patients, some of whom are disturbed and disturbing, an equally wide range of treatment techniques may have to be made available, including drug therapy and individual psychotherapy. But, even so, the group remains the point of reference, the main arena for interaction, and the enduring source of support.

As patients interact with one another in psychotherapy or activity groups, they reveal patterns of behaviour which are characteristic of them. Some such patterns may be damaging to self or others, as already noted above. The theme of *reality-confrontation* comes into play in ensuring that the deviant conduct is reflected back to the patient so that he may modify it. Experience shows that confrontation and interpretation of this kind is usually accepted more readily from peer group rather than from staff. But at times the ego-strength of the group is low and staff have to accept the task of confrontation and boundary-keeping. The use of video-tape, which may capture such behaviour in a group setting, is a valuable (if sometimes time-consuming) technique. The tape, when played back, adds immediacy and force to comment and interpretation. The method may be used not only in small groups but also in marital and family therapy. In this fashion, as Hogan (1972) has discussed, the person concerned develops a more accurate self-image. He is encouraged to compare his inner experience with outer behaviour, as seen by his own eyes. This may lead him to recognize and redress the discrepancy between what he feels and how he thinks he is behaving, on the one hand, and the reaction of those around him, on the other.

The theme of *communalism* serves to underscore the sharing nature of the enterprise. This is encouraged by a lowering of status barriers and an avoidance of ceremony. For example, nurses do not wear uniforms, first names are generally used by all, and staff and patients share facilities and functions to some extent at least. This may be done in a contrived and gimmicky fashion; but it may be used, equally well, as a genuine way of examining and changing outdated and inhibiting views of authority figures. It also helps to overcome the fear of being physically and emotionally close to others and in dealing with special phobias and taboos.

In the setting of the therapeutic community certain techniques of treatment deserve identification. Clearly the system depends a great deal on group methods of one kind or another, but this does not mean the exclusion of other methods when they are appropriate, for example, individual psychotherapy, behaviour therapy or drug therapy. In addition activity methods such as sociodrama, encounter and work therapy are particularly valuable in bringing to light the problems of patients who are reluctant to talk about them.

To illustrate how such methods are brought together in the treatment and rehabilitation of long-standing neurotics, the practice of the Unit which is run on these lines in the Ross Clinic, Aberdeen, will be cited. Obviously local conditions determine very largely what is possible. Besides that, the staff of the Ross Clinic Unit are well aware of how performance so often fails to live up to expectation. Nevertheless, by describing the routine of this particular therapeutic community, it is hoped to give a clearer picture of aims and methods.

The Unit consists of a day hospital which can accommodate around 35 patients, a ward of 19 in-patient beds, and out-patient facilities. Since Unit Staff participate in the whole catchment area psychiatric service, they take part in emergency and consultation services. They also have access to the hospital's occupational therapy and industrial therapy departments, as well as a sheltered workshop (Unicorn Enterprises) sited in the town. Although it has altered in size and composition over the twelve years of its life, the Unit has maintained its basic aims and style. They may be summarized as follows:

(1) To treat on a day basis patients who would otherwise require in-patient admission or very frequent out-patient attendance. Day care, it is thought, is less regressive than in-patient care, keeps the individual in close touch with family and community, and so obviates some rehabilitation problems.

(2) The therapeutic community style means, for example, that patients are asked to share responsibility for their own treatment processes; and all staff members, according to their abilities, are given active therapy roles within the framework of a multidisciplinary team.

(3) The involvement of family members is recognized as important, both in the social crisis which often precipitates the patient into care, and also in the treatment and rehabilitation process. For this reason, marital and family therapy are given high priority.

(4) Liaison with caring agencies in the outside community is fostered as far as possible, for example, General Practitioners, Health Visitors, Social Workers, Disablement Resettlement Officers, Marriage Guidance Counsellors, employers, clergy and schoolmasters.

All patients who come to the Unit are assessed for participation in the psychotherapeutic programme. Since it is a wide range of patients that presents, some are judged unsuitable for an intensive psychotherapeutic approach and may be given more time in activity groups or less demanding talking groups. The others follow a daily routine which may include large and small group experiences, a work group, a regular encounter group, and other activities that might be called occupational and recreational therapy.

Case Reports

Jim first presented ten years ago, aged 51, with complaints of depression, backache and dyspepsia. He had become bad-tempered with his wife and had just lost his job through a quarrel at work. The referring GP described him as presenting 'a pathetic picture' and gave a history of recurrent episodes of anxiety and depression starting at the time he was invalided from the Forces because of 'nerves'. Over the years he had been prescribed many different sedatives and tranquillizers. Jim informed us that he was finding it impossible to work because of his agitation and he felt his marriage and family life were suffering. Arrangements were made for him to attend the day hospital and marital therapy was also recommended. He attended for only ten days, maintained a highly defended attitude and, while demonstrating feelings of inferiority and anger, refused to discuss them. He left to take up his trade as bricklayer with a new employer.

Six weeks later he was referred again by his GP with similar symptoms and the suggestion that the patient had benefited so much from his previous attendance at the day hospital that he wished to come back! Jim had lost his job once more and expressed the view that he 'just can't cope'. On this occasion he was able to join in treatment. He gave an account of his war experiences, his difficulties with wife and children, and his problems at work. However, he had a repeating tendency, in the face of minor stress at home or in the groups, to escape from constructive action into tears and self-pity. His wife expressed great reluctance to attend for marital therapy. Jim, for his part, seemed willing to settle down in the day hospital as a way of life and leave responsibility to others. In regular meetings that included the DRO he showed no desire to plan ahead. His treatment routine was therefore altered. While continuing to attend group therapy in the mornings, he also started work at the hospital car-wash and spent each afternoon there.

This regime brought his relationship difficulties more into the open and it proved possible to understand them and help him to 'work through' at least some of them. For example, he told in great detail and with considerable emotion, how he broke down under the stress of combat while serving in the Second World War. He was accused of cowardice by his NCO and, when he reported sick, of malingering by the Medical Officer. He was finally discharged from the army with the label of psychoneurosis. He felt guilty and ashamed; but he also recognized feelings of resentment and anger at being misunderstood, misrepresented and unaided. In fact, such feelings were echoes from previous experiences in his family of origin and were reverberating also with current feelings regarding his wife and daughters, who did not show him the respect and affection he craved. His conflicts also showed up at the car-wash in relation to his workmates and to authority figures. He was all too ready to hear criticism or rejection and tended to explode into tears or tempers.

He made some definite improvement at this time and this derived from his willingness to make connections between his feelings, on the one hand, and his symptoms and behaviour on the other. He also accepted the relevance of past experience being projected into present relationships. His therapeutic relationships in the Unit allowed him to deal more constructively with the anger he found so dangerous in himself. He gained self-confidence and became more cheerful and assertive. Things improved at home. A meeting of the whole family took place with some consequent betterment of general communications, but no formal marital or family therapy was possible.

Five months after his referral Jim was able to find suitable employment which he has held ever since. He still reacts to minor crises by becoming anxious and depressed, but he is able to deal with most of these occurrences himself. Only occasionally do I see him individually as an out-patient, at long intervals, and one or two visits are enough to reassure him.

Two further cases are briefly described to illustrate other aspects of the therapeutic regime.

Max was a young man of 22 who was referred by a psychiatric colleague. He had been under treatment for depression for nearly two years with little response. Since his early teens Max had felt shy and ill-at-ease with people. He entered University, but shut himself in his room, avoided company, and missed many of his classes. He failed his examinations and became severely depressed and caught up in ruminations. He agreed to attend the day hospital and, not unexpectedly, found group meetings very anxiety-provoking. He revealed a particular fear of being touched in encounter groups. However he was motivated enough to attend the weekly swimming-group in order to learn how to swim. There he allowed himself to be supported in the water by fellow-patients and members of staff. This marked a new departure. He became available both in therapy and during informal social occasions. At this time he made his first relationship with a girl and, although some symptoms remained, he was able to leave treatment and return to University.

The third case is that of Bill, an American oilman of 40, who became bored and depressed between jobs and ran up a bill of £2000 in two weeks at a local hotel. A large proportion of this sum was spent on whisky. Always a heavy drinker, he had increased his intake over the past year following the collapse of his marriage. He was earning a high salary as an oilman, but finding no satisfaction in life. He was admitted as an in-patient for detoxification and subsequently attended the psychotherapeutic programme. It became apparent that he was suffering from a long-standing personality disorder. He had endured a deprived and unhappy childhood, being brought up apart from his parents. All his life he had found it difficult to communicate with people, especially the opposite sex. His marriage had never been a success. There were no children and he was without close relatives. He welcomed 'the family' of the Unit, but kept his relationships at a safe and superficial level. He appeared anxious to please and be liked. The death of a fellow-patient upset him greatly but, at first, he denied his feelings. This resulted in an angry exchange with the senior therapist in the large group to whom he had always shown an exaggerated respect. This seemed to breach a defence and he became much more open and available for therapeutic relationships. He experienced a sort of re-parenting. He also became involved with a number of young female patients in the Unit and began to handle such relationships more comfortably. During the two months he was under treatment he abstained from alcohol altogether and took his discharge to return to the oil industry.

Framework for Therapy

These three cases illustrate the principles and practices of the Unit and, in particular, our belief that psychotherapy and sociotherapy may be combined with advantage. Indeed, like treatment and rehabilitation, the two approaches interlock and one facilitates the other. If psychotherapy is concerned with the modification of behaviour by way of *intra*personal processes, then sociotherapy does so by *inter*personal processes. Combining the two in a dynamic fashion is what the psychosocial approach is all about. The therapeutic community offers a suitable framework within which individuals can experiment with behaviour and relationships and try out new roles.

Bennett (1977), discussing the rehabilitation of the mentally ill, emphasizes the concept of role and how an individual's role performance may be upset in different ways by psychiatric disorder. He also points out how secondary disabilities occur in the mentally ill caused by social inactivity, absence of responsibility and increasing dependence on others. 'It is important to remember', he says, 'that an environment which demands too little of the patient will handicap him as much as one which expects too much.' Awareness of this has led psychiatrists in the past twenty years to attend more closely to the milieux in which long-stay patients are treated. There has been a growth in industrial therapy, sheltered workshops, remedial education, social skills training and placements in hostels and group homes. This has been particularly the case in the rehabilitation of chronic schizophrenics. But the patient diagnosed as suffering from neurosis or personality disorder is still often given hospital treatment which enhances rather than challenges his dependency and his avoidance of responsibility. The very fact of hospital admission tends to encourage a regressive attitude. Doctors and nurses are quick to accept tasks which would be better retained by the patient and his family. The advantages of a day hospital setting in keeping the patient's home contacts alive are still not fully appreciated, and in Britain we admit too readily to in-patient care. An insightful appreciation of the use of milieu and group therapy is also often lacking or the methods are openly disparaged. Yet the case-histories cited indicate how the culture of a unit, and an event or new relationship in it, may be therapeutically advantageous, even critical, if the signifiance of the experience is recognized and the opportunity used.

Yalom (1975) has noted how social learning operates in all therapy groups, 'although the nature of the skills taught and explicitness of the process varies greatly depending upon the type of group therapy'. When resources allow, it is of benefit to organize within the same unit a small range of groups with rather different aims and expectations. It must be confessed, however, that it is sometimes difficult to assess patients quickly and place them in the group which is appropriate to their needs and abilities. A group may set as its explicit goal the development of social skills. Recourse may be had to role-playing or sociodrama—sometimes using video play-back to aid patients in their approach to prospective employers or, for example, to help an adolescent gain confidence in inviting a girl on a date. Another group may set out to engage in intensive psychotherapy, with emphasis on the unravelling of memories, conflicts and resistances, attention being given to defence mechanisms and interpretation of transference. But it is in the nature of groups that here too important social learning occurs as frequent feedback gives patients information about themselves and their impact on others.

For some isolated individuals the group is their first real experience of intimate relationships, and the support they feel may allow and help them to see themselves in its reflecting mirror. For patients who gain experience of a group over time there may accrue learning of a less obvious kind, but important enough to be called personality change. They may become more aware of themselves and of others. They are more sensitive and helpful, less prone to rush to judgement, and more likely to resolve conflict in a co-operative and constructive way. The hope is that such a change is carried over to family and outside society.

Yalom (1975) has also sought to identify the curative factors, so-called, which operate in group therapy. He names twelve such factors and discusses them in considerable detail. Here they need be mentioned but briefly. He labels them: interpersonal input, catharsis, cohesiveness, self-understanding, interpersonal output, existential factors, universality, instillation of hope, altruism, family re-enactment, identification, and guidance. These factors tend to group themselves into two broad categories, one of which might be called supportive, and the other confronting. Here again are two linking concepts. Patients in groups need to feel supported and understood in order to face the risk of new experience and learning.

How far each of these twelve factors comes into play depends on a number of variables, for example, the goal of the group, its composition, the style and skill of the therapist, and how long it has been in existence. It is important to strike a balance between the reassurance provided by supportive factors and the anxiety generated by new learning. As far as possible the therapists must consider this in each group and for each patient. It is often suggested that for short-term patients it is supportive factors only that come into play and help in the relief of symptoms; and only longer-stay patients experience, because they alone will tolerate, mechanisms like reality-confrontation, modelling, and family re-enactment, which bring new learning. This may well be true of out-patient groups meeting weekly. But, in the daily interactions of a therapeutic community, patients may show rapid progress, at least those who are well motivated. So it is that corrective emotional experiences and the exploration of new behaviour possibilities need not wait the passage of months. It is a fact, however, that some patients find change very difficult and a proportion are likely to be unresponsive to any psychotherapeutic approach. Other patients, being poor verbalizers, find formal talking groups quite threatening, but may be able to express themselves in activities which can then be reviewed with some hope of social learning and insight.

The theme of social learning by way of interpersonal relationships has been explored by Cox (1973). He states, 'An individual develops his own sense of identity in sequential interpersonal interactions which begin at the moment of birth.' And further, 'If a group is the milieu in which the original defining process takes place, then, *ipso facto*, the group will also be the milieu in which redefinitions occur.' In taking this stance neither Cox, nor indeed the present writer, is supporting an exclusively determinist view of behaviour, nor denying the importance of intrapsychic phenomena. Rather the suggestion is being made that an interactionist perspective is useful in understanding and treating neurotic behaviour and personality disorder. In the assessment of such patients, therefore, one may have in mind such questions as, 'What style of behaviour has this individual adopted and why?' or 'How has he failed in his social roles, i.e. his capacity to live and work with others?' In the Ross Clinic Unit, we are accustomed to think in terms of psychosocial diagnosis and treatment prescription when assessing new patients (Morrice 1974). This routine encourages staff to identify the goals of treatment and rehabilitation in terms of the patient's role-relationships and to recognize success and failure by the same tokens. Although change of this sort is notoriously difficult to measure, a group of patients and staff experience how an individual member alters in his self-esteem, his understanding and self-identity, through group processes.

Group therapy brings factors into play which encourage a patient to experience what Malan (1979) has called the 'triangles of insight'. These two triangles represent the aims of most dynamic psychotherapy in reaching beyond defence and anxiety to hidden feelings, which are to be seen as having past origins but present effects. A patient is impelled towards experiencing the here-and-now in terms of the there-and-then, and vice versa. So, as a member of a group, all of whom are sharing something of the same experience, a patient's perceptions become less fixed and positive change is reinforced. With group support, the individual should be able to explore what he is and what he is not, in a process of redefinition. Support and new learning thus go hand-in-hand. As Thompson and Kahn (1970) have said, 'The very factors that support and sustain the individual member support and sustain him in order to expose him to increasing stress and pain. As his endurance increases, so he is given more to endure.' It is possible then, with the skilful and diligent application of such methods, to alter behaviour and personality structure.

As already hinted, the patient's family do not always welcome the change in him, no matter how positive it may appear to staff. Group therapy tends to encourage the growth of ego strength. The individual becomes more aware of his own needs and his own value. The husband who has been unduly tolerant may begin to stand up for himself, to his wife's dismay. For such reasons, it is wise to involve spouse and other significant family members from the beginning of treatment. If the marriage or family is conceptualized as a social system, this helps to initiate and maintain the process of constructive change.

The same approach should be possible, at least theoretically, in terms of the patient's work-group. Only occasionally, in this writer's experience, does this occur and it proves possible to have a full discussion with employer and colleagues about an individual's return to factory, office or department. On the other hand, some employers and personnel officers are extremely sympathetic and concerned to facilitate the return of an employee who has suffered a breakdown. Trade unions appear largely uninterested in such matters, in what seems to be their exclusive concern with material benefits.

Over the years, the attitude of Employment Rehabilitation Centres has also been disappointing. Their focus on technical skills seems often to blind them to the difficulties and special problems of the mentally ill. However competent a tradesman a patient may become, he has to be able to get along with his fellow-workers and conform to the expectations of his employers in terms of time-keeping and speed of production. A sheltered workshop or industrial rehabilitation unit like Unicorn Enterprises, which is run by NHS staff under the auspices of Grampian Health Board, is able to attend to such aspects of rehabilitation. The individual's attendance record, type of task, hours of work, productivity, social relationships and special problems are all kept in view. Levels of payment are dependent on assessment of each person's performance. Moreover, an attempt is made to place patients in suitable outside employment when the rehabilitation period is complete.

As Wansbrough and Cooper (1980) point out, working for a living is a basic activity and determines a person's income, status, self-esteem and friendship patterns. Yet these same authors ask the provocative question, 'Why work?' They comment that job satisfaction varies with occupation and social class. They quote research to show that some 80 per cent of mathematicians, lawyers and journalists would choose the same work again, compared to under 22 per cent of unskilled car and steel workers. It is evident that many working-class patients do not revel in their labour and that the sick-role offers them a way of avoiding monotonous and unsatisfying tasks. Many people accept work as simply a means of providing themselves with goods, services and leisure opportunities. For the mentally ill, work carries all the same implications. But, in addition, rehabilitation has to take account of the less positive attributes of the Welfare State, which may tend to sap individual initiative and effort. Difficulties are also provided by periods of national economic stress and high levels of unemployment. At the same time it is possible to overemphasize the work ethic and neglect education for the constructive use of leisure. Social clubs run by experienced mental health workers may encourage the isolated discharged patient to find friends, recreational pursuits and more enjoyment in life.

'The ability to hold a job, have a family, keep out of trouble with the law, and enjoy the usual opportunities for pleasure'—this is the definition of mental health offered by Baroness Wootton (1959). As a straightforward goal for psychotherapy and rehabilitation it still has much to recommend it. The methods described in this chapter are one way of helping patients towards that objective.

References

Bennett, D H (1977). The Mentally Ill. In: *Rehabilitation Today* (ed. S Mattingly). Update Publications, London

Brown, G W, Bhrolchain, M N and Harris, T (1975). Social class and psychiatric disturbance among women in an urban population. *Sociology* **9,** 225

Clark, D H (1964). *Administrative Therapy.* Tavistock, London

Cox, M (1973). Group psychotherapy as a redefining process. *International Journal of Group Psychotherapy* **23,** 465

Henderson, S, Duncan-Jones, P, McAuley, H and Ritchie, K (1978). The patient's primary group. *British Journal of Psychiatry* **132,** 74

Henderson, S, Byrne, D G, Duncan-Jones, P, Scott, R and Adcock, S (1980). Social relationships, adversity and neurosis. *British Journal of Psychiatry* **136,** 574

Hinshelwood, R D and Manning, N (1979) (eds). *Therapeutic Communities: Reflections and Progress.* Routledge & Kegal Paul, London

Hogan, P (1972). The Use of Videotape Playback as a Technique in Psychotherapy. In: *Innovations in Psychotherapy* (eds. Goldman and Milman). Charles C Thomas, Springfield, Illinois

Jones, M S (1952). *Rehabilitation in Psychiatry.* WHO/Ment/30

Jones, M S (1968). *Beyond the Therapeutic Community.* Yale University Press, London

Jones, M S (1976). *Maturation of the Therapeutic Community.* Behavioural Publications Inc, New York

Kreeger, L (1975) (ed.). *The Large Group.* Constable, London

Malan, D H (1979). *Individual Psychotherapy and the Science of Psychodynamics.* Butterworths, London

Morrice, J K W (1973). A day hospital's function in a mental health service. *British Journal of Psychiatry* **122,** 307

Morrice, J K W (1974). Life crisis, social diagnosis, and social therapy. *British Journal of Psychiatry* **125,** 411

Morrice, J K W (1976). *Crisis Intervention: Studies in Community Care.* Pergamon Press, Oxford

Rapoport, R N (1960). *Community as Doctor.* Tavistock, London

Stanton, A H (1964). In: *Ego and Milieu* (by J and E Cumming). Tavistock, London

Thompson, S and Kahn, J H (1970). *The Group Process as a Helping Technique.* Pergamon Press, Oxford

Wansbrough, N and Cooper, P (1980). *Open Employment after Mental Illness.* Tavistock, London

Wootton, B (1959). *Social Pathology and the Concept of Mental Health.* Allen and Unwin, London

Yalom, I D (1975). *The Theory and Practice of Group Psychotherapy.* Basic Books, New York

7 Drug Treatment in Chronic Neurosis

Peter Tyrer, MD, MRCP, FRC Psych
Jennifer Hughes, BM, BCh, BSc, MRCP, MRC Psych

Neuroses are commonly felt to be minor disorders and psychoses major ones, and similarly neuroses are often felt to be acute whereas psychoses are said to be chronic. Rehabilitation necessarily is associated with chronic disorders and so it might be thought that rehabilitation of neuroses would be a comparatively small subject. This is far from being the case, as chronic neurosis abounds although it frequently remains untreated. The division between neuroses and psychoses is also inappropriate in many cases. Many authorities explicitly (Foulds 1976) or implicitly (Wing *et al* 1974) support a hierarchical model of psychiatric illness in which the higher levels automatically take precedence over lower ones. Thus major psychoses are regarded as having many of the symptoms of minor illnesses but the delusions and hallucinations of the major psychiatric disorder dominate the clinical description. Whether or not one believes this model, there is no doubt that patients with serious psychiatric disorder pass through a phase during their rehabilitation in which their only symptons are those of the neuroses. Drug treatment is often given during these phases and because of the chronic nature of these disorders is likely to be given long-term.

Although psychopharmacology has made great advances in the last thirty years its main thrust has been in the field of acute therapy. More recently maintenance therapy of the affective psychoses and schizophrenia has been studied in some depth but there is a surprising lack of information about maintenance therapy in neurotic disorders. There are dangers in resorting to anecdotes in describing the subject but as much as possible in this chapter we shall confine ourselves to evidence from published studies. We shall follow the subdivision of neurotic disorders described in the International Classification of Diseases (WHO 1979) in this account as this is probably the best known.

Anxiety Neurosis

Although there are many effective pharmacological treatments for the immediate relief of anxiety there are no drugs that can be administered with equanimity on a long-term basis. In rehabilitation practice long-term prescription is more likely to be required and particular care is needed over the choice of drug.

Barbiturates

Barbiturates have no place in the drug treatment of anxiety and their use can only be defended in the treatment of epilepsy and anaesthesia. Unfortunately there is a sizeable minority of patients who were first prescribed barbiturates as hypnotics in the years before there were other effective drugs available and many of these patients have become dependent on their barbiturates. It was only in the recent past that most patients requiring a hypnotic drug in hospital were prescribed a barbiturate as a matter of course. These patients in psychiatric hospitals who have progressed towards rehabilitation have frequently continued their barbiturate because of their protestations that no other drug helps them to sleep. This statement is not necessarily true, as when these patients are withdrawn from their barbiturates they show mild withdrawal reactions, including insomnia. The new substitute drug is unfairly criticized for causing these reactions and is not given a fair trial. With such patients it is always better to replace gradually the barbiturate with a safer drug such as a benzodiazepine. A good formula is to replace every 100 mg of butobarbitone (or equivalent barbiturate) with 5 mg of diazepam (or equivalent benzodiazepine) and for the change to be made over a period of several weeks to keep withdrawal symptoms to the minimum (Anon. 1976).

Benzodiazepines

The benzodiazepines have gradually replaced the barbiturates as the drug treatment of choice in anxiety and for the last ten years their use has become so widespread that they have become top of the league of prescribed drugs (Skegg *et al* 1977). There are many reasons why they are preferred to the barbiturates but in summary they are safer, more effective and more selective. Unlike the barbiturates they act specifically on the functional systems of the brain concerned with anxiety whereas barbiturates are generalized cerebral depressant drugs. The recent discovery of benzodiazepine receptors in the central nervous system (Möuler and Okada 1977) confirms this selective action. In addition to their anxiety-reducing effects benzodiazepines have other properties which may assist in the treatment of anxiety. These include anti-aggressive, muscle-relaxant and anti-convulsant properties. This has led to benzodiazepines being used in the treatment of spasticity, epilepsy, other disorders in which muscle spasm is prominent and tetanus. They have also become important in anaesthesia, both for premedication and induction of sleep, when intravenous injections are used.

The benzodiazepines are incredibly safe and to date there are no instances recorded in which an overdose of a benzodiazepine alone has been fatal. However, when taken with other cerebral depressant drugs (including alcohol) an overdose can be fatal. The main reason for this excellent safety record is the lack of serious depressive effect on the heart and the cardiorespiratory centres. Unfortunately the excellent safety record of the benzodiazepines has perhaps led to cavalier prescribing and a massive increase in their prescription that has caused widespread concern (Trethowan 1975). There are several possible reasons for this increase in prescribing (Leading article *Lancet* 1978) and it would be wrong to jump to conclusions that medical irresponsibility is the prime cause.

Long-term prescription of benzodiazepines is one factor that tends to increase the total number of prescriptions. If a sizeable proportion of all new patients receiving benzodiazepines continued to take them chronically then the total number of prescriptions is bound to rise by a 'ratchet effect' even if the number of new patients receiving a benzodiazepine does not increase. There is some evidence that chronic benzodiazepine prescription is the norm with some groups of patients (Balter and Levine 1969; Tyrer 1978).

There is some argument over the risk of pharmacological dependence developing in patients taking benzodiazepines for long periods. Considering the extent of benzodiazepine prescription there are relatively few reports of classical pharmacological dependence (Marks 1978). In such cases drug-seeking behaviour, tolerance and a dramatic increase in dosage are associated with a severe abstinence syndrome on withdrawal, in which paranoid symptoms, hallucinations and confusion can occur (Fruensgaard 1976; Preskorn and Denner 1977). Most patients on benzodiazepines are in no danger of falling into this category but are more likely to be taking benzodiazepines in low dosage over a long period. Although the risk of classical pharmacological dependence in this group is so low as to be infinitesimal (Marks 1978), there is increasing evidence that a definite withdrawal syndrome follows the stopping of benzodiazepines in a substantial minority of such patients. The symptoms include perceptual distortion of movement, hypersensitivity to noise, touch and smell, and severe mood disturbance amounting to dysphoria, as well as typical somatic and psychological symptoms of anxiety (Pevnick *et al* 1978; Winokur *et al* 1980; Tyrer *et al* 1981; Lader 1981). Withdrawal symptoms occur in a substantial minority of patients taking benzodiazepines for six months or longer, possibly as high as a third (Tyrer *et al* 1981). A similar phenomenon after withdrawal of benzodiazepine hypnotics has been termed 'rebound insomnia' (Kales *et al* 1978). As withdrawal symptoms are immediately relieved by taking the benzodiazepine again it is not surprising that patients continue taking their drugs regularly and regard the initial symptoms they get if they stop therapy as evidence of recrudescence of their original anxiety.

A large number of patients attending the rehabilitation unit of psychiatric hospitals are taking benzodiazepines regularly, either as hypnotics or anti-anxiety drugs. Many will have had their benzodiazepines prescribed by general practitioners rather than psychiatrists as indeed by far the greatest number of benzodiazepines are given in primary care. Often the original reason for prescribing the benzodiazepine disappeared several years ago and patients continued receiving the drug in the absence of clear instructions to the contrary. It has been shown in those general practices in which repeat prescribing is carried out without any contact between doctor and patient a much larger proportion of patients continue drugs for long periods than in other practices where repeat prescribing is closely monitored (Dennis 1979).

At some point during rehabilitation these patients will have lost all or most of their anxious symptoms and withdrawal can then be considered. It is probably unwise to stop the drugs abruptly; although some patients have no ill-effects there is evidence that a rapid fall in plasma benzodiazepine levels is more likely to lead to withdrawal symptoms (Tyrer *et al* 1981). For the same reason it is also preferable to change patients on short-acting benzodiazepines, such as lorazepam, to a long-acting benzodiazepine such as diazepam (Table 7.1) before effecting withdrawal. The long-acting

Table 7.1 Short-acting and long-acting benzodiazepines

Short-acting	Long-acting
triazolam	chlordiazepoxide
lorazepam	diazepam
temazepam	flurazepam
oxazepam	chlorazepate
clobazam	ketazolam
	medazepam
	nitrazepam

All benzodiazepines (or their active metabolites) with an elimination half-life of 24 hours or more are included in the long-acting group.

benzodiazepines (or their metabolites) have elimination half-lives of 24 hours to several days and their slow excretion accounts for a delay of between 3 and 5 days in the onset of withdrawal symptoms when these drugs are stopped. The beta-adrenoceptor blocking drug, propranolol, or a similar beta-blocking drug such as oxprenolol, may also be helpful in attenuating some of the withdrawal symptoms after stopping benzodiazepines (Tyrer *et al* 1981). Only a small dose (e.g. 40–80 mg/day of propranolol) is necessary and can be stopped without difficulty after the withdrawal period is over. A suggested procedure to effect withdrawal of benzodiazepines while minimizing the risk of adverse effects is illustrated (Figure 7.1).

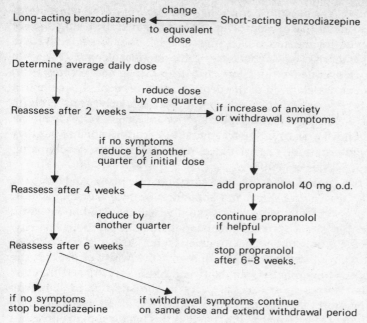

Figure 7.1 A scheme for withdrawal of benzodiazepines

When benzodiazepines have been withdrawn completely a small proportion of patients will still come back repeatedly and ask for more. It would be too puritanical to deprive all of these from further prescriptions of benzodiazepines, particularly if alcohol or other potentially more dangerous drugs are being taken in their place. If patients are represcribed benzodiazepines it is best to adopt a flexible dosage regime up to an agreed maximum (seldom more than 15 mg diazepam daily or equivalent) and to take the drug intermittently with periods of abstinence. This is also a valuable strategy when initially prescribing benzodiazepines in patients who have not yet become dependent. This procedure is likely, but not necessarily certain, to prevent dependence from developing.

Other Anti-anxiety Drugs and Hypnotics

But for the problem of dependence there would be no real rivals to the benzodiazepines as anti-anxiety drugs. In patients who have been seriously dependent on benzodiazepines and those who have been dependent on other drugs (including alcohol) in the past it may be considered too risky to prescribe benzodiazepines. Unfortunately most of the other drugs available carry some risk of dependence and it is very difficult to decide on the relative order of risk for an individual drug. The propanediol group of

drugs used to be very popular before the introduction of the benzodiazepines but only one of these, meprobamate, is still generally used. It is not
really a substitute for the benzodiazepines as it is rather less effective and
also carries some risk of dependence. Chlormethiazole also carries a
definite risk of dependence (Hession *et al* 1979; Gregg and Akhter 1979)
but as it has been widely used in the detoxification of alcoholic patients it
has perhaps been exposed to a population that is much more likely to
develop drug dependence. The chloral group of drugs (e.g. dichloral-
phenzone) still have a place in the treatment of chronic insomnia but they
are best given intermittently as tolerance to their effects can develop after
chronic therapy (Kales *et al* 1970).

There are two groups of drugs that carry no risk of dependence, the
neuroleptic (antipsychotic) drugs and beta-adrenoceptor blocking agents.
Neuroleptic drugs in low dosage are mildly sedative and it is worth
stressing that this effect is quite independent of antipsychotic activity,
which in any case is only obtained with much higher dosage. Trials of these
drugs against benzodiazepines suggest that any superiority of benzodiazepines in efficacy is marginal (Greenblatt and Shader 1974) and they are
acceptable alternatives to benzodiazepines in the short term. Unfortunately after long-term therapy they carry some risk, albeit a small one, of
tardive dyskinesia (Marsden *et al* 1981) and as this handicapping iatrogenic
syndrome is so difficult to treat everything possible should be done to avoid
creating it. It is therefore unwise to continue low doses of neuroleptic drugs
regularly for a long period. For those who have recurrent episodes of
anxiety, and this can be quite common in patients undergoing rehabilitation when exposed to new life stresses, a short course of a neuroleptic drug
(e.g. trifluoperazine 1 mg b.d.) may be the most appropriate way of
treating the anxiety. The related thioxanthene antipsychotic drug, flupenthixol, in doses of 1–2 mg daily may also be of value in treating coexisting
depressive as well as anxiety symptoms (Young *et al* 1976) and has
energizing properties that may be helpful in apathetic patients.

Beta-adrenoceptor blocking drugs are effective in relieving a small
proportion of patients with anxiety neuroses who have predominant
somatic anxiety (Tyrer and Lader 1974). Such patients often complain of
both anxious and hypochondriacal symptoms. Many of them pass through
the hands of specialists in other medical disciplines before being seen by
psychiatrists and in dynamic terms they tend to repress and deny the
psychological aspects of their condition. Beta-adrenoceptor blocking drugs
attenuate somatic and autonomic symptoms that result from stimulation of
beta-receptors, particularly in heart and skeletal muscle. Thus symptoms
such as awareness of the heart beating fast, palpitations, flushing and
tremor are mainly relieved. It has been shown that beta-blockade improves
the performance of anxious musicians (James *et al* 1977) and this is likely to
be due to reduction of tremor. The mechanism of this reduction in anxiety
is almost certainly peripheral rather than central (Lader and Tyrer 1972;

Tyrer 1976a) and in such patients a reduction in physical symptoms is regarded as equivalent to alleviation of anxiety (Tyrer 1973). Only a low dose of beta-adrenoceptor blocking drug is needed (e.g. propranolol 40–120 mg daily) and if necessary this can be continued long-term.

Hysteria

There is no place for drug treatment in the management of hysteria except possibly through the judicious use of placebos.

Phobic Anxiety

Phobic anxiety is a common problem in patients undergoing rehabilitation. Agoraphobia and social phobia are particularly handicapping as they may lead to complete isolation from society for many years. The pathway towards reintegration is a difficult one and pharmacological assistance is often necessary. Long-term treatment lasting several years often turns out to be needed if not planned for at the outset. Pharmacological treatment therefore needs to be not only effective in the short-term but capable of maintaining improvement and having no adverse sequelae in chronic dosage.

The benzodiazepines have already been discussed. They are effective in phobic anxiety but the case for intermittent therapy is much stronger than in anxiety states. Phobic anxiety means situational anxiety, which clearly demarcates calm situations from anxious ones. It is therefore inappropriate to take benzodiazepines regularly with the aim of producing constant anti-anxiety effects. It is preferable to take the benzodiazepine intermittently and for its ingestion to be timed in relationship to the feared situations. There is some argument over exactly when the timing of this should be. Some work suggests that the benzodiazepine should be taken about four hours before phobic exposure so that its main effect is on anticipatory anxiety (Marks *et al* 1972) but others have failed to replicate this (Hafner and Marks 1976). It is reasonable for patients to experiment in the timing of their dosage to determine which is best for the individual. Because shortlived anxiety relief is usually necessary there are advantages in choosing a short-acting benzodiazepine for relief of phobias. These benzodiazepines have a duration of action of a few hours and cumulation does not occur to any significant degree after repeated dosage in young healthy individuals.

Beta-adrenoceptor blocking drugs might be expected to be of value in phobic disorders but with the exception of common acute phobias such as public speaking and examinations (Somerville *et al* 1973; Conway 1971) their effects have not been impressive. In agoraphobia (Hafner and Milton 1977) and spider and snake phobias (Bernadt *et al* 1980) beta-blockade has not reduced subjective anxiety.

Monoamine oxidase inhibitors have been used for the treatment of agoraphobia and social phobias for some years. Early reports that they were effective treatment (Kelly *et al* 1970) have been confirmed by controlled trials (Solyom *et al* 1973; Lipsedge *et al* 1973; Tyrer *et al* 1973) and improvement in phobic symptoms appears to be quite independent of depressed mood (Tyrer *et al* 1973). Earlier reports suggesting that MAOIs were relatively ineffective did not take into account their anti-phobic effects which may often be more potent than their antidepressive ones. Improvement may be delayed for several weeks when a hydrazine MAOI such as phenelzine or isocarboxazid is used (Tyrer *et al* 1973) but is more rapid if the non-hydrazine, tranylcypromine, is given or if the hydrazine MAOI is prescribed in a higher dose (Tyrer *et al* 1980a).

It is difficult to decide whether to stop an MAOI after improvement has been achieved, and the question of withdrawal often comes up during rehabilitation after some progress in overcoming fears has been made. There are strongly held views that the drugs need to be continued for many months or years (Sargant *et al* 1972) but in most cases the drug can be withdrawn before a year's continuous therapy without ill-effects (Tyrer and Steinberg 1975). Nevertheless, a small proportion of patients relapse no matter when their drugs are withdrawn and in this respect phobic patients are more prone to a return of symptoms than are depressed ones (Tyrer 1981). It is difficult to know whether such relapse indicates pharmacological dependence or a return of phobic symptoms. True pharmacological dependence has been reported with MAOIs (Ben-Arie and George 1979) and it is possible that a similar syndrome to that of benzodiazepine withdrawal can occur in patients on long-term MAOIs without preceding evidence of tolerance or increased dosage.

Tricyclic antidepressants have sometimes been used for treating phobias (Klein and Fink 1962) although Klein regards their effectiveness as primarily due to reduction of panic rather than a specific anti-phobic action (Klein 1976). The only published comparison of tricyclic antidepressants (imipramine) and MAOIs (phenelzine) in phobic states has shown a slight superiority for phenelzine (Sheehan *et al* 1980).

Often the decision about continuing or stopping an MAOI or a tricylic antidepressant in phobic disorders has to be made by a doctor who did not know the patient's symptoms when he was prescribed the drug. In such instances the natural reaction is to continue the drug rather than 'rock the boat'. This negative attitude is not satisfactory, particularly with the MAOIs, as their interaction with foodstuffs and other drugs makes them potentially dangerous compounds and may create problems when, for example, patients have to undergo a general anaesthetic for surgery. It is best to reduce the drug gradually with the intention of stopping it altogether if there are no adverse effects. When doing this it is important to remember that the effects of MAOIs last up to several weeks after the drug is withdrawn, so (pharmacological) changes will not be shown immediately.

Obsessional Neurosis

Obsessional neurosis is usually a chronic or a relapsing condition. Most cases start in adolescence or early adult life and symptoms may get worse in middle age. Relapses and remissions may occur in response to external circumstances, symptoms being exacerbated by anxiety-provoking stress but sometimes ameliorated by new responsibilities which are well within the patient's capabilities. In some cases fluctuations in severity appear to follow a pattern which is independent of environmental factors and is regarded as endogenous. About two thirds of cases with mild symptoms have improved or recovered after several years' follow-up, but only about a quarter of cases with severe symptoms will improve. Longstanding cases have a poor prognosis. Obsessional personality traits, which may be difficult to distinguish from symptoms of the illness itself, are probably a good prognostic factor if not unduly severe.

Chronic obsessional neurosis is a severely disabling condition. Rituals may be a gross impediment to the simplest activities of daily life, and the high degree of insight present tends to intensify patients' distress. About 1 per cent of patients commit suicide.

The treatment of obsessional neurosis is not one of psychiatry's triumphs. No drug therapy can be regarded as entirely satisfactory in this group of disorders but there are several agents which are useful adjuvants to other approaches. The tricyclic antidepressants are the most commonly used drugs and one of these, clomipramine, has been studied most closely. The evidence that it is superior to other tricyclic antidepressants in obsessional states is tenuous, and the findings with clomipramine may well apply to other antidepressant drugs.

Early studies with clomipramine suggested its effectiveness in obsessional disorders (Walter 1973; Capstick and Seldrup 1973) but, as obsessional symptoms are common in depressive illness (Gittelson 1966), the improvement might be a consequence of its antidepressant effects rather than due to any specific anti-obsessional action. By far the most comprehensive study to date, in which assessments were made over eight months, has been that reported by Professor Marks and his colleagues (Marks *et al* 1980). Comparisons were made between clomipramine and placebo and between relaxation therapy and exposure *in vivo*. Clomipramine in doses between 150 and 225 mg daily produced significant improvement in obsessional rituals, social adjustment and mood but only in those patients who initially had depressed mood. This effect was maximal between the 10th and 18th weeks of treatment and afterwards slowly declined. After eight months drug treatment was stopped, but the superiority of the clomipramine group over the placebo one continued up to one year. Nevertheless, in patients who were initially depressed there was often a return of symptoms after stopping clomipramine.

The authors concluded that the case for a specific antiobsessive effect for clomipramine was yet to be proved. This is not to say that clomipramine (and other tricyclic antidepressants) have no value in obsessional illness, as depression frequently coexists with obsessional symptoms. The benefits of exposure *in vivo*, the most effective of the treatments, and those of clomipramine, are additive and apparently independent, so that clomipramine alone may be considered in the absence of facilities for behaviour therapy.

Patients with obsessional neurosis who have responded to clomipramine (or another antidepressant) and who have mood disturbance associated with their obsessional symptoms are therefore more likely to need long-term treatment than those who have relatively 'pure' obsessional symptoms.

Monoamine oxidase inhibitors have been used in the treatment of obsessional neurosis (Philpott 1976) but there are no formal studies of their effectiveness. Benzodiazepines are also used to relieve coexisting anxiety and they may be of special value in patients whose obsessional rituals are carried out as anxiety-relieving manoeuvres. If a small dose of a benzodiazepine will reduce the anxiety just as easily it may well replace the rituals.

Depressive Neurosis

The argument over the classification of depressive illness is relevant to this chapter, as by definition the non-neurotic conditions now commonly described as depressive psychosis, unipolar depression or the depressive phase of manic-depressive (bipolar) psychoses are beyond its brief. Those who regard depressive illness as a continuum dislike this categorization but some form of clinical separation is necessary before deciding on drug treatment.

Tricyclic Antidepressants

The main use of tricyclic antidepressants is in the treatment of acute depressive illness. Their value in other psychiatric illnesses is less clearly established, but claims have been made for their efficacy in chronic depressive, phobic and obsessive-compulsive neuroses. Frequently these drugs need to be continued for months or years to prevent relapse, and the long-term use of tricyclic drugs is associated with several hazards. Tricyclic antidepressants are the established drug treatments prescribed for depression. Most studies show that depressive neurosis is less likely to respond to tricyclics than depressive psychosis. Kiloh, Ball and Garside (1962) found that 84 per cent of patients with depressive psychosis but only 42 per cent of patients with depressive neurosis responded to imipramine. Similarly, Paykel (1972), after categorizing depressive symptoms using a cluster analysis technique, found that depressive psychosis responded to amitriptyline better than did other types of depression, and that the presence of anxiety predicted a poor response. Rogers and Clay (1975) come to similar conclusions in reviewing various trials assessing the efficacy of imipramine in different types of depressive illness.

The relatively poor results of drug treatment in depressive neurosis may be explained by the frequency of abnormal premorbid personality traits and environmental problems in these conditions. The group is also heterogeneous diagnostically. If drugs are to be used, tricyclics are felt to be generally superior in moderate depressive illness (Young *et al* 1979) although monoamine oxidase inhibitors may be more appropriate for some patients with additional anxiety, phobic or hypochondriacal symptoms (Tyrer 1976b). Only two controlled trials have compared the efficacy of monoamine oxidase inhibitors and tricyclic antidepressants in depressive neurosis (as opposed to depressive illness in general) and both have shown no superiority of either drug group (Nies and Robinson 1981; Rowan *et al* 1981).

An adequate dose of the tricyclic must be given for four weeks before its efficacy can be assessed. If the depression responds, it is necessary to decide how long to continue medication by weighing up the benefits of a sustained antidepressant action against possible ill-effects of long-term treatment, considering the natural history of the illness. The course of the single episode, and the likelihood of further attacks, depend on the personality of the patient and on external circumstances. Most episodes of depressive neurosis, even if not treated, improve after a few months, but may not recover completely. Most of such patients are prone to react adversely to unpleasant life events, and those whose life circumstances continue to be stressful may become chronically depressed. The frequency and severity of episodes often increase in middle life. The prospect of complete recovery, with or without treatment, is less good than for an episode of psychotic depression. About 10 per cent of patients commit suicide.

Continuing a tricyclic for several months after apparent recovery from a depressive illness protects against relapse during that time. Mindham and his colleagues (1973) assigned patients whose depression had improved with imipramine or amitriptyline to one of two groups. One group continued the active drug for six months in a dosage of 75–150 mg daily, and the other received a placebo. 22 per cent of patients on active drug relapsed, and 50 per cent of patients on placebo. A similar study was carried out with patients whose depression had responded to amitriptyline.

None of those who remained on the drug in a dose of 150 mg daily relapsed, but 42 per cent of those given placebo did so, usually within six months (Coppen *et al* 1978).

There is no risk of dependence after long-term therapy with tricyclic antidepressants and even sudden withdrawal does not lead to an increase in symptoms (Tyrer 1981). This does not necessarily prevent some patients from becoming psychologically dependent after many months of therapy. Unwanted effects may interrupt treatment and be a reason for stopping continued prescription.

The cardiac side effects of tricyclics, which have not attracted much attention until recently, may prove the most serious contra-indication to their long-term use. The ECG shows tachycardia and prolongation of A–V conduction time in most subjects receiving tricyclic antidepressants. These effects are dose-related, and are less with the newer antidepressants such as doxepin than with amitripytline, imipramine or nortriptyline (Burrows *et al* 1976). Postural hypotension, arrhythmias, conduction defects, and congestive cardiac failure are observed occasionally with therapeutic doses, especially in patients with pre-existing cardiac impairment (Rose 1977). Tricyclics may also predispose to myocardial infarction. Sudden deaths are more frequent in patients with cardiac disease who are taking amitriptyline than in those who are not (Coull *et al* 1970). Against this, untreated depressed patients have an increased mortality both from suicide and other causes including cardiovascular disease, and this high mortality outweighs the risk of death from antidepressant drug treatment (Avery and Winokur 1976).

Other side effects of tricyclics may also be a problem with long-term administration. Their anticholinergic properties increase the risk of acute glaucoma, retention of urine and paralytic ileus in patients who are predisposed to these conditions for medical reasons or because they are taking other anticholinergic drugs. Pre-existing liver damage and epilepsy may be exacerbated. Less serious but often troublesome side-effects, particularly anticholinergic ones, may continue with prolonged use. The most common are dry mouth, blurred vision, constipation, impaired ejaculation, sweating, drowsiness, confusion, insomnia, headache and weight gain. There is, however, a tendency for unwanted effects to decrease after chronic dosage and in one recent study dry mouth was the only side-effect which patients on long-term tricyclics experienced with significantly greater frequency than patients on placebo (Mindham *et al* 1973).

Other Antidepressants

Unwanted effects with tricyclic antidepressants may be a reason for changing to one of the newer tricyclic-like drugs. Although there is no good evidence that these new drugs are more effective than the originals, in general they have fewer side-effects and for this reason may be preferred. Mianserin and nomifensine may be used with relative safety in patients with cardiac disease and nomifensine in patients with epilepsy as it is a mild anticonvulsant as well as an antidepressant (Trimble *et al* 1977).

Some other newer antidepressants, including viloxazine, dothiepin and doxepin, have fewer anticholinergic effects and the newest antidepressant, trazodone, is alleged to have no anticholinergic effects at all.

To summarize, only some of the depressive disorders classified as neurotic are responsive to drug therapy and they are not easy to identify. It is more difficult to decide to which category a patient belongs when he presents himself to a rehabilitation unit several months or years after starting antidepressant therapy in another treatment setting. It is most likely that such patients will be taking tricyclic antidepressants and a decision is needed about their continuation or substitution. If the patient has cardiac disease or epilepsy substitution may be indicated. If, however, the patient is healthy and has been taking the antidepressant for six months or less it is reasonable to continue this. After six months' therapy the decision becomes a lottery and, provided that the patient is symptom free, it is reasonable to reduce the drug dosage gradually while watching for any signs of relapse. The continuation of drug therapy does not in any way prevent other types of treatment being given, particularly psychotherapy, which interacts with drug treatment positively (Rounsaville *et al* 1981).

Neurasthenia

Some may think it odd that such an archaic diagnostic term should still be in the International Classification of Diseases; it describes a condition 'characterized by fatigue, irritability, headache, depression, insomnia, difficulty in concentration and anhedonia' (WHO 1979). It has some merit and many patients attending rehabilitation departments satisfy this description. In two words they 'lack motivation'. Drug therapy has relatively little part to play in their management but the energizing effects of the MAOIs or flupenthixol may prove useful. Minor tranquillizers should in general be avoided as these patients are prone to dependence.

Depersonalization Syndrome

Depersonalization is relatively rare as a primary diagnosis but frequently occurs as a symptom in depressive illness, phobic and free-floating anxiety and in schizophrenia. As a primary disorder the condition tends to follow a chronic course (Shorvon 1946) but is rarely a serious handicap. Although in the past stimulant drugs such as amphetamine and methylphenidate were recommended in depersonalization their addiction potential definitely contra-indicates their use.

Hypochondriacal Neurosis

Hypochondriasis is also a disorder that is more commonly found as a secondary condition than as a primary one. Care must be taken to exclude depressive illness, anxiety states with somatic emphasis, 'hysterical hypochondriasis'—now officially recognized as Briquet's syndrome in the United States (Perley and Guze 1962) and personality disorders in which anankastic, anxious and hypochondriacal traits predominate. It is also relevant to mention the range of psychosomatic disorders classified in the International Classification of Diseases as 'physiological malfunction arising from mental factors' (WHO 1979). These include torticollis, hyperventilation syndrome, neurocirculatory asthenia, hyperdynamic heart syndrome, pruritus ani and aerophagy. Why some patients present their psychological problems in these curious ways is far from clear although social class, illness behaviour, dynamic conflicts and physiological idiosyncrasy all play a part (Mayou 1976). Many patients with chronic neurotic disorder have such symptoms and in time may come to tolerate if not overcome them. Whilst psychopharmacology has relatively little to offer this group of patients it would be wrong to reject drug treatment altogether.

Treatment offered with the sole aim of alleviating the symptoms is reckoned by some to be bad psychiatry as it connives with the patient's distorted view of his disorder. Even if one decides that his perception is sadly awry it may still be appropriate to give symptomatic treatment as in the patient's view the symptom is the sole manifestation of illness (Tyrer 1973). Recent evidence that the hypochondriac's complaints frequently have a physiological basis and can be explained by heightened awareness of normal function (Tyrer *et al* 1980b) supports the case for symptomatic treatment. Codeine phosphate for intestinal hurry, propranolol for palpitation, chlorpheniramine or promethazine for nausea, and charcoal for aerophagy all have a respectable place in therapy. They are rarely the sole treatment but by alleviating the patient's immediate concern they allow other approaches to work more effectively.

Summary

Drug therapy in chronic neurosis is no easy option, although the relative simplicity of drug prescribing may make it appear so. Too casual prescribing may lead to serious problems and, as with all iatrogenic disease, this is impossible to defend unless even more serious illness would ensue in the absence of treatment. This case cannot be made out in most of the patients with neurotic disorders involved in rehabilitation, and in most instances one could achieve the same therapeutic results without any drug therapy. But this does not mean that drugs are useless in the rehabilitation of chronic neurosis. They enable the therapist to speed recovery and take short cuts.

The rehabilitation team should look on drug therapy in neurosis in the same way that the good gardener looks on chemical fertilizers. With an abundance of rehabilitation facilities (or unlimited rotted farmyard manure) all chemical treatments are unnecessary. But these ideals are almost impossible to achieve in practice and the chance of success is usually greater when pharmacological treatments are used judiciously. If they are used carelessly new diseases are produced that cancel out any gains that may have been made. So a constant monitoring of dosage and effect is needed by both doctor and gardener.

There is a final point that needs emphasis. Before a patient is discharged from a rehabilitation service some decision should be made about the continuation of drug therapy. It is not a subject that can be shelved or left to the general practitioner. Sometimes the decision may be a pessimistic one, that for the indefinite future there is no alternative to continuation of a drug, but usually drug withdrawal can be achieved. This is best done before final discharge but, if not, then clear instructions are needed for the GP or the new medical attendant. If this is forgotten or ignored it is more than likely that prescription will continue indefinitely without any plan. Even if this does not create new disease it is not conducive to positive health, because the regular consumption of psychotropic drugs is a procedure that reinforces the sick role. Drug treatment should be finite in neurosis and there are few experiences more satisfying in our branch of the profession than sharing the pleasure of a recovered chronic patient who is now taking no drugs, pleasure enhanced by the knowledge that it is entirely free of any artificial aid.

References

Anonymous (1976). How to get patients off barbiturates. *Drug and Therapeutics Bulletin* **14,** 11

Avery, D and Winokur, G (1976). Mortality in depressed patients treated with electroconvulsive therapy and antidepressants. *Archives of General Psychiatry* **33,** 1029

Balter, M B and Levine, J (1969). The nature and extent of psychotropic drug usage in the United States. *Psychopharmacology Bulletin* **5,** 3

Ben-Arie, O and George, G C W (1979). A case of tranylcypromine ('Parnate') addiction. *British Journal of Psychiatry* **135,** 273

Bernadt, M W, Silverstone, T and Singleton, W (1980). Behavioural and subjective effects of beta-adrenergic blockade in phobic subjects. *British Journal of Psychiatry* **137,** 452

Burrows, G D, Vohra, J, Hunt, D, Sloman, J G, Scoggins, B A and Davies, B (1976). Cardiac effects of different tricyclic antidepressant drugs. *British Journal of Psychiatry* **129,** 335

Capstick N and Seldrup, J (1973). Phenomenological aspects of obsessional patients treated with clomipramine. *British Journal of Psychiatry* **122**, 719

Conway, M (1971). Final examinations. *Practitioner* **206**, 795

Coppen, A, Ghose, K, Montgomery, S, Rama Rao, V A, Bailey, J and Jorgensen, A (1978). Continuation therapy with amitriptyline in depression. *British Journal of Psychiatry* **133**, 28

Coull, D C, Crooks, J, Dingwall-Fordyce, I, Scott, A M and Weir, R D (1970). Amitriptyline and cardiac disease. *Lancet*, ii, 590

Dennis, P J (1979). Monitoring of psychotropic drug prescribing in general practice. *British Medical Journal* **2**, 1115

Foulds, G A (1976). *The Hierarchical Nature of Personal Illness*. Academic Press, London

Fruensgaard, K (1976). Withdrawal psychosis: a study of 30 consecutive cases. *Acta Psychiatrica Scandinavica* **53**, 105

Gittelson, N L (1966). The effect of obsessions on depressive psychosis. *British Journal of Psychiatry* **112**, 253

Greenblatt, D J and Shader, R I (1974). *Benzodiazepines in Clinical Practice*. Raven Press, New York

Gregg, E and Akhter, I (1979). Chlormethiazole abuse. *British Journal of Psychiatry* **134**, 627

Hafner, J and Marks, I (1976). Exposure *in vivo* of agoraphobics: contributions of diazepam, group exposure and anxiety evocation. *Psychological Medicine* **6**, 71

Hafner, J and Milton, F (1977). The influence of propranolol on the exposure *in vivo* of agoraphobics. *Psychological Medicine* **7**, 419

Hession, M A, Verma, S and Mohan Bhakta, K G (1979). Dependence on chlormethiazole and effects of its withdrawal. *Lancet*, i, 953

James, I M, Pearson, R M, Griffith, D N W and Newbury, P (1977). Effect of oxprenolol on stage-fright in musicians. *Lancet*, ii, 952

Kales, A, Allen, C, Scharf, M B and Kales, J D (1970). Hypnotic drugs and their effectiveness: all-night EEG studies of insomniac patients. *Archives of General Psychiatry* **23**, 226

Kales, A, Scharf, M B and Kales, J D (1978). Rebound insomnia: a new clinical syndrome. *Science* **201**, 1039

Kelly, D, Guirguis, W, Frommer, E, Mitchell-Heggs, N and Sargant, W (1970). Treatment of phobic states with antidepressants: a retrospective study of 246 patients. *British Journal of Psychiatry* **116**, 387

Kiloh, L G, Ball, J R B and Garside, R F (1962). Prognostic factors in treatment of depressive states with imipramine. *British Medical Journal* i, 1225

Klein, D F (1976). Diagnosis of anxiety and differential use of antianxiety drugs. In *Drug Treatment of Mental Disorders* (ed. L L Simpson), pp. 61–72. Raven Press, New York

Klein, D F and Fink, M (1962). Psychiatric reaction-patterns to imipramine. *American Journal of Psychiatry* **119**, 432

Lader, M (1981). Benzodiazepine dependence. In *Use and Misuse of Psychotropic Drugs* (eds R Murray, H Ghodse, C Harris, D Williams and P Williams). Gaskell Books, Royal College of Psychiatrists, London

Lader, M H and Tyrer, P J (1972). Central and peripheral effects of propranolol and sotalol in normal human subjects. *British Journal of Pharmacology* **45**, 557

Leading article (1978). Stress, distress and drug treatment. *Lancet*, ii, 1347

Lipsedge, M S, Hajioff, J, Huggins, P, Napier, L, Pearce, J, Pike, D J and Rich, M (1973). The management of severe agoraphobia: a comparison of iproniazid and systematic desensitisation. *Psychopharmacologia* **32,** 67

Marks, J (1978). *The Benzodiazepines: Use, Overuse, Misuse, Abuse.* M T P Press, Lancaster

Marks, I M, Viswanathan, R, Lipsedge, M S and Gardner, R (1972). Enhanced relief of phobias by flooding during waning diazepam effect. *British Journal of Psychiatry* **121,** 493

Marks, I M, Stern, R S, Mawson, D, Cobb, J and McDonald, R (1980). Clomipramine and exposure for obsessive-compulsive rituals: 1. *British Journal of Psychiatry* **136,** 1

Marsden C D, Mindham R H S and Mackay, A V P (1981). Extrapyramidal movement disorders produced by antipsychotic drugs. In *Pharmacology and Treatment of Schizophrenia* (eds P D Bradley and S R Hirsch). Oxford University Press, London

Mayou, R (1976). The nature of bodily symptoms. *British Journal of Psychiatry* **129,** 55

Mindham, R H S, Howland, C and Shepherd, M (1973). An evaluation of continuation therapy with tricyclic antidepressants in depressive illness. *Psychological Medicine* **3,** 5

Möuler, H and Okada, T (1977). Benzodiazepine Receptor: Demonstration in the central nervous system. *Science* **198,** 849

Nies, A and Robinson, D S (1981). Comparison of clinical effects of amitriptyline and phenelzine treatment. In *Monoamine Oxidase Inhibitors—The State of the Art* (eds M B H Youdin and E S Paykel), pp. 141–8. John Wiley, Chichester

Paykel, E S (1972). Depressive typologies and response to amitriptyline. *British Journal of Psychiatry* **120,** 147

Perley, M J and Guze, S B (1962). Hysteria—the stability and usefulness of clinical criteria. *New England Journal of Medicine* **266,** 421

Pevnick, J S, Jasinski, D R and Haertzen C A (1978). Abrupt withdrawal from therapeutically administered diazepam. *Archives of General Psychiatry* **35,** 995

Philpott, R (1976). The assessment of drugs in obsessional states. *British Journal of Clinical Pharmacology* **3,** Supplement 1, 91

Preskorn, S H and Denner, L J (1977). Benzodiazepines and withdrawal psychosis: report of three cases. *Journal of the American Medical Association* **237,** 36

Rogers, S C and Clay, P M (1975). A statistical review of controlled trials of imipramine and placebo in the treatment of depressive illnesses. *British Journal of Psychiatry* **127,** 599

Rose, J B (1977). Tricyclic antidepressant toxicity. *Clinical Toxicology* **11,** 391

Rounsaville, B S, Klerman, G L, and Weissman, M M (1981). Do psychotherapy and pharmacotherapy for depression conflict? *Archives of General Psychiatry* **38,** 24–9

Rowan, P R, Paykel, E S, Parker, R R, Gatehouse, J M and Rao, B M (1981). Tricyclic antidepressant and MAO inhibitor: are there differential effects? In *Monoamine Oxidase Inhibitors—the State of the Art* (eds M B H Youdin and E S Paykel), pp. 125–39. John Wiley, Chichester

Sargant, W, Slater E and Kelly, D (1972). *An Introduction to Physical Methods of Treatment in Psychiatry,* 5th edition. Churchill Livingstone, Edinburgh

Sheehan, D V, Ballenger, J and Jacobsen, G (1980). Treatment of endogenous anxiety with phobic, hysterical and hypochondriacal symptoms. *Archives of General Psychiatry* **37,** 51

Shorvon, H J (1946). The depersonalisation syndrome. *Proceedings of the Royal Society of Medicine* **39,** 779

Skegg, D C G, Doll, R and Perry, J (1977). Use of medicines in general practice. *British Medical Journal* **1,** 1561

Solyom, L, Heseltine G F D, McClure, D J, Ledwidge, B and Steinberg, G (1973). Behaviour therapy versus drug therapy in the treatment of phobic neurosis. *Canadian Psychiatric Association Journal* **18,** 25

Somerville, W, Taggart, P and Carruthers, M (1973), Cardiovascular responses in public speaking and their modification by oxprenolol. In *New Perspectives in Beta-blockade* (eds D M Burley *et al*). CIBA, Horsham

Trethowan, W H (1975). Pills for personal problems. *British Medical Journal* **3,** 749

Trimble, M R, Meldrum, B S and Anlezark, G (1977). The effect of nomifensine on brain amines and epilepsy in photosensitive baboons. *British Journal of Clinical Pharmacology* **4,** Supplement 2, 101S

Tyrer, P J (1973). Relevance of bodily feelings in emotion. *Lancet*, i, 915

Tyrer, P (1976a). *The Role of Bodily Feelings in Anxiety*. Oxford University Press, London

Tyrer, P (1976b). Towards rational therapy with monoamine oxidase inhibitors. *British Journal of Psychiatry,* **128,** 354

Tyrer, P (1978). Drug treatment of psychiatric patients in general practice. *British Medical Journal* **2,** 1008

Tyrer, P (1982). Consequences of withdrawing monoamine oxidase inhibitors and tricyclic antidepressants after prolonged therapy. (to be published)

Tyrer, P J and Lader M H (1974). Response to propranolol and diazepam in somatic and psychic anxiety. *British Medical Journal* **2,** 14

Tyrer, P and Steinberg, D (1975). Symptomatic treatment of agoraphobia and social phobias: a follow-up study. *British Journal of Psychiatry* **127,** 163

Tyrer, P, Candy, J and Kelly, D (1973). A study of the clinical effects of phenelzine and placebo in the treatment of phobic anxiety. *Psychopharmacologia* **32,** 237

Tyrer, P, Gardner, M, Lambourn, J and Whitford, M (1980a). Clinical and pharmacokinetic factors affecting response to phenelzine. *British Journal of Psychiatry* **136,** 359

Tyrer, P, Lee, I and Alexander, J (1980b). Awareness of cardiac function in anxious, phobic and hypochondriacal patients. *Psychological Medicine* **10,** 171

Tyrer, P, Rutherford, D and Huggett, T (1981). Benzodiazepine withdrawal symptoms and propranolol. *Lancet*, i, 540

Walter, C J S (1973). Clinical impressions on treatment of obsessional states with intravenous clomipramine (Anafranil). *Journal of International Medical Research* **1,** 413

Wing, J K, Cooper, J E and Satorius, N (1974). *The Measurement and Classification of Psychiatric Symptoms*. Cambridge University Press, London

Winokur, A, Rickels, K, Greenblatt, D J, Snyder, P J and Schatz N J (1980). Withdrawal reaction from long term, low dose, administration of diazepam. *Archives of General Psychiatry* **37,** 101

World Health Organisation (1979). *International Classification of Diseases, Injuries and Causes of Death*. 9th Revision. WHO, Geneva

Young, J P R, Hughes, W C and Lader, M H (1976). A controlled comparison of flupenthixol and amitriptyline in depressed out-patients. *British Medical Journal* **1,** 116

Young, J P R, Lader, M H and Hughes, W C (1979). Controlled trial of trimipramine, monoamine oxidase inhibitors and combined treatment in depressed outpatients. *British Medical Journal*, ii, 1315

8 Head Injury, Its Psychological Sequelae, and Compensation Neurosis

A A McKechnie, MD, FRC Psych, DPM

Legal Aspects

The concept of compensation for injury or for impaired capacity to earn a living through injury or illness has been a major preoccupation of legal and social justice systems. The fear of impairment of capacity to earn a living is also the basis of insurance policies, including those now associated with variations on provisions made by the State. Liability is a crucial question. The historical roots of civil liability in tort lie in the earliest tradition common to many societies of paying a forfeit for harm done. The following quotation sums this up well:

> Under the customary European systems including those of England and Scotland there was no clear distinction between crime and tort and where personal injury or death occurred a single proceeding served for buying off the vengeance of the injured person or his family and placating the king or lord for the disturbance of the peace. The amount of payment reflected the affront to the dignity or rank of the person injured rather than the actual loss occasioned by the injury. (Pearson Report 1978)

Several aspects need to be highlighted in this very important paragraph

(1) the concept of vengeance as a result of the injury to the person or his family;
(2) the question of placating the king or lord; and
(3) finally and perhaps most importantly of all the amount of payment reflected the affront to the dignity or rank of the person injured rather than the *actual loss occasioned*.

These observations seem to have much more bearing on an understanding of compensation and neurosis than any of the many articles which have appeared in relation to the psyche of the injured person. Of equal importance is that, on actuarial principles, the longer an individual is off sick the greater the chance of tort. The conclusion therefore must be that length reflects the severity of disability and the longer the disability has lasted the greater the likelihood of compensation. Two opposing trends are apparent—a lawyer sees no settlement without clinical finality but a doctor sees no clinical finality without settlement (Miller 1961).

Other aspects need to be considered, for example the age-old concept of alms for the sick and needy which has developed slowly into statutory payment of cash or kind to those in want as a result of incapacity or loss of a breadwinner. In the seventeenth century compensation liability could be paid without fault—initially compensation for disabled soldiers and sailors. Later nineteenth-century developments provided for compensation for injury at work, again without any necessity for fault or blame. From the eighteenth century there was the development of personal insurance against impaired capacity to earn, by and on behalf of, an individual and/or his dependants.

Compensation therefore can at the present time be paid:

(1) as a result of a civil action;
(2) as a result of a criminal action where the State pays an injured individual (Criminal Compensation Act);
(3) industrial injury compensation;
(4) health insurance payment—private insurance payment;
(5) payment under a non-contributory pension for disability.

The arrangements by which individuals can be compensated for impaired capacity or 'gain' financially from being ill have therefore become increasingly complex in recent years.

It is important to realize that compensation is not just a question of litigant and defender. Several other bodies become involved. Traditionally the family always suffered—and one could argue that professional organizations and trade unions act *in loco parentis*. Secondary beneficiaries are clearly the legal profession both defending and prosecuting and expert witnesses—in this instance doctors who may be called upon to make comment about the nature of an illness and prognosticate about the degree of disability. Individuals, families, trade unions or professional organizations may well pursue the same action of 'buying off the vengeance' of the injured person or his family. The concept of an affront to the dignity of an individual, his family or his representative has always been as important as the actual degree of injury sustained.

Table 8.1 sets out some of the terms which are commonly used in relation to aspects of compensation. Compensation can be seen as providing adequate financial redress, absolving the individual from personal neglect or negligence and serving as a token to others that the injured party was not at fault—the concept of visible proof.

Clinical Aspects

The full range then of what might be termed 'post-traumatic problems' would include not just those in which there was a question of liability or

Table 8.1   Terms used in aspects of compensation

(*a*) Compensation neurosis	A genuine neurosis which develops in an injured person while a tort claim is outstanding and which tends to prolong illness
(*b*) Delict	Scots term for tort
(*c*) Tort	A wrongful act or omission in respect of which damages can be claimed but not including a breach of contract as such
(*d*) Damages	Reparation is a sum paid to compensate for the injury
(*e*) Non-pecuniary loss	Non-patrimonial loss (Scots)—the intangible results of injury often summarized as pain and suffering and loss of amenities
(*f*) Solatium	Compensation paid to an injured person for non-pecuniary loss. Scots term initially used. Compensation paid to a relative of a deceased person in recognition of his grief subsequently abolished and replaced by the entitlement to a loss of society award. Alternatively, compensation paid to an injured person for non-pecuniary loss

Other definitions which may be of interest are contained in the Glossary of the Royal Commission Report pp 514–16 from which Report these have been abstracted ('Pearson' Report 1978).

pursuit of damage but also those where secondary gain comes from the inability to work. This becomes more complex once the concept of payment without liability is accepted. Post-traumatic problems therefore would include:

(1) psychological sequelae of actual brain damage;
(2) affective illness;
(3) compensation neurosis.

Head Injury

Injury to the head and neck may result in open or closed injury to brain substance, concussion, loss of consciousness or symptoms which appear unrelated to any measures of actual brain trauma. Head injury may be a result of industrial, road, home or sporting accident, and may follow an assault.

Incidence

Trauma now accounts in advanced countries for much mortality and morbidity especially in younger males. Lewin (1970) estimated that 7500 people each year in Britain sustained major head injuries with a post-traumatic amnesia (PTA) of more than 24 hours. Steadman and Graham (1970) reported almost 400 cases of head injury admitted in one year from a population of approximately 250 000. Of these 20 per cent were reported on admission as drowsy or unconscious or had a PTA of at least 24 hours' duration. This extrapolated to a population of 50 000 000 gives an annual incidence of about 10 000 new cases per annum. Kerr *et al* (1971) found that in admissions to a Regional Neurological Centre (Newcastle upon Tyne) the rate was 5·6 per 10 000 population at risk but in this series over half of those admitted were fully conscious.

Phillips (1967) stressed that even after prolonged coma of up to five weeks there may still be capacity for good recovery. He said that generally recovery could take two to three years. It appears to be accepted that continued recovery or adaptation may continue in certain instances for as long as five years (Miller 1966). The outcome with regard to return to employment has been reported as generally favourable. Miller and Stern (1965) and Lewin (1970) estimated that 20 per cent would be unemployed or have to seek lower employment status. A less favourable response appears to be the outcome in the USA.

The frequency then of major head injury and the lengthy time which may lapse before recovery ceases make a considerable demand in relation to resources.

Predisposing Factors, Including Previous Personality

Lishman (1968) found no evidence that previous intellectual level or socio-economic status was associated with increased psychological symptoms. Taylor (1967) in reviewing post-concussional sequelae concluded that there was no correlation between post-traumatic sequelae and a history of previous psychiatric illness but did state that this excluded litigants.

Alcohol-related Problems

Alcohol is of course a major contribution in its own right to organic brain damage. Alcohol-related problems contribute to road traffic accidents, to accident and emergency department referrals and constitute in Scotland 50 per cent of male admissions to psychiatric admission units; alcohol is a major factor in causing brain damage directly or indirectly. Kerr *et al* (1971) found that recent consumption of alcohol was noted in a consecutive series of admissions to a Regional Neurosurgical unit—29 per cent of males and 10 per cent of females. It was commonest in domestic accidents and assaults and one quarter of pedestrians were affected by alcohol.

More recent work has identified subtler forms of impairment of function as well as the more generally recognized and accepted consequences of prolonged and severe alcohol abuse, e.g. Korsakov's Psychosis. The principles of rehabilitation, especially with regard to length of recovery, are as apposite to alcohol-related damage as they are to trauma.

The continued abuse of alcohol may impede or indeed worsen recovery from brain injury especially where there is epilepsy. Reduced tolerance to alcohol has also been quoted to the author as one of the more dire consequences of accidental brain injury and in some families at least has been of the greatest concern. Advice which has recommended abstinence has not been accepted graciously.

Psychiatric Disability

The severity of psychiatric disability has been shown by Lishman (1968) to relate to the extent of brain damage measured by the duration of post-traumatic amnesia and the development of post-traumatic epilepsy. Retrograde amnesia and actual duration of unconsciousness appear to be less reliable indices. The type of psychiatric disability was related to generalized cerebral damage, injury to specific areas of the brain or it may present where no objective signs or symptoms of brain trauma were identified.

He found that intellectual disorders and behavioural disorders had close association with brain damage and showed that left rather than right cerebral hemisphere damage was associated with a higher incidence of psychiatric disability. He stated that affective disorders or somatic complaints were less firmly related to organic brain damage.

Depressive Illness
Miller (1961) identified a group of people in his series with depressive illness. He stated that they were the only patients in his whole series who exhibited a favourable response of psychiatric symptoms to treatment (9 cases out of 200).

Frontal Lobe Syndrome
Frontal lobe lesions present with euphoria, lack of judgement, reliability or foresight, facile or childish behaviour, disinhibition and an increased propensity to criminal offences. Wounds of the convex lateral surface of the frontal lobe appear associated with intellectual abnormality whilst orbital lesions show emotional disorder.

Convex lesions show lack of productive thinking, indifference, euphoria and incapacity for decisions. Orbital lesions do not show defects on formal tests of intellectual impairment but are more prone to develop radical personality changes. These latter included failure to maintain satisfactory human relationships. They tend to lack perseverance, are demanding, disinhibited, interfering and aggressive. They demonstrate increased libido and potency, often with scant regard for their marital partners. Criminal offences have been shown to be more prevalent in this group and this often in the form of social offences.

Temporal Lobe Injury
Injuries to the temporal lobe are more frequently associated with atypical psychoses and with schizophreniform psychoses as well as temporal lobe epilepsy.

Basal Injury
Injuries to the midbrain, hypothalamus and adjacent area show sluggishness, apathy and disturbances of fundamental drive. Patients may have disorders of appetite, thirst and increased somnolence.

Sensory Defects
Sensory defects and lesions producing visual field defects are associated with increased psychiatric disability. Lesions which produce dysphasia are also associated with increased psychiatric disability. Parietal lobe lesions of the right cerebral hemisphere are associated with sensory defects which may be mistaken for functional symptoms.

Emotional Rage
Trethowan (1970) stressed some very important nonspecific sequelae of head injury. He identified these as emotional incontinence, irritability, a lowered tolerance of frustration and explosive outbursts. Panting and Merry (1972) recorded that in a large proportion of their cases, outbursts of vivid emotional rage were common and the frequency and severity of their outbursts diminished as the patient himself progressed.

Compensation Neurosis

An important sequel to injury is that found in relation to compensation, accident, traumatic or litigation neurosis. These terms appear to describe similar syndromes and the terms reflect, often in a prejudicial manner, the issue of litigation. They have been defined by Hudderston (1932) as 'A psychogenic or non-structural nervous disorder shortly following a physical injury and complicated or not by structural changes in the central nervous system or elsewhere.'

Miller (1961) reported on 200 consecutive cases seen in relation to medico-legal examination. He found 50 cases in whom gross psychoneurosis was present. In none of these was there any objective evidence of serious head injury. This latter feature has been a consistent finding elsewhere (Parker 1977; Braverman 1978; Lloyd 1980). Other authors do relate brain injury to neurosis. Taylor (1967) reported a higher rate of neuroticism after head trauma than trauma to other parts. Whiplash injuries of the neck (La Rocca 1978) also appear associated with a high incidence of neurotic symptomatology.

Miller (1961) and Lloyd (1980) identified those at risk from demonstrating features of compensation neurosis as being of lower socio-economic status and with a previous history of prolonged sick leave after episodes of illness. Both found it commoner amongst men. Kay *et al* (1971) found psychosocial factors were associated with post-concussional syndromes. Amongst these factors were lower socio-economic status, having suffered an industrial accident, being male, middle-aged and married and having had previous psychiatric illness.

Factitious illness, malingering and hysteria are all highly emotional labels. Munchausen's syndrome is a cause of much difficulty in acute general hospitals but does not appear specifically related to injury as such. Naish (1979) has some forceful remarks with regard to deception in medical practice and concludes 'if our profession as a whole can be persuaded to abandon the disease model as applied to games of deceit and manipulation, individual doctors would soon learn to be more proficient in helping their fellow humans'.

Miller (1961), Parker (1977) and Braverman (1978) warn however that malingering is seldom if ever diagnosed. Braverman has reviewed this aspect in relation to 2500 cases of injury of whom 50 were treated by him. He found that a tendency to overvalue, to be excessively preoccupied with and to exaggerate symptoms, was very common. He identified different types of malingering.

One type is psychotraumatic malingering after factual, threatened or imagined injury but where the individual believes ('knows') injury in fact does not exist. Braverman described a conscious exaggeration, preservation and extension of psychiatric symptoms. He said such true, deliberate or fraudulent malingering was uncommon. He gave a useful description of those likely to be in this category with gross evidence of psychopathy, no binding ties with family or friends, transient work pattern and demands for quick settlement with intolerance of time-consuming legal proceedings. He also described the cover-up or decoy malingerer—a person who has received relatively severe injury to the head or from industrial chemicals which he believes has resulted in very serious disease (e.g. cancer), the discovery of which he wants to avoid at whatever cost. Such patients may identify a symptom remote from the area of concern, a near total lack of relationship being common.

Bennet (1946), in his review of psychiatric syndromes simulating organic disease, defined a specific type as peculiarly difficult to help. Such a person is always 'rational', often rather clinical in manner; he sticks to an account of symptoms in great physical detail and consistently denies other concerns or anxieties. Bennet's description is useful, especially so in the area related to organic physical illnesses—an area of obvious concern to psychiatrists but which also has relevance to the sequelae of head injury.

Whatever the aetiology (in Scotland one can always return a not proven verdict) the syndrome exists and has been well identified by Miller (1961) who described the following clinical features.

He noted that those referred to him invariably attended late for interview and were always accompanied by relatives who insisted on coming in with the patient. The patient's attitude was characterized by a hostile, martyred look and a tendency to blame others. Miller identified a gross dramatization of symptoms; head pains graphically described, exertional or postural dizziness, irritability, failure of concentration and restlessness. There was usually some insomnia with difficulty in getting off to sleep, restless sleep and often nightmares related to the accident. They tended to complain of intractable pain following physical injury with an absolute refusal to admit to symptomatic improvement and an unshakeable conviction of unfitness to work. There was a subjective complaint of amnesia. Finally, whilst there were complaints of anxiety there were no objective signs of such at interview.

Rehabilitation

The functions under which the various aspects of patient care can be subsumed are as follows:

Assessment or Diagnosis:	Defining a category of symptoms, identifying a syndrome
Treatment:	The provision of drugs or other specific measures
Rehabilitation:	Aiding a full recovery or compensating for lost ability
Monitoring:	Checking and supervision of progress or outcome
Care and Support:	Providing of help and care, accepting a degree of irreversible disability
Education:	Trying to prevent illness or its recurrence

These functions are closely interwoven and the elements, once identified, need constant review. They usually need attention at one and the same time. The problem orientated approach has theoretical advantages in such a complex system (Weed 1971).

Rehabilitation can be considered under the following headings:

(1) Return to full normal function—relearning of lost skills;

(2) the development of additional skills to compensate for lost capacity;
(3) learning to cope with permanent loss of ability or capacity without losing so much heart that all other aspects of ability are forgotten;
(4) restoration of self-confidence.

Rehabilitation is essential in relation to the neuroses and especially there is a need to return the individual to independence rather than allowing him to rely on others for support. Crutches are valuable, but undue dependence on them can be more crippling than the original disorder which called for their use and could disguise the fact that greater potential recovery was possible than the individual or his family appreciated.

Rehabilitation in relation to the psychological sequelae of brain injury has received scant attention in the literature especially that emanating from psychiatrists; and this is despite the extent of the problem and the length of time, measured in years rather than months, before the recovery process has ceased.

Vandyk (1975) has some trenchant remarks to make:

Too often in the past attention to the rehabilitation problems has gone by default and valuable time and opportunities lost. Early attention to these matters may actually speed up general recovery because optimism on the patient's part is encouraged with the knowledge that his problems are receiving recognition, he is not alone in facing them and that there is a future for him even if it is on different lines from previous plans. . . . It is not satisfactory to rely on doctors for advice on social employment and welfare matters. They have enough to do with the medical side without dabbling in the areas where they are untrained. In many instances a straightforward medical case may prove to be a complex rehabilitation one.

These comments stress the need for a multispecialty and multidisciplinary approach. This has led to the appointment of Consultants in Rehabilitation Medicine in recent years in a number of countries.

Lewin (1970) has stressed the need for close contact between the neurosurgical team and psychiatrists. Psychologists have long been accepted in the management of the brain injured. There is extensive literature relevant especially to the intellectual deficits associated with trauma but sparse information with regard to personality factors. Bond (1975) criticized the undue dependence on physical disability in rehabilitation with little attention to the serious emotional and intellectual handicaps incurred.

Panting and Merry (1972) emphasized the problems which beset families faced with a member with moderate or severe brain damage. They found that 61 per cent of the relatives—usually spouse or mother—had needed supportive treatment with tranquillizers and sleeping tablets which had not been necessary previously. They also reported that families had 'an enormous prejudice' against psychiatry especially in lower socio-economic groups. They favoured medical social work involvement especially in a co-ordinating role.

Treatment or rehabilitation has not appeared to influence the outcome of compensation or accident neurosis. The outcome appears to be favourable once litigation has been resolved although, in some, intractable symptomatology may follow on unsuccessful claims.

Over the past 20 years crisis intervention has had its disciples. More recently the initial enthusiasm has been tempered by better evaluation. Bordon and Porritt (1979) working in Australia applied this methodological approach to subjects admitted to hospital for treatment of road trauma. Their subjects were suffering from bony injury—usually people with fracture of leg or pelvis—and did *not* specifically have brain injury. Bordon and Porritt had identified the following indications of better outcome:

(1) willingness to acknowledge openly realistic difficulties and personal upset;
(2) the ability to resume gradually social roles after a period of reduced performance;
(3) the availability of practical help; and
(4) the availability of people who listen caringly and understand and accept expressions of hurt, anger and confusion.

In their controlled trial they demonstrated that crisis intervention was effective in returning patients to normal functioning after injury and may have reduced length of hospitalization. At follow-up patients not receiving intervention were as disturbed as typical psychiatric out-patients. Their paper indicated that doctors were perceived by patients as not understanding and social agencies as not caring genuinely. They concluded that static services which wait for people at risk to make contact, miss major parts of the need that exists in their community.

These conclusions are of great relevance and are similar to those shown to influence outcome in regard to recovery from myocardial infarction (Schiller and Baker 1976; Philip *et al* 1979) and to have reduced the incidence of psychiatric morbidity in patients suffering from cancer (Maguire *et al* 1980). From these reported findings there appears to be evidence that intervention at an early stage of established physical illness may lessen the likelihood of subsequent emotional or psychological morbidity. This may well be of equal relevance with regard to recovery from brain injury.

Psychiatric expertise in rehabilitation has been well established in the last 20 years or so in relation to recovery from the major functional psychoses. Given the size and extent of the problem which is seen in relation to major brain trauma it is evident that psychiatric hospitals already have to play a part in the management and care of brain-damaged patients. Far too frequently such care and treatment has taken place in overcrowded wards with a wide mixture of patient categories. This has perhaps jaundiced too many psychiatrists against involvement in an area where it would seem that the psychiatric team does have a role to play as part of a multidisciplinary approach.

In conclusion far too much has been made of the problems of compensation neuroses. It has been amply demonstrated by Miller that this group recover very well after the compensation issue has been settled and without specific treatment. Miller also clearly identified in his series—and this has been borne out by other investigations—that psychological sequelae are common especially after severe brain damage and may present with severe management problems. The ultimate prognosis does appear to be reasonably good though the time scale is protracted. It is to be hoped that there will be a major contribution from psychiatrists as part of a multidisciplinary team but not, of course, either at the expense of existing patients or, in the all too common tradition of psychiatric hospitals, of making do with inadequate premises and very poor staffing ratios.

References

The author would like to thank Dr Raymond Antebi for valuable suggestions and much help in providing references.

Bennet, A E (1946). Faulty management of psychiatric syndromes simulating organic disease. *Journal of American Medical Association* **130**, 1203–8

Bond, M R (1975). Assessment of the psychosocial outcome after severe head injury. In *Outcome of severe damage to the central nervous system.* Ciba Foundation Symposium 34. Elsevier, Amsterdam

Bordon, S and Porritt, D (1979). An experimental evaluation of crisis intervention. *Social Science Medicine* **13a (3)**, 251–6

Braverman, M (1978). Post injury malingering is seldom a calculated ploy. *Occupational Health Safety* **472**, 36–48

Hudderston, J H (1932). Accidents, neuroses and compensation. Quoted by Mulcahy, M (1966). Accident Neurosis. *Journal of Irish Medical Association* **58**, 197–201

Kay, D W J, Kerr, T'A and Lassman, L P (1971). Brain trauma and the post concussional syndrome. *Lancet* **ii**, 1052–3

Kerr, T A, Kay, D W K and Lassman, L P (1971). Characteristics of patients, types of accident and mortality in a consecutive series of head injuries admitted to a neurosurgical unit. *British Journal of Preventive and Social Medicine* **25**, 179–85

La Rocca, H (1978). Acceleration injuries of the neck. *Clinical Neurosurgery* **25**, 209–17

Lewin, W (1970). Rehabilitation needs of the brain injured patient. *Proceedings of the Royal Society of Medicine* **63**, 28–32

Ley, P (1976). Towards better doctor patient communication. In *Communication between doctors and patients* (ed. A E Bennet). Oxford University Press

Lishman, W A (1968). Brain damage in relation to psychiatric disability after head injury. *British Journal of Psychiatry* **114,** 373–410

Lloyd, J H (1980). Compensation neurosis. *Australian Family Physician* **9**

Maguire, P, Tait, A, Brooke, M, Thomas, C and Sellwood, R (1980). Effect of counselling on the psychiatric morbidity associated with mastectomy. *British Medical Journal* **281,** 1454–6

Miller, H (1961). Accident neurosis. *British Medical Journal* **1,** 919–25

Miller, H (1966). Mental sequelae of head injury. *Proceedings of the Royal Society of Medicine* **59,** 257–61

Miller, H and Stern, G (1965). The long term prognosis of severe head injury. *Lancet* **i,** 225–9

Naish, J M (1979). Problems of deception in medical practice. *Lancet* **ii,** 139

Panting, A and Merry, P H (1972). The long term rehabilitation of severe head injuries with particular reference to the need for social and medical support for the patient's family. *Rehabilitation* **82,** 33–7

Parker, N (1977). Accident litigants with neurotic symptoms. *Medical Journal of Australia*, 318–22

Pearson Report (1978). Royal Commission on civil liability and compensation for personal injury, Vol I. HMSO, London

Philip, A E, Cay, E L, Vetter, N J and Stuckey, N A (1979). Personal traits and the physical, psychiatric and social state of patients one year after a myocardial infarction. *International Journal of Rehabilitation Research* **2** (4), 479–87

Phillips, D G (1967). Long term problems and prognosis on head injuries. *Hospital Medicine*, 913–22

Schiller, E and Baker, J (1976). Return to work after myocardial infarction: evaluation of planned rehabilitation and of a predictive rating scale. *Medical Journal of Australia* **1,** 859

Steadman, J H and Graham, J G (1970). Head injuries: an analysis and follow-up study. *Proceedings of the Royal Society of Medicine* **63,** 23–8

Taylor, A R (1967). Post concussional sequelae. *British Medical Journal* **2,** 67–71

Trethowan, W H (1970). Rehabilitation of the brain injured; the psychiatric angle. *Proceedings of the Royal Society of Medicine* **63,** 32–6

Vandyk, N D (1975). *Accidents and the Law*. Law Society, by Oyez Publication, London

Weed, L L (1971). *Medical records, medical education and patient care, the problem oriented record as basic tool*. Press of Case Western University, Cleveland

Part 3 **Alcohol and Drug Abuse**

9 Alcoholism

P W Kershaw, MD, FRCPE, FRCPsych, DPM, DObst, RCOG

Rehabilitation, from the verb rehabilitate defined as 'to make fit, after disablement or illness, for earning a living or playing a part in the world' (*Chambers Twentieth Century Dictionary*, 1977 edn) is, in the alcoholic, especially difficult to distinguish from 'treatment'. Many writers talk of 'treatment and rehabilitation' while others apparently use the word interchangeably; for example, in a recent publication entitled *Alcoholic Rehabilitation* it is stated: 'treatment of alcoholism as a disease rather than as a symptom of something else has been the cornerstone of most successful Rehabilitation Centres' (Groupé 1978). In 1972 James *et al* implied that rehabilitation in the alcoholic was 'post-hospital'. They included out-patient groups and occupational therapy as well as 'social and spiritual re-awakening'. More recently Polich *et al* (1980) refer to rehabilitation as meaning 'improvement in social characteristics'. It is the author's contention that, though rehabilitation in the alcoholic can begin at the first contact and that full assessment is the essence of the management of the alcoholic, most rehabilitation begins after drying out and, hence, detailed references to detoxification will not be made. The emergency management and the treatment of physical and psychiatric complications in the alcoholic will not be included. However most other aspects of 'treatment' will be described. Most of this 'rehabilitation' can be performed by personnel other than doctors but some patients as part of the rehabilitative process will require the use of drugs and hence a doctor. Sometimes this will be a psychiatrist, who may then co-ordinate the aspects of care necessary. At other times the specialized services of clinical psychologists, social workers, nurses, health visitors and occupational therapists will be equally necessary.

It is only over the last 25 years that there has been widespread interest in alcoholism on the part of health care personnel and a mushrooming of services in Britain. There is evidence that this is a result of an increase in the number of alcoholics and of the problems caused by drinking to excess. In view of the apparent increased drinking in the young and of the length of time that it takes a person to become an alcoholic, unfortunately this increase will continue for some time. Ironically, at a time when public and political awareness and concern is growing there is a great deal of questioning concerning the efficacy and, hence, the cost effectiveness of alcoholism treatment. The development of the various treatment services has been admirably summarized by Orford and Edwards (1977). Although other indirect figures indicate a real increase in alcoholism, they argue that the increased supply of services for alcoholics may have generated an increased demand for these services. The increased admission figures may thus be illusory unless the treatment services are efficient. This suggestion may be at least partly correct. Kershaw and Timbury (unpublished) have shown that the work-load in a general psychiatric service grows in relation to the growth in personnel and to specific policy changes, partly confirming Orford and Edwards' contention. However, the relatively late development of specific alcohol treatment services at Gartnavel Royal Hospital in Glasgow was prompted by an increase in referrals of alcoholics which accounted for 20 per cent of all male referrals. The lack of commitment and the pessimism in some members of the hospital staff made the development of a specialized treatment service necessary though this development could well have caused an increase in the number of referrals.

Most psychiatrists have in recent years used the 1952 WHO definition of alcoholism:

> alcoholics are those excessive drinkers whose dependence on alcohol has attained such a degree that it shows a noticeable mental disturbance or interference with their bodily or mental health, their interpersonal relations and their smooth social and economic functioning or who show the prodromal signs of such development.

Edwards and Gross (1976) considered that this definition was over-inclusive and proposed to stress the dependence as opposed to socio-economic consequences. As a result they suggested the term 'alcohol dependence syndrome' as a group of variable symptoms which are then influenced by social and cultural factors. These comprise narrowing of the drinking repertoire, salience of drink-seeking behaviour, increased tolerance to alcohol, repeated withdrawal symptoms, relief avoidance of withdrawal, subjective awareness of compulsion to drink and reinstatement of the syndrome after alcohol. The main triad is: the recognition of repeated alcohol withdrawal symptoms by the patient, the recognition that he will drink occasionally and frequently to relieve this and the recognition that such drinking will effectively provide relief within a short period (Edwards 1977). The alcohol dependence syndrome should be differentiated from 'alcohol related disabilities' which include the broad categories of physical, psychological, social and interpersonal problems. These ideas have been stated in a WHO report (Edwards *et al* 1977) and they have received some support of a scientific nature (Hodgson 1980; Polich *et al* 1980). Hodgson and his colleagues have developed a questionnaire to measure the severity of alcohol dependence (Stockwell *et al* 1979) and have demonstrated that those who are more dependent drink faster, and in a separate follow-up study showed that those who were more severely dependent tended either to be abstinent or totally uncontrolled, whereas those who were moderately dependent could achieve a controlled drinking goal. Similarly Polich *et al* (1980) suggested, in their four-year follow-up study of alcoholics treated at alcohol treatment units in the United States where abstinence was the aim, that the older, more dependent men appeared to do better with abstinence whereas the younger less dependent men achieved 'non-problem drinking'.

These latter workers have also confirmed the hypothesis that alcoholics can move in and out of excess drinking. They state 'alcoholism is a chronic unstable condition' and 'remissions are frequent but are generally intermittent rather than stable'. This obviously makes the assessment of both treatment results and the facilities for treating alcoholics extremely difficult. It also suggests the practical point that many patients only seek help at times of stress and, if this is adequately provided, then they may need very little rehabilitation as such.

The author believes that most alcoholics are 'normal' people who drink excessively. Possibly a more elegant way of stating this is 'alcoholics are different in so many ways but it makes no difference' (Keller 1972). In a large series of alcoholics admitted to a general hospital psychiatric unit in Glasgow, reference was made to underlying personality or neurotic traits or psychosis in only 15 per cent of patients (Kershaw 1973). This is confirmed by Syme (1957) who failed to demonstrate differences in personality traits between alcoholic and non-alcoholic populations and by Horne *et al* (1974) who demonstrated such a great diversity in personality structure that it was impossible to find specific personality attributes, traits or mechanisms that would predict alcoholism. This does not refute the idea that some alcoholics cut across the three major diagnostic categories of neurosis, psychosis and personality disorder, but these groups are relatively small. Nor does it imply that alcoholics do not have interpersonal problems and neurotic symptoms brought about by their heavy drinking and its consequences. It is obviously essential in the management of any alcoholic patient to determine the presence of neurotic or psychotic features and to assess the personality structure as clearly as possible.

Assessment

Probably the most important aspect in dealing with the alcoholic is the initial assessment. This is obviously impossible if the patient is drunk and it may require a period of sobriety for any underlying neurotic traits, personality abnormalities or even psychotic features to be elicited. A psychiatrist is the obvious person to carry out this part of the assessment when for example subtle paranoid ideas, affective and phobic symptoms may be documented. The other points to be brought out in assessment relate to the drinking history, the abnormal drinking, and the degree of dependence. Possible problem areas such as physical symptoms, psychological problems and social difficulties require to be elicited and during the initial interview an attempt should be made to assess the degree of motivation. Where possible, as part of the assessment, the spouse, near relative or friend closely acquainted with the patient should be interviewed. Ideally this assessment should probably be performed by a multi-disciplinary team consisting of psychiatrist, social worker, psychologist, nurse, occupational therapist and other personnel who might be available as part of the specialized alcohol treatment unit, but anyone attempting to assess an alcoholic should remember the principal areas of evaluation.

Mention has been made of the difficult task of appraising motivation. Most patients attend as a result of external pressure. Roizen (1977) is quoted by Room (1980) as saying that alcoholics come to treatment because of the 'four l's'—liver, lover, livelihood and the law. However it seems likely that as well as seeking help as a result of these pressures, the patient's acceptance of his problems, and insight into his condition has already been developing. Some will require much time for insight to develop and certainly the assessment of motivation may require drying out of the patient before it can be reasonably evaluated. Possibly much of the rehabilitation may be a gradual process of developing insight, which in alcoholism refers to the patient's ability to appreciate that his alcohol intake is causing his symptoms and problems. If the detoxification is carried out in an alcoholism treatment unit where staff are attuned to notice attitudes and casual statements, this may assist the assessment of motivation but this still remains difficult. As there is as yet no scientific measurement of motivation and insight in the alcoholic, the intuition and attitudes of staff may be of as much importance as the patient's characteristics. In a very detailed recent review it was concluded that we are no nearer to assessing motivation despite much apparent work on the subject than we were some years ago (Ogborne 1978). Motivation however is a very flexible concept, but clinical experience would suggest that it can be engendered by treatment and rehabilitation.

The aim of the whole assessment is to formulate goals of treatment for each patient which should be clear to each member of the team, after discussion, and to the patient. It may be that the initial goal may be purely drying out and then reassessment following this period, though usually much more specific aims are necessary. Pattison has written extensively on this subject in the last 15 years, most recently in 1979. He has stressed the importance of matching sub-populations of alcoholics with the most appropriate facilities, methods and treatment personnel. He has pointed out that the aims of treatment are not the same in each patient or group of patients and that these aims may change through time. Thus the professional man who has few problems will require certain facilities which will be totally different from those needed by the patient from 'Skid Row'.

However, eventually the 'Skid Row' patient may achieve sufficient progress to require a totally different set of facilities. Pattison points out that matching the patient with a certain type of treatment is essential to achieve most effective results and the outcome of success is maximum if the expectation of the patient and the facility can be matched. Similarly, treatment programmes can achieve maximum effectiveness by clearly specifying what population they propose to serve, what goals are feasible with the population and what methods can be expected to best achieve these goals. None the less, he concludes, our current state of knowledge about treatment is still too global and imprecise to formulate exact treatment guidelines. Our measurement and evaluation methods are too crude to assess our methods accurately. These sentiments are echoed repeatedly in almost every treatment paper on alcoholism. However Pattison does say that comprehensive treatment programmes vary from community to community and depend largely on the social system characteristics of the community. In approaching the individual patient van Dijk (1975) illustrates how the vicious circles of addiction, cerebral damage, psychological factors and social factors caused by the excessive use of alcohol reinforce each other, but how by assessing each one in a many-sided approach, the resources and techniques of medicine, psychology and social work can be utilized. Most workers would agree that this multi-modal approach is the most optimistic to date.

Despite these comments, as will be seen later, there are many questions being asked about the efficacy of the expensive treatment provided by hospital-based alcohol treatment units. One alternative is the primary health care team of general practitioner, health visitor, district nurse, and social worker who should be ideally placed to recognize the problems caused to the patient and his family by alcohol (Shaw *et al* 1978; Advisory Committee on Alcoholism 1978). Unfortunately these services feel they lack the knowledge and support that are necessary for them to be effective. Shaw and his co-workers describe the community alcohol team, or variants on it, who can train and give specialist support to the primary care team. These teams would vary from place to place depending on local conditions. They consider that psychiatric resources have tended to be used in an inefficient and inappropriate manner but they point out that the nucleus of the community alcohol team should be, ideally, a psychiatrist and a social worker. They state that

whatever the case, any psychiatrist hoping to provide role support would have to spend more of his time than usual in casualty departments, general medical wards, health centres, social work area team offices, probation departments, prisons, day hospitals, hostels, marriage guidance clinics and reception centres to appreciate the range and variety of drinking problems, to comprehend the responses made to them by different agencies and to learn how best to assist other agents.

While this consultative work would seem to be essential it is feared that without some hospital back-up all the community agencies mentioned might still feel they do not have the skills that they require. As pointed out by Cartwright (1980), the issues relating to the attitudes of community workers are complex and may require national guidelines. It seems that a practical alternative is for existing alcohol treatment units to move gradually into the community and support existing agencies who then acquire a confidence and expertise in dealing with the problems themselves. Possibly the aim is for alcohol treatment units gradually to 'do themselves out of business', provided they are able to stimulate enough facilities in their area. At the moment, what is essential is for all workers in the field, both primary and secondary, to be aware of the facilities available locally, and to become aware of each others' services and needs.

Detoxification

As indicated it is not possible to complete the assessment of many patients until they have dried out. Although some alcoholics who are drinking excessively require specialized treatment for their withdrawal, presumably many more do this satisfactorily on their own without any professional help or with minimal help only. Even then, many of those who are admitted require only minimal use of tranquillizing agents (Olbrich 1979; Arroyave et al 1980). Similarly, despite the fact that all admissions to the Alcohol Treatment Unit at Gartnavel Royal Hospital were for detoxification most patients showed surprisingly little features of physical withdrawal. Though minor tranquillizers were given routinely, a short-term trial resulted in eight patients receiving no medication, only one required treatment and one other asked for drugs. Of 675 alcoholics admitted to a general hospital psychiatric unit 40 per cent showed no withdrawal, 25 per cent showed mild withdrawal, 20 per cent showed moderate to severe withdrawal and 15 per cent had delirium tremens (Kershaw 1973). The use of drugs in the withdrawal period should therefore be kept to a minimum, be reviewed on a daily basis, and only maintained for a few days.

Alcoholism Treatment Units

Alcoholism treatment units in Britain have developed over the past 25 years on the basis of the model created by Glatt at Warlingham Park (Glatt 1955). This was a specialized in-patient unit in which patients stayed for three months with group therapy and Alcoholics Anonymous being the main therapeutic tools, though a wide range of other facilities were utilized. There was a tendency for social classes I and II to be over-represented in such treatment, a trend which has been repeated in many units since (Hore and Smith 1975). The Warlingham Park unit appeared to be successful and as a result the Ministry of Health recommended in the early 1960s the setting up of further units, of which various descriptions and experiences have been documented (Ritson and Hassall 1970; James *et al* 1972; Hore 1976). However, in the early 1970s there was a change in emphasis to a much more community-based service. This type of unit had been described by Davies *et al* (1956) in the Maudsley Hospital where, though patients were admitted to a general psychiatric ward, there was more stress on out-patients and community involvement. At the same time there has been constant questioning about all aspects of alcoholism, the aims, treatment and facilities and especially of the value of 'treatment' (Clare 1977; Edwards *et al* 1977). This change in attitudes has partly resulted from the involvement of psychologists and sociologists and has considerably widened the horizons for rehabilitation. As a result it is impossible to be dogmatic and difficult to be comprehensive in the description of these units. Despite the trend towards out-patient treatment and community involvement almost all units, whether in-patient or day-patient in type, still use group work of some kind. The length of stay in treatment units varies from two weeks to three or more months, though there is no good evidence for prolonged length of stay in treatment units. The form of groups ranges from the psychotherapeutic, which would have been in the majority just over a decade ago, to the informative–educative type of groups, which are probably now beginning to be the most popular. The units that run as in-patient psychotherapeutic based groups tend to perform as therapeutic communities and in some centres there is much stress on patients running the units with little interference and minimal supervision from staff. Physically the units are of great variety. Some are part of hospital buildings, others are quite separate units situated a considerable distance from the hospital with which they have contact. Some are purpose built such as those in Manchester and Newcastle. In Britain most are under the National Health Service but there are a few privately run alcohol treatment units. In the United States there are many private or non-statutory treatment units and a recent publication has described some of them (Groupé 1978). Many of these units are run by ex-alcoholics and some have a large Alcoholics Anonymous commitment. The variations in alcohol units would appear to depend on many factors, such as the ideas of those who have played a part in their individual development, personnel, local socio-cultural groups and local expediency.

   The alcoholism treatment unit at Gartnavel Royal Hospital was a relatively late starter. Gradually developing since 1973, it has been able to utilize many of the new concepts. Hence it seems worth while to illustrate the methods of rehabilitation used there. It serves a population of approximately a quarter of a million which includes part of the West End of Glasgow, two large burghs including Clydebank, which has one of the highest unemployment rates in the country, and two dormitory suburbs.

There is also a rural area extending to the edge of Loch Lomond. There is a wide social mix in the catchment area; referrals to the alcohol unit tend to mirror this, so that there is certainly no over-representation of social classes I and II. We accept referrals from any agency as well as self-referrals. About half the referrals are separated, divorced or never married at referral and nearly 50 per cent are unemployed. A weekly multi-disciplinary out-patient clinic is held. Originally it was intended that all patients would be seen there; however only about 60 per cent of referrals are seen at the clinic, with the remainder being seen on home visits by members of the unit (6 per cent) and 34 per cent are seen as emergencies by other members of the hospital staff.

When the clinic started nearly 50 per cent of new referrals did not attend the clinic but this was reduced to 25 per cent by shortening the length of waiting time (Hyslop and Kershaw 1982). Most patients are now seen within one week of arrival of the referral letter. We are currently trying to accept phoned referrals in an attempt to shorten referral time even further and at the same time to evaluate home visiting.

There are only six beds for male patients in the unit which are used for 'drying out', patients being admitted only for about one week. Females are admitted to a general psychiatric ward under the care of the same consultant. Patients are admitted to this 'detoxification' part of the unit on the assumption that they require specialized facilities for detoxification, though, as already stated, this is not always very easy to assess. However as Arroyave et al (1980) have indicated, this type of unit serves a useful bridge to rehabilitation and we consider that it is useful for the staff of the unit to help a patient through his withdrawal. Increasingly we are relying on out-patient, day-patient or home detoxification with visits by the community nurse. There is a six-week day programme where patients attend for five days a week, though occasionally some will come to the unit at weekends for two or three weeks.

All units have some selection procedure; for example some would not admit patients who still have a court-case pending and, as a result, some units are considered by outside agencies to be highly selective. However we tend to accept a wide range of patients, again similar to Arroyave et al (1980). Patients who are overtly psychotic, who have severe memory impairment, are deaf, blind or dysphasic find it difficult to take part in the programme and are hence excluded, though patients with all these disabilities have been referred for consideration by other members of hospital staff or outside agencies. After completion of detoxification patients who are on no medication, are prepared to attend for six weeks and to remain abstinent will usually be accepted. Patients are not usually readmitted to the programme within a year of previous attendance.

Although the programme is a six-week 'course' with a special emphasis for each week, in view of the impracticality of asking patients to wait for six weeks before attending, patients start at any one of the weeks. As a result groups are open and constantly changing and hence vary in character and cohesiveness. This also makes it difficult for patients to play an active part in decision-making in the unit. However, patients have their own once-weekly meeting where a chairman is chosen for that week, and where they can discuss with staff the policy and practical arrangements of the unit. Although there are patients who do not complete the programme the group size remains reasonably constant at between 10 and 14.

The aims of the programme are to encourage sobriety, to lead a life without alcohol and to regain personal and social responsibility. There is considerable variety in the groups; some are purely education/information, others are of a more diffuse nature where patients are encouraged to discuss their own problems. Various members of the unit take the groups with obviously considerable different emphasis. Various sessions are spent on occupational, recreational and physical therapy, supervised by the occupational therapist. Many sports and pastimes are covered in an attempt to stimulate the patient into finding something which will help fill the time previously spent drinking. As a result patients go swimming and play badminton and football; jogging is also held. As far back as 1972 it was suggested that cardiovascular fitness and self-esteem of hospitalized alcoholics improved if they jogged one mile for twenty days, and they also slept better (Gary and Guthrie 1972). More recently circuit training has also been recommended in alcoholics (Piorkowski and Axtell 1976). Time is spent on social skills therapy usually in groups, but occasionally individually. Video-tapes with patients acting out various situations have been used but these have not been very popular with patients. Relaxation techniques are also taught. Films are shown to provide discussion for the group and visits are made to a day centre, to any suitable exhibitions or relevant plays both within and outwith the usual hours.

Each patient is given a 'key worker' who will see the patient once weekly and more if necessary to discuss any difficulties. Obviously each member of the multi-disciplinary team is available for individual interviews.

All patients are encouraged to attend Alcoholics Anonymous who meet twice weekly in the hospital. One group is held weekly by an ex-alcoholic who has had experience of Alcoholics Anonymous and is also a counsellor with Clydebank Council on Alcoholism.

During the early part of their attendance a visit is made to the patient's home by the charge nurse or social worker, or contact is made with spouses of relatively recently separated families. The value of involving the family in the rehabilitation of the alcoholic would appear to be important, and will be discussed later. Some units successfully manage to have groups where spouses attend with their alcoholic partner. Others have whole families attending on certain days. Certain patients for whom this would appear to help would include those whose interpersonal relationships and communications in the family have deteriorated considerably. This aspect of therapy is currently very fashionable though scientific evidence of its usefulness is not yet clear. We have not yet successfully arranged such groups though we have tried on more than one occasion. However spouses are encouraged to attend Alcoholics Anonymous which again meets once weekly in the unit.

As patients are constantly leaving the group the threat of separation may not be as strong as in a closed group. None the less some patients have a great deal of anxiety about retaking their own total responsibility and independence, and much time is spent discussing this aspect. A continuation group is held twice weekly at lunch time. Originally this was a relatively small group of patients who were having difficulty in finding employment. Because of the recent increase in unemployment more patients are keen to continue to attend and, as a result, there are now two groups which are constantly enlarging. Hence we are keen to encourage the recent development of day centres in the area. These are progressing and will be discussed later.

Patients obviously welcome continuing contact with a hospital-based specialist service where doctors, social workers, and nurses are easily seen in an atmosphere which is well known to them. The problem of over-dependence on the unit has to be constantly borne in mind and at the same time, for some patients, the therapeutic value of this contact can help retain sobriety; and, similarly, long-term support to some families may be necessary. It is important to remember that these services are relatively expensive and recent papers have questioned the value of 'intensive treatment' of alcoholics. There are various accounts of specific comparisons, which suggest for example that the length of stay is not important for success in the treatment of alcoholics (Willems *et al* 1973) and that out-patients do just as well as in-patients (Edwards and Guthrie 1967). Most recently Edwards *et al* (1977) have shown in a 12-month follow-up that for married male alcoholic patients there is little difference whether they received 'treatment' which involves several months of in- and out-patient treatment or purely 'advice' which involved one assessment and counselling session. The various papers which question our methods of treatment have been reinforced by the work of Polich *et al* (1980), already quoted, in which abstinence as a goal can still lead to non-problem drinking. In our programme abstinence is the aim and the only condition of attendance is of sobriety as it is considered that the patient should be totally dried out for reassessment. During this period it is hoped that physical damage will improve and as far as possible the patient should remain clear thinking to understand the nature of the groups. Discussion of controlled drinking used to be part of the group work but appeared to cause more confusion than was necessary. In view of the fact that most of the patients who attend this day programme appear to have a fairly high dependence on alcohol, the abstinence approach would appear to be the most appropriate.

Although the day-patient programme would appear to be a 'blunderbuss' type of rehabilitation, it is difficult from a practical point of view to isolate bits of the programme for groups of people, though individual therapy is given when it is considered necessary. A recent paper by Ewing (1977) describes a comprehensive alcoholism service allowing access to various types of treatment, with examples and type of personnel needed. In group A there is suggestion and support, medications, Alcoholics Anonymous, family therapy, and insight therapy, group B behaviour therapy, patients' clubs and in group C encounter therapy, occupational therapy and rehabilitation, and psycho-drama. He considers that the programme should offer at least three of those in Group A, one of Group B, plus C items if available. He stresses the importance of follow-up, the disengagement process and a flexible approach. He calls this system the Cafeteria System as there is choice within certain modalities of treatment.

As well as the day programme of groups a female out-patient group is held once a week. Though originally there was an evening out-patient group, this was found to be redundant in view of the development of nightly meetings of local Councils on Alcoholism. There has been long-term contact with these local Councils and at present three staff members act as counsellors, and we are gradually increasing our community services. Clydebank Council on Alcoholism has in association with the unit developed two male and female halfway houses. Day centres are in the process of being evolved in the area. Home visits are made as part of the family assessment but more patients are being seen initially at home.

Follow up of referrals is at six months and, if there has been little other contact with the patient, involves a home visit. We have held study days for local health visitors and social workers and these personnel are encouraged to visit the unit for the out-patient assessment clinic. The consultant at the unit has a general psychiatric out-patient clinic in one of the Health Centres and has frequent contact with many of the general practitioners there, so that patients are able to influence and aid the various services of the primary care team. Other groups of health care personnel have been involved in various teaching/training sessions, usually including students visiting the unit from the Alcohol Studies Centre at the Paisley College of Technology.

I have described the work of the unit in broad outline, including some deficiencies. Ewing (1977) and many other workers have stressed the importance of remaining flexible and open minded in our approaches to the alcoholic while providing a wide range of treatment modalities.

The Use of Drugs

Minor tranquillizers and anti-depressants have little place in the rehabilitation of the primary alcoholic. If after some weeks of definite alcohol withdrawal, the patient remains anxious or depressed it then becomes a calculated decision on the part of the doctor whether to treat this appropriately. It must be remembered that the alcoholic patient can become readily addicted to drugs other than alcohol and that he has an increased risk of suicide. These drugs should be avoided as much as possible.

Disulfiram (Antabuse) and Calcium carbimide (Abstem)

Disulfiram has been used in the treatment of alcoholics since 1948. The main action is to inhibit the oxidation of acetaldehyde and hence cause in effect acetaldehyde poisoning if alcohol is taken, resulting in effects which can be severe, such as nausea, sickness, headache, flushing, hypertension and even cardiovascular shock, heart failure, fits or death. The drug requires to be given for a few days before there is sufficient accumulation in the body and usually the effects last for three to four days. Results from the use of Disulfiram have varied from very good (Wallerstein *et al* 1957) to less than good (Baekeland *et al* 1971). In the latter study older men who were socially stable and motivated did best, but this is usually the case in any form of management. In view of the toxic effects, the screening of patients for disease of heart, chest, liver and kidneys is a wise precaution and may tend to emphasize to the patient the point of taking the Disulfiram and its dangers. There are a few side-effects from taking Disulfiram such as somnolence, bad taste and occasionally impotence. As a result calcium carbimide (Abstem) which has similar properties but which is said to have slightly fewer side-effects can be used. The drug can be given in the drying-out period, but its main use is either as a long-term adjuvant to the various other rehabilitative measures or occasionally at times of crisis or stressful drinking periods, such as New Year, Christmas, holidays and special occasions. The use of Disulfiram by the patient must be a positive act which enables him to achieve sobriety and enhance other measures. Disulfiram has also been implanted under the skin but blood levels would suggest that the effect is more psychological than pharmacological (Malcolm *et al* 1974).

Metronidazole (Flagyl)

This drug was used some years ago as it was suggested that it caused sensitivity to alcohol in some people and it was said to decrease the craving for alcohol. When put to the test of controlled trials however it was found to have no efficacy in the treatment of alcoholism.

Psychological Methods of Treatment

Behavioural psychologists have been the recent motivators of much stimulating work in the rehabilitation of the alcoholic. Nathan and Briddell (1977) and Miller (1977) have both reviewed comprehensively behavioural techniques.

Aversion therapy which has been utilized in alcoholics for 50 years—either electrical, inducing pain, or chemical, inducing nausea and vomiting—has lost its popularity. Covert sensitization (Cautela 1970), a form of verbal aversion therapy, tries to evoke unpleasant thoughts such as nausea, vomiting, or even losing a job, in association with imagined scenes of drinking while the patient is relaxed. Patients theoretically can be taught to use this method whenever they feel the urge to drink. Nathan and Briddell consider it offers only modest gains to the alcoholic but Miller feels that it could be used as a method of temporarily suppressing alcohol abuse before other more positive means are achieved.

Operant methods of conditioning, modifying the drinking response by manipulating its consequences, have been recently used in a variety of ways. The assumption is that these consequences may be positive reinforcers tending to increase the probability of drinking again. After careful behavioural assessment several techniques may be used to reduce the reinforcing mechanisms. While some of these methods involve the use of controlled drinking programmes, others do aim at abstinence. Thus 'contingency contracting' can be used for either, and includes contracting to certain behaviour, even in some cases signing an actual contract and having it witnessed. The general approach is one of direct symptom attack, so that the drinking behaviour of the patient is the essential form of assessment and subsequent intervention. Throughout the treatment much emphasis is placed on making the patient responsible for his behaviour and making him understand those situations likely to lead to excessive drinking. Assertive training can also be of relevance to the treatment of alcoholics and could be combined with social skills training. In both, the lack of self-esteem, the previous use of alcohol to inhibit feelings and frustrations, and the inability to cope with social pressures to drink can all be altered if the alcoholic can be taught to be sensitive to his own feelings and to the needs and feelings of others. Much of this assertive and social skills training involves gradual re-learning in many situations, first, in theory and, secondly, in practice. This can be used in groups and can involve role-playing and the use of video-tapes. At the moment there has been no detailed study of the effectiveness of such techniques even though in its simplest form, helping the social isolation of some alcoholics, it can be seen to be valuable.

These various techniques do not necessarily work alone and most psychologists would recommend a combined approach with considerable flexibility. Certainly they offer some advantages in that large numbers of alcoholics may be able to be treated. Reliable follow-up of treatment is assured, assuming the regular return of the patient to the treatment facilities. In so far as careful analysis of the individual's behaviour is essential these recent treatments do offer a return to the study of the individual.

Controlled Drinking

Through the use of a behavioural model it should theoretically be possible to train an alcoholic to drink normally. This idea has gained enthusiastic credence from various workers (Lovibond and Caddy 1970 and Sobell and Sobell 1973 especially). They use the term controlled drinking to describe the achievement of a remarkable number of their alcoholic patients who resume drinking without causing deterioration in the social, physical or interpersonal aspects of their life.

Davies (1962) had originally found that some patients can return to 'normal drinking'. More recently Polich *et al* (1980) have labelled this as 'non-problem drinking'. They have found in their four-year study of a cohort of 758 men treated in alcoholism treatment units throughout the United States of America, that 18 per cent of the 548 they were able to trace and who were still alive, were apparently drinking but were not having problems, even though the original aim in treatment had been abstinence. They are quite clear that alcoholism is a chronic and unstable condition but that remission can occur as 'non-problem drinking'. They point out however that the result of treatment may depend on previous characteristics of the alcoholic or any environmental change as he enters treatment. What is depressing in the context of the present account is that social rehabilitation was not as successful in their patients as remission of alcohol problems. These results are obviously not comparable to others where the aim is controlled drinking, whatever the technique used to attempt this. The enthusiasm of this approach has been criticized by Arroyave and McKeown (1979) who consider that treatments advocating controlled drinking appear as warm, humanitarian, progressive and attractive and reduce tensions in the relationship between the alcoholic and his helpers. On the other hand the concept of abstinence is made to appear old-fashioned, punitive, prejudiced, harsh and unsupportive. They argue that those who promulgate the idea of controlled drinking should identify the alcoholics that can be helped by it and demonstrate the final outcome as effective in terms of quality of life. Polich *et al* (1980) would certainly suggest that male alcoholics under the age of 40 and of low dependence appear to do better, in terms of non-relapsing by non-problem drinking, whereas those over 40 with a high degree of dependence appear to do better by abstinence. A recent work by Heather and Robertson (1981) has produced an authoritative review of the whole subject. At the moment it seems important to keep a balanced view and hope that the continued stimulus of workers in this field will help us clarify our goals for the individual patient, aiming at abstinence in patients who are severely dependent on alcohol and contemplating controlled drinking in those not so dependent, assuming that the patient is keen. The use of the Severity of Alcohol Dependence Questionnaire may be useful in assigning patients to abstinent or controlled drinking goals (Stockwell *et al* 1979).

Alcoholics Anonymous

The development of Alcoholics Anonymous has been and remains of extreme importance in the rehabilitation of the alcoholic. While the primary aim of the Fellowship of AA is sobriety which is achieved by members learning to live their lives again and 'be at peace with themselves and with others', its philosophy can be clearly seen to be derived from its historical context. Its founders were a New York stockbroker, Bill W., and a Ohio surgeon, Dr Bob. Both had had some contact with the Oxford Group, an evangelical organization which was the forerunner of the Moral Rearmament Movement. They first met through the Oxford Group in 1935 and assimilated the concepts which were taking shape concerning alcoholism as a disease which had medical interest in the era following prohibition. At this time the American Medical Council on Alcoholism was founded and shortly after the *Quarterly Journal of Studies on Alcohol* had its first issue. As a result alcoholism was seen as a disease, and an all-or-nothing phenomenon where sobriety was the only goal. Alcoholics Anonymous believe that the alcoholic can reach and treat fellow-sufferers as no one else can and they affirm that it gives contact and hope. They realize that by making the alcoholic admit his problems he will reverse the years of denial. The meetings retain some of the Oxford Group's characteristics: they have a 'closing prayer' and there are the Twelve Steps and Twelve Traditions. They have references to 'a power greater than ourselves' and 'God as we understand him'. All these factors stress the spiritual reawakening of the individual and one of the founders talked of his 'conversion'.

The growth of Alcoholics Anonymous has been prodigious. There are now over 28 000 in the world and in the Glasgow area, for example, there are about 200 groups. Thus it is easy for any alcoholic to attend a local meeting and, in a large city such as Glasgow, to find a meeting each night of the week within easy access. Many newcomers go to Alcoholics Anonymous to find a 'sponsor' who is able to introduce him, to help him through his drying out process and is someone to contact at times of difficulty. However the main aim of the sponsor is to enable the newcomer to get the most out of his new way of life, or as stated by Norris (1978) 'to build a bridge of understanding'.

In view of the nature of AA, which has been described as 'an Open Group with no leader', its anonymity and its evangelical appeal, it is difficult to find clear evidence of its effectiveness. There have been claims of success rates of 66 per cent but on careful analysis the success may be nearer that of other agencies of about 33 per cent. This aspect of the literature has been reviewed by Bebbington (1976) who considers that scientific assessment is not possible. Leach and Norris (1977) have positively reviewed all aspects of AA and include more than 700 references. On the other hand Tournier (1979) has recently criticized the rigidity of the organization which tends to reject any innovation, has limited treatment strategies, and apparently precludes early intervention in the alcoholic. He fears that the AA philosophy has been generalized to all interventions with deleterious effects. Perhaps his criticisms are more valid in the United States of America where the influence of AA is stronger in general than in Britain. Whatever the criticisms, not only has AA become a world-wide organization whose significance to the individual alcoholic can be pre-eminent, but it has also directly influenced the development of similar self-help groups for gamblers, neurotics and many others. Most patients should be told of the organization and encouraged to attend for as yet there is no clear indicator as to which alcoholics achieve their sobriety through it.

Councils on Alcoholism

The growth of these non-statutory agencies has been rapid in the last 17 years. Their influence has become of great importance nationally, as well as locally, as they have been encouraged and supported by governmental and statutory bodies, which at the same time have taken note of their recommendations. In view of current trends in governmental policy their growth will presumably continue. Although Councils are set up locally there are now 23 in Scotland and 33 in England and Wales. They have the backing of the Scottish Council on Alcoholism in Scotland and the National Council on Alcoholism in England and Wales. The aims of these National Councils are very wide:

to promote . . . an increased awareness within the whole community of the severity and far reaching nature of the problems of alcoholism and to promote co-ordination and unity of effort in striving for solutions, the study and research into the nature and extent of alcoholism and to promote its prevention, early diagnosis and treatment, the provision by both statutory and voluntary bodies of adequate levels of integrated alcoholism services and facilities for the humane management of the alcoholic,
a national network of local councils on alcoholism, education of the public and young people and the training of professional and lay persons in alcohol and its misuse, the illness of alcoholism and the availability of treatment,
the adoption of policies on alcoholism and programmes of recovery within industry and commerce,
the development of policies to deal with problems of alcoholism of an endemic nature which are national issues and to advise government accordingly.
Further aims are to publish advisory and informative material and to

liaise and interchange views with other concerned bodies in and outside the United Kingdom.

(Scottish Council on Alcoholism 1975)

In the last five years each one of these aims can be said to have been effected in part though presumably they will never be totally achieved. Each local Council is ideally placed to be able to assess the individual needs in that locality and to try and deal with the problems it finds in a gradual way. Kenyon (1972) has described the development and function of the first Regional Council on Alcoholism in the country, in Liverpool. He points out that, though education and publicity are very important, establishment of services to deal with the manifold problems of the active alcoholic is the first priority. He describes how over the years the organization has been built up, based upon demand and experience. He stresses the need for full-time professional staff to give a good counselling service, the access to hospital beds when needed and the co-operation with other non-statutory agencies. Initially the tendency is to have a 'shop front' where alcoholics or their families can go for advice and guidance (in Liverpool about half the cases originate with a third party inquiry). Following this, it is common to develop group counselling and thereafter a wide variety of functions including the setting up of day centres, halfway houses, and liaison with industry and with the courts. Education and research are equally possible and have been achieved by various local Councils on Alcoholism though obviously much co-operation with the statutory services is necessary.

It is difficult to assess the value of the various Councils on Alcoholism, but they have apparently not yet been criticized. Madden and Kenyon (1975) have given an account of 98 alcoholics who received group counselling at the Merseyside Council on Alcoholism with follow-up of between six months and three years. Half the patients were said to be abstinent and 64 to have 'recovered'. These results are obviously superior to many agencies but they point out that there is considerable selection and self-selection and 36 of the clients were in social classes I and II. The group had relatively high social stability scores.

The other encouraging aspect of the Councils on Alcoholism is that some alcoholics seem more willing to attend them than a statutory agency. Recently the Merseyside and Somerset Councils on Alcoholism have both suggested that they have a female: male referral rate of 1:1, whereas most alcohol treatment units have rates remaining between 1:3 and 1:5.

Halfway Houses/Hostels

Although in this country there is little difference between the term halfway house and hostel, most of those for alcoholics are in effect halfway houses in so far as they are not totally 'long term'. The aim is to discharge to other accommodation, even though the range of stay can vary from weeks to years. Madden (1979) has pointed out also that, in the United States, the term hostel implies a shelter for the homeless and vagrant, so that in the American literature the term halfway house is invariably used. As almost invariably in the alcoholism field, the development of this facility was pioneered in the United States so that by the mid-70s there were reported to be more than 500 halfway houses for alcoholics there. The theory of social rehabilitation inherent in the Halfway House Movement is a means of bridging the gap between an institution, usually prison or hospital, and the community. The concept is to encourage social adaptation and organization in an atmosphere which appears to be home-like, and hence relatively small, where staff and residents can communicate easily. They provide an environment away from alcohol and yet where there is a great deal of support.

There are many varieties of halfway house, from those taking vagrant alcoholics to some taking for a brief time patients who have a home to go to but who require some support between drying out and achieving reintegration into the family. It is important therefore to ascertain the local situation in regard to halfway houses and have a working knowledge of the type of patient they might accept. Most hostels demand clients to be dried out before admission so that this part of the treatment will require to be organized. This is one of the reasons why patients are admitted to the Alcohol Treatment Unit at Gartnavel Royal Hospital. Inevitably most hostels tend to be in large towns, and the psychiatric hospital may be approached to dry out the patient, or the general practitioner may prefer to, or have to, achieve this at the patient's home or in a bed supervised by himself.

Some detoxification centres which by their name imply they cater for the vagrant alcoholic, or the 'habitual drunken offender', will, if there seems to be desire on the part of the client, arrange for transfer to halfway houses, which may be run by the same organization. This facility can be the start of a lengthy rehabilitative process for the vagrant alcoholic. One such in Glasgow is the Talbot Centre, which initially does not necessarily demand sobriety, provided the client is not aggressive or violent. The homeless alcoholic may use a large hall as a meeting and eating place during the day and, by the provision of mats at night, the hall can be used as a dormitory. If he expresses the desire to stop drinking he may be dried out on the premises in a ward-like dormitory where a few drinking alcoholics may also be admitted for minor illness. A local general practitioner visits this unit regularly as it is obviously essential to enable this function to exist. After this there is a rehabilitation service in the building which runs as a self-help unit with separate sleeping and living areas and kitchen. Clients who have successfully achieved sobriety can then be moved to a few houses situated in various parts of Glasgow which offer flat-type accommodation with shared facilities, in which one resident will act as Warden. These latter facilities can obviously be considered 'long-term' and hence the houses are true hostels. This model offers as total a rehabilitative service as possible, usually with the help of Alcoholics Anonymous. Under these circumstances hospitals are only used for patients who have physical or psychiatric problems.

Another fairly typical halfway house is run by Clydebank Council on Alcoholism with some support from Gartnavel Royal Hospital, Alcohol Treatment Unit. When it was set up in 1974 the aim was to have a halfway house with patients who, after drying out in hospital for some two to three weeks, would be transferred to the house for three to six months, during which time they would initially attend the hospital as day-patients. They would spend brief periods at home and later they would work from the halfway house, returning home for longer periods or finding other accommodation before finally living at home. Although this service was thought to be what the patients wanted, in fact it tended to be refused by the patients, who on discharge from hospital wished to go home, rather than to a halfway house relatively near their own house. As a result patients admitted were usually homeless and as such required a considerably longer period of residence than was originally planned, sometimes even for nearly three years. Many patients are still admitted via the Alcohol Treatment Unit after drying out but some are admitted direct from the Council, others by social workers from other hospitals or prison. Occasionally it is used as a temporary shelter for those rejected by their families on account of drinking.

Initially there was a resident warden and groups were organized most days by either counsellors or the hospital service. Gradually it was realized that a warden was not strictly necessary and for a period of two years the hostel ran without one. This was found to be possible because of the relative stability of some of the residents who had been sober for about two years. In that period the turnover was slow, only 12 admissions per year. However, when this stable group left, and the length of sobriety was less, it was found that some residents began drinking *in situ* and a warden had to be reinstated. Since the period without a warden internal groups have not been held with such frequency, but this has been offset by daily groups being held by the Council, one of which is held in the hostel. Residents are also encouraged to attend AA. Although the atmosphere has always been informal, it has become even more so with fewer groups. Visits are made regularly by various counsellors, recovered alcoholics, ex-residents and members of the Alcohol Treatment Unit. Because of the length of time such homeless alcoholics seem to require to achieve stability, a small house which had three rooms and shared facilities was taken over for residents who were working. Until recently most patients stayed there for a year or more before moving on to their own flats or marrying. As a result of recent unemployment residents of this house have not found work and have not progressed to other accommodation.

In the last year a hostel for females has been opened with up to 10 beds. This has served a much wider area and residents are usually admitted at the request of the social work departments in the region. Ironically, compared to the hostel for males it was felt necessary to have three staff and the degree of support which has been found to be necessary to the homeless female has warranted this. The number of referrals is much greater than can be accepted and these are vetted by an assessment committee, though occasionally it has been found possible to admit as a relative emergency. The warden has to have considerable skills and support to be able to liaise with housing authorities, social workers, children's panels and foster homes. It has been found that when male residents relapse they have tended to leave and not return, or occasionally to drink surreptitiously. Females however tend to become inebriated locally and return to the halfway house causing serious problems. In neither of the houses has it been found particularly useful to re-accept someone who has been discharged because of drinking, though resident groups always want to give them 'another chance'.

There has been a steady growth in the number of halfway houses for alcoholics in Scotland. At present there are 14 of which three are in Edinburgh, one in Peterhead and the rest in the West of Scotland. However, as well as the usual difficulty in assessing effectiveness there is the added problem of attempting to measure such things as 'atmosphere' (Orford *et al* 1975; Otto and Orford 1978; Rubington 1979; Annis and Liban 1979). Annis and Liban (1979) in Toronto monitored three detoxification centres, followed up men transferred to five different halfway homes and compared them with a control group who did not go to such places. At three months follow-up, and on purely official data which cover drunkenness, arrests and readmissions, they found some differences in the groups. In the men who went to halfway houses 6 per cent had drunkenness arrests compared with 32 per cent of the control sample. There was no difference in readmissions or in the total number of drunkenness episodes so that the halfway house sample apparently learnt to return to some form of drying out rather than commit offences when they relapsed. They suggest that in place of the short-stay rehabilitative halfway house a more realistic approach to this group of clients would be the more humanitarian long-term type of hostel. Rubington (1979) concludes that halfway houses with an informal home-like atmosphere appear to be more effective than those with a more institutional type of atmosphere. Orford *et al* (1975), studying one halfway house in England, have shown that the attitudes of staff and residents are more related to a normal and everyday social relationship than to those of skilled technicians. Rubington (1977) has given a full account of his social theories in regard to the halfway house. He divides his residents into groups which he calls 'loners', 'mixers', 'company men' and 'regular guys'. He considers that, because of different patterns of authority in the different types of halfway houses found in the United

States, that is, private, state-funded and church-run halfway houses, these different groups will relate differently in each and this will influence their outcome. He points out the relatively poor outcome in general and stresses the need to study these facilities carefully. Certainly in Clydebank, about 50 per cent of those admitted left the hostel for an unknown destination presumably to drink again, yet there have been many individual dramatic successes, and the halfway house remains an integral part of the rehabilitation process which aims at re-socializing the alcoholic who is homeless.

Day Centres

Until relatively recently the idea of a day centre consisted basically of a 'soup kitchen', a haven for down and outs which might offer washing and laundering or even recreational facilities; but day centres have now become relatively sophisticated, aiming at as full a rehabilitation programme as possible. Although various non-statutory organizations have taken up the challenge and provided facilities for alcoholics under this broad heading, there has also been an increase in the interest of the social work departments in this development. This is encouraging, and it is hoped that these centres will eventually take over the functions of the more expensive hospital-based service. Some of the day centres have developed because of increasing unemployment, with the problem of boredom for the alcoholic, so that a meeting place and recreational area where drink is irrelevant have become important. It is possible that Alcoholics Anonymous and Councils on Alcoholism may be able to use the facilities at night. In Scotland in 1978 there were 11 such centres as well as other soup kitchens. However a further eight have opened or are in the process of opening in the Strathclyde region under the auspices of the social work department.

In Glasgow Alban House is one such centre. This was originally conceived as a dry social club where no special reference to drinking or alcoholism was made, but where alcoholics could obviously meet and relax. Regular dances and socials were held and there were facilities for pool, table-tennis, cards and a television room. It became difficult not to enlarge to include an Alcoholics Anonymous meeting and Gamblers Anonymous asked to use the premises. As a result the original concept has changed somewhat so that it has become a day centre for alcoholics with a large conference area and exhibition rooms for aspects of alcoholism. These facilities can be used by any organization which wishes to disseminate information on the subject. Two counsellors have been appointed to be available daily and day programmes are running for alcoholics. Clients are taken either on self-referral or from social work, general practitioners or hospital. Some of the clients live in halfway houses nearby. It is hoped that habitual drunken offenders may be able to attend regularly and that this will play a part in the decriminalization of the alcoholic.

Employment

The basic nature of rehabilitation requires that the patient should be fit for employment, and this is therefore one of the main aims in the rehabilitation of the alcoholic. Unfortunately finding employment in an area of high unemployment is more difficult for the patient than for his non-alcoholic counterpart. This disheartening aspect of present-day rehabilitation means that the main aim is to maintain the alcoholic in any existing employment. Obviously this aspect of the problem varies from area to area but it illustrates how social change can clearly influence rehabilitation. Whereas previously anyone working in the drinks industry would be recommended to change their employment, today this would be debated in view of the problems which beset someone who is unemployed.

Assuming that the alcoholic patient is employed, it may be necessary to consult with his employer, who may well have had great difficulties with him and may have come to the end of his patience. None the less this effort has to be made. The approaches are best achieved either through a social work agency or when available an Industrial Alcohol Team. The important positive message to be made to employers is that, given the co-operation of the alcoholic, it is better to retain him as someone who has perhaps given years of good service before his gradual decline than to retrain someone else. It has taken years for this attitude to bear fruit in Britain, though forty years ago employees assistance programmes originated in the United States of America. Nowadays various companies including many large corporations have realized this and have organized programmes in their firms with the assistance of the Industrial Alcohol Units, Local Councils on Alcoholism, local AA groups and with the co-operation of the unions. Although this insight has not been uniform it is still increasing despite unemployment. The main aim of such a programme is to enable alcoholics to seek help in the confines of work, both individually through a counsellor from one of the organizations mentioned above, or by group meetings which may be held on the premises, for example at lunch-time. It is usually made a condition of continued employment, following an initial individual warning and then a warning when a union member is present, that the alcoholic should attempt to stop drinking by attendance at some programme. Referrals to the health service appear to be increasing from this source.

At a managerial level the private nursing homes are being utilized, presumably financed through private health schemes as part of the employee's conditions of service. Freedberg and Johnston (1980) have recently shown that, using an assisted treatment programme for employed alcoholics, about 80 per cent of referrals could be retained in the same company by using a behavioural approach to rehabilitation. They divided them into two groups: 370 sought help after being threatened with dismissal; this group had more problems with work; 58 sought help voluntarily and their problems were mainly psycho-social. However, there was no difference as assessed by work performance at follow-up. Many alcoholics are unemployed by the time they seek help. As stated, nearly 50 per cent of referrals to the Alcohol Treatment Unit were unemployed, though loss of job is one of the common reasons for the actual referral. As a result much effort is expended by social workers and Disablement Resettlement Officers in finding employment. Retraining programmes of various sorts may be found necessary.

At present in an area of high unemployment alcoholics are often tempted to seek work away from home, for example in oil-related industries. Unfortunately there are many pitfalls, and unless the alcoholic has sufficient confidence to face up to many unfamiliar situations that confront him then relapse may well take place. It is almost the social norm for workers on returning from the oil rigs to drink heavily as alcohol is not allowed on the rigs. Plant (1979) has shown that there are more alcoholics in those jobs in which travelling away from home is an integral part. All these problems should be discussed either individually or in groups before the alcoholic leaves to find work. It is in this area that social skills therapy, such as interview role playing, may be of especial benefit.

Families

One of the few apparently good predictors of recovery in the alcoholic is being married or, more accurately, having a stable home life. Thus it is important to retain the family and its support. Unfortunately many alcoholics have lost this support and 50 per cent of referrals to Gartnavel Royal Hospital Alcohol Treatment Unit are not married. Threats of separation and actual separation are a common reason for referral. Contact with the patient's family is necessary as soon as possible and should be part of the assessment process. If not, then an early interview, usually at home, is of value to assess the problems which have to be faced.

Family attitudes vary considerably and are obviously complex. The attitude of the spouse may vary from total compliance and denial, to passive acceptance of the alcoholic, through to rejection and hostility. At times, joint interviews with the alcoholic and spouse can be useful to discuss conflicts and problems. If this is not possible in the clinic or day centre, social workers, health visitors or community nurses who have developed special skills necessary in making contact at home should utilize this contact to help the family and the patient. Social workers especially are concerned with the family and there are signs that, with increasing knowledge, their confidence in dealing with this common problem is increasing. Thus some of the day centres which are being set up in the West of Scotland will have as their basis the management and involvement of the whole family. Some treatment units utilize group therapy either for the spouses of alcoholics or for both spouses and their alcoholic partners. Other units have families visiting the unit as part of the programme. The aim is to reduce the many aspects of stress that have accrued in the family as a result of the alcoholic. Family problems change as the drinking continues. Initially there is confusion as to what is going wrong, and then the wife may attempt to control the patient's drinking while taking over part or the whole of his role in the family. Gradual social isolation may develop and, later, feelings of hopelessness and fear about being able to cope and, as a result, outside help is sought. Orford *et al* (1976) have shown that when wives coped by developing some sort of engagement with the husband, even if this was a stormy relationship, the prognosis was better over the next twelve months than when their behaviour involved avoidance or disengagement, for example, when she told the alcoholic he must leave or when she felt too frightened to do anything. They point out that these behaviour patterns might be artificial and merely a sign of the severity of the problem. Most of the research work has been done on wives of alcoholic husbands but equally there are problems in the families of alcoholic mothers and, although there has been much speculation as to the effect on the children of alcoholic parent or parents, there remains little study of a scientific nature. Obviously there are many complicated areas to discuss and deal with in the family. Even when the alcoholic assumes sobriety there are other problems, such as taking over functions within the family again and the re-learning of trust by family members. Much help will be needed at times of relapse, and here the contact with an agency may be helpful to retain the stability of the marriage and help the alcoholic family through the crisis. Steinglass (1977) has extensively reviewed the concept of 'family therapy' in the alcoholic and concludes that there is guarded optimism about application of these techniques in the treatment of alcoholism, while pointing out that there is little hard evidence demonstrating the actual efficacy of it. He appears to suggest that, far from the alcoholic being dealt with in the conventional alcohol treatment unit, it is possible that more use should be made of family therapy units which deal with the family as a whole and treat the alcoholism only as a secondary problem.

One common area of dysfunction in the alcoholic is of course related to sexual problems. A drunk and impotent partner confronting a fearful and uninterested spouse can lead to difficult problems and occasionally to the development of morbid jealousy. This latter condition must be dealt with as a problem the seriousness of which depends on the risk to the spouse. However, at the other end of the spectrum, when the alcoholic is improving then it becomes important to use a variety of techniques to enable the marriage to become sexually viable again. Occasionally conjoint marital therapy may be necessary, though usually encouragement is sufficient as this dysfunction may need some weeks abstinence before improvement. Potensan forte may sometimes be of benefit as a very short-term measure, but how much the effect of this is psychological and how much physical is extremely difficult to decide.

Al-Anon/Alateen

As groups of AA members met throughout the USA they were obviously accompanied by relatives who therefore met each other, with the realization that they had many common problems. They gradually met more formally and in 1951 scattered family groups came together and named themselves 'Al-Anon Family Groups'. Their aim was to help the families of alcoholics by using the twelve steps and twelve traditions adopted from Alcoholics Anonymous. Obviously these groups had some concern with the special problems of young people and had meetings which discussed these. In 1957 the first Alateen Group was formed in California by Bob, teenage son of AA/Al-Anon parents. There has been a gradual growth of these groups which are usually formed out of Al-Anon groups and are, in fact, Al-Anon groups for teenagers. As can be imagined there are many difficulties in forming such a group and in keeping it going. However by 1973 there were 6500 Al-Anon groups and 1000 Alateen groups throughout the world. Basically the purpose of the groups is to help the families and children of alcoholics. However, as has been shown for nearly 20 years (Jackson 1954) the stress that the alcoholic puts on the family further pushes the alcoholic into persisting with his drinking. If the family can gain help in any way this may assist the alcoholic and can in fact be the start of his improvement. As a result, it can be of great value to recommend to spouses of alcoholics to attend Al-Anon if these groups are available, even if the alcoholic is denying his problem. Occasionally the patient, by his mechanism of projection, may well suggest that all Al-Anon does is to cause further break-up of the family.

Special Groups

As Pattison (1979) points out, simple psychological and social data can provide better indicators for treatment selection than many available complex tests and measurements. In view of the evidence mentioned previously, the degree of dependence is also important to assess (Stockwell *et al* 1979). It may be useful to attempt to indicate the special needs of other groups, however, so that it may be clearer how to match the client population with the facilities available.

Female Alcoholics

Although there is evidence that there is an increase in the number of female alcoholics this is not yet clearly borne out by referrals to statutory agencies. None the less one would expect an increase in female alcoholism in view of the increased freedom of women which results in 'equality' with the disadvantages of being male as well as the advantages. If younger women are drinking more than their elders, the male:female alcoholic ratio will presumably reach 1:1. What is more worrying is that, although in general women present with very similar problems to men as a result of excess drinking—though with an increase of cirrhosis and dementia (Kershaw 1973; Wilkinson *et al* 1969)—they will have been drinking less alcohol for a shorter time. Pessimistically therefore one may expect more serious physical problems at an earlier age. Although much has recently been written about the female alcoholic and her separate problems, it is difficult not to see this as a measure of political movement, rather than as a result of any great indicators that suggest female alcoholics need special treatment approaches. None the less the female alcoholic still finds it difficult to make her problems known and her abnormal drinking in a solitary surreptitious fashion might suggest a different approach. Similarly there is evidence that alcoholic women have increased behavioural disturbance, depression or abnormal personality adjustment (Rathod and Thomson 1971; Sclare 1970), though Saunders (1980) reviewing this topic considers that socio-cultural factors are more important. Some women find it difficult to talk about their problems in groups which are dominated by men. They can certainly have extra problems in relation to family care. Consequently it may be useful to be able to discuss their various problems in a separate forum. At Gartnavel Royal Hospital we have developed a weekly female group run by a female psychologist and this is appreciated by the patients who feel they can discuss some problems in a much more relaxed way. Home visiting by a social worker or other counsellor may be just as important in the female alcoholic as in the male, and can possibly give an indication of how she is functioning in her family role. Sheehan and Watson (1980) point out that it is important to include the husband, family or boyfriend in the female alcoholic's rehabilitation and that long-term support may be necessary. They also point out that there should be greater individualization of response to women and greater flexibility of treatment towards the specific needs of each woman. While this is perfectly true it is equally true in the case of men. Annis (1980) states that the female alcoholic population is not homogeneous and obviously a single form of treatment will not be fully efficacious, just as with men, and pooling results across all female alcoholic patients may obscure significant improvement within sub-groups, just as with men.

Young Alcoholics

There appears to be an increase in the number of young alcoholics, usually defined as under 30 years though by some workers defined as under 24 years. There is a suggestion that even at this age they may have very severe problems, yet it is very difficult for them to accept that abstinence is essential for the rest of their life. This may explain why Rathod *et al* (1966) have suggested there is a poorer prognosis in the young alcoholic. Fischer and Coyle (1977) describe a specialized treatment service for young problem drinkers in which they have both individualized treatment and twice weekly group meetings. Controlled drinking may be of value for this group especially, and, even if this is not considered useful, re-learning procedures such as taking a group to the pub but drinking soft drinks may help. Gwinner (1977) has described in-patient treatment for young alcoholics. There is hope for the future that there may be a clearer management strategy for this group.

Elderly Alcoholics

Perhaps because the incidence of alcoholism in the elderly is relatively low (6·5 per cent of alcoholic referrals to Gartnavel Royal Hospital were between the age of 60 and 69 years and only 1·2 per cent over 70 years), this diagnosis may go unsuspected. The problems have not yet been extensively studied. However, the elderly are unable to take as large a quantity of alcohol as young people and difficulties may arise as a result of this. Glatt (1978) considers that they respond well to the same comprehensive approach which proves useful in other age groups. He does state however that alcohol misuse in the elderly is often symptomatic of underlying socio-psychological changes. Hence it is important to give support to improve self-esteem and self-respect, and also self-expression. Social work help is essential for economic difficulties and, for example, introduction to local community groups. Similarly Zimberg (1978) feels that elderly alcoholics are unwilling to be involved in the usual programmes and stresses that effective home care is important.

Middle Class Alcoholics

There is reference in American literature (Groupé 1978) to an increase in facilities for residential and day care for middle class alcoholics. In this country the growth of private clinics catering for professional and middle class would confirm this. In the West of Scotland there appears to be initial resistance to attending the various health service facilities provided, though some appear to do well with out-patient care alone. The middle class alcoholic who eventually accepts these facilities usually has taken the first step to his successful rehabilitation.

Skid Row Alcoholics

Although the numbers of Skid Row alcoholics is relatively small, their impact on the community and the concern they engender are great. Their problems have been well documented in America and were only originally brought to notice in Great Britain by Edwards *et al* (1966). This was followed by the 1971 report *Habitual Drunkenness Offenders* (Home Office 1971), which recommended the setting up of hostels and urged the decriminalization of the alcoholic offender. The importance of hostels and halfway houses in the rehabilitation of such patients has been discussed. With the recent Criminal Justice Acts, and the provision of detoxification centres this decriminalization should in theory be much nearer completion, though a great deal of co-operation will be required from the police. These centres are probably useless without rehabilitative support to back them (Hore 1977; Hamilton *et al* 1978).

Personnel in Alcoholic Rehabilitation

It must be obvious that, although much research is in progress bearing on results of treatment, the attitudes of the individual person treating the alcoholic must have a great deal of influence, and references have already been made to an increasing awareness of this problem (Orford *et al* 1975; Shaw *et al* 1978). There are special difficulties because of the multi-disciplinary nature of the rehabilitative programme and the degree of co-operation which is essential between the disciplines, in which quite different models of management are found. Kalb and Propper (1976) suggest that the professional worker adopts a 'scientific' model, while the para-professional worker uses a 'craft' model. They pessimistically suggest that the two cannot profitably co-exist when it is quite clear that they have to achieve co-existence and a great deal of tolerance is important.

What can be difficult is the relationship with non-statutory bodies when ex-alcoholics play their role in rehabilitation. Under these circumstances confidentiality is essential, as often patients are prepared to talk fully to anyone that they think is going to help them. A few patients require the absolute confidentiality that is necessary in medical practice and it is important that this confidentiality is maintained. There is a growing literature (e.g. Cartwright 1980; Shaw *et al* 1978) which shows that support and supervision are essential for the alcoholism counsellor and greater emphasis needs to be placed on the Alcohol Treatment Unit staff supporting primary workers.

The final difficulty is in relation to other medical workers. There are still negative attitudes to be overcome with one's non-psychiatric colleagues. This is well illustrated by Hamilton *et al* (1978) who experienced difficulties in setting up a detoxification unit in a Regional Poison Centre in a general hospital.

Conclusions

The aim of this account has been to provide an over-view of recent literature concerning rehabilitation of the alcoholic, together with an account of the workings of the facilities available in part of a country where alcoholism and alcohol-related disabilities occur in 5 to 10 per cent of the male population (Saunders and Kershaw 1978).

A careful assessment to ascertain the needs of the individual patient should be followed by discussion of the aims of rehabilitation for the patient. A working knowledge of the facilities available is essential so that they can be utilized most effectively and most efficiently. Despite aiming at matching client for facility, scientific data have still not clarified this issue, though one or two guidelines have been stated. A description such as this would appear to make the patient a passive recipient of treatment, yet rehabilitation implies the patient playing an active role and developing responsibility for his recovery. It is possible that much of the rehabilitative process relates to the patient remaining in contact for sufficient length of time to learn social readjustment. It seems important to have flexible concepts and remain questioning but hopeful, remembering that it is important not to over-treat. Finally, it must not be forgotten that the therapist's attitudes may be more important in treatment than the actual facilities available.

Edwards (1980) reviewing the whole alcoholism treatment field states 'we might be seen as having reached a stage of discontent with old ways and sensed a need for change'. However, in the management of the alcoholic patient we can do no better than to remember Thomas Trotter's advice in 1812:

I have mentioned above the necessity of studying the patient's temper and character, that we may acquire his confidence. These will lead us to the particular cause, time and place of his love of the bottle. The danger of continuing his career may be then calmly argued with him, and something proposed that will effectually wean his affections from it, and strenuously engage his attention. This may be varied according to circumstances, and must be left to the discretion of the physician.

Appendix

Various bodies provide useful lists of facilities for the rehabilitation of the alcoholic:

Scottish Council on Alcoholism
49 York Place
Edinburgh EH1 3JD
(this provides an excellent Register
of Alcoholism Services in Scotland,
2nd edn. 1981)

Scottish Health Education Unit
Woodburn House
Canaan Lane
Edinburgh EH10 4SG

Alcohol Studies Centre
Paisley College of Technology
72 George Street
Paisley
Renfrewshire PA1 2LF

Medical Council of Alcoholism
8 Bourdon Street
London W1X 9HU

Health Education Council
78 New Oxford Street
London WC1

National Council on Alcoholism
3 Grosvenor Crescent
London SW1X 7EE

Alcoholics Anonymous
11 Redcliffe Gardens
London SW10 9BG

Al-Anon Family Groups
6 Great Dover Street
London SE1 4YF

Alcohol Education Centre
Maudsley Hospital
99 Denmark Hill
London SE5 8AQ

References

Advisory Committee on Alcoholism (1978). *The Pattern and Range of Sources for Problem Drinkers*. Report to the Department of Health and Social Security and Welsh Office

Annis, H M (1980). Treatment of Alcoholic Women. In *Alcoholism Treatment in Transition* (ed. G Edwards and M Grant). Croom Helm, London

Annis, H M and Liban, C B (1979). A follow-up study of male halfway-house residents and matched non-resident controls. *Journal of Studies on Alcohol* **40**, 63–9

Arroyave, F and McKeown, S (1979). Controlled drinking—a perspective. *British Journal of Hospital Medicine* **22(6)**, 604–7

Arroyave, F, McKeown, S and Cooper, S E (1980). Detoxification—an approach to developing a comprehensive alcoholism service. *British Journal of Addiction* **75**, 187–95

Baekeland, J, Lundwall, L, Kissin, B and Shanahan, T (1971). Correlates of outcome in Disulfiram treatment of alcoholism. *Journal of Nervous and Mental Diseases* **153**, 1–9

Bebbington, P E (1976). The efficacy of Alcoholics Anonymous. The elusiveness of hard data. *British Journal of Psychiatry* **128**, 572–80

Cartwright, A K (1980). The attitudes of Helping Agents towards the alcoholic client: the influence of experience support training and self-esteem. *British Journal of Addiction* **75**, 413–31

Cautela, J R (1970). The treatment of alcoholism by covert sensitization. *Psychotherapy: Theory Research and Practice* **7**, 86–90

Clare, A W (1977). How Good is Treatment. In *Alcoholism New Knowledge and New Responses* (ed. G Edwards and M Grant). Croom Helm, London

Davies, D. L (1962). Normal drinking in recovered alcohol addicts. *Quarterly Journal of Studies on Alcohol* **23**, 94–104

Davies, D L, Shepherd, M and Myers, E (1956). The two year prognosis of 80 alcohol addicts after treatment in hospital. *Quarterly Journal of Studies on Alcohol* **17**, 485–502

van Dijk, W K (1975). Vicious circles in alcoholism—many sided approach to therapy. *Medicine 2nd Series* **13(1)**, 598

Edwards, G (1977). The Alcohol Dependence Syndrome: Usefulness of an Idea. In *Alcoholism New Knowledge and New Responses* (ed. G Edwards and M Grant). Croom Helm, London

Edwards, G (1980). Alcoholism treatment between guesswork and certainty. In *Alcoholism Treatment in Transition* (ed. G Edwards and M Grant). Croom Helm, London

Edwards, G and Gross, M M (1976). Alcohol dependence: provisional description of a clinical syndrome. *British Medical Journal* **1**, 1058–61

Edwards, G and Guthrie, S (1967). A controlled trial of inpatient and outpatient treatment of alcohol dependency. *Lancet* i, 555–9

Edwards, G, Gross, M, Keller, M, Moser, J and Room, R (1977). Alcohol Related Disabilities. *World Health Organisation Offset Publication* no 32 Geneva

Edwards, G, Hawker, A, Williamson, V and Hensman, C (1966). London's Skid Row. *Lancet,* 249–52

Edwards, G, Orford, J, Egert, S, Guthrie, S, Hawker, A, Hensman, C, Mitcheson, M, Oppenheimer, E and Taylor, C (1977). Alcoholism: a controlled trial of 'treatment' and 'advice'. *Journal of Studies on Alcohol* **38(5)**, 1004–31

Ewing J A (1977). Matching therapy and patients: the cafeteria plan. *British Journal of Addiction* **72**, 13–18

Fischer, J and Coyle, B (1977). A specialised treatment service for young problem drinkers: treatment results obtained during the first six months of the treatment programme. *British Journal of Addiction* **72**, 317–19

Freedberg, E J and Johnston, W G (1980). Outcome with alcoholics seeking treatment voluntarily or after confrontation by their employer. *Journal of Occupational Medicine* **22**, 83–6

Gary, V and Guthrie, D. (1972). The effect of jogging on physical fitness and self concept in hospitalised addicts. *Quarterly Journal of Studies on Alcohol* **33**, 1073–8

Glatt, M M (1955). A Treatment Centre for alcoholics in a public mental hospital: its establishment and its working. *British Journal of Addiction* **52**, 55–92

Glatt, M (1978). Experience with elderly alcoholics in England. *Alcoholism: Clinical and Experimental Research* **2(1)**, 23–6

Groupé, V (ed.) (1978). Alcoholism Rehabilitation Methods and Experiences of Private Rehabilitation Centres. *Alcoholism Treatment Series No 3* NIAAA–RUCAS, New Brunswick, New Jersey

Gwinner, P D V (1977). The Young Alcoholic Approaches to Treatment. In *Alcoholism and Drug Dependence A Multidisciplinary Approach* (eds J S Madden, R Walle and W H Kenyon). Plenum Press, New York

Hamilton, J R, Griffith, A, Ritson, B and Aitken, R C B (1978). Detoxification of habitual drunken offenders *Scottish Health Service Studies No 39*. Scottish Home & Health Department

Heather, N and Robertson, I (1981). *Controlled Drinking*. Methuen, London

Hodgson, R (1980). Treatment strategies for the early problem drinkers. In *Alcoholism Treatment in Transition* (ed. G Edwards and M Grant) 162–78. Croom Helm, London

Home Office (1971). *Habitual Drunkenness Offenders.* Working Party Report. HMSO, London

Hore, B (1976). *Alcohol Dependence.* Butterworth, London

Hore, B (1977). Setting Up Detoxification Centres. In *Alcoholism New Knowledge and New Responses* (ed. G Edwards and M Grant). Croom Helm, London

Hore, B and Smith, E (1975). Who goes to alcoholic units. *British Journal of Addiction* **70,** 263–70

Horne, J L, Wanberg, K W and Adams G (1974). Diagnosis of alcoholism factors of drinking background and current conditions in alcoholics. *Quarterly Journal of Studies on Alcohol* **35,** 147–75

Hyslop, A and Kershaw, P (1982). Non-Attenders at an Alcoholism Referral Clinic. *Health Bulletin* **39,** 314–19

Jackson, J K (1954). The adjustment of the family to the crisis of alcoholism. *Quarterly Journal of Studies on Alcoholism* **15,** 562–88

Jackson, P and Oei, T P S (1978). Social skills training and cognitive restructuring with alcoholics. *Drug and Alcohol Dependence (Lausanne)* **3,** 369–74

James, W P, Salter, C E and Thomas, H G (1972). *Alcohol and Drug Dependence Treatment and Rehabilitation.* King Edward Hospital Fund for London

Kalb, M and Propper, M S (1976). The future of alcohology craft or science? *American Journal of Psychiatry* **133,** 641–5

Keller, M (1972). The oddities of alcoholics. *Quarterly Journal of Studies on Alcoholism* **33,** 1147–8

Kenyon, W H (1972). A Regional Council on Alcoholism. In *Notes on Alcohol and Alcoholism* (ed. S Caruana). London

Kershaw, P W (1973). Unpublished MD thesis, University of Edinburgh

Kershaw, P W and Timbury, G C (1982). In preparation

Leach, B and Norris, J L (1977). Factors in the development of Alcoholics Anonymous (A.A.) In *The Biology of Alcoholism Vol 5 Treatment and Rehabilitation of the Chronic Alcoholic* (ed. B Kissin and H Begleiter). Plenum Press, New York

Lovibond, S H and Caddy, G (1970). Discriminated aversive control in the moderation of alcoholics' drinking behaviour. *Behaviour Therapy* **1,** 437–44

Madden, J S (1979). *A Guide to Alcohol and Drug Dependence.* John Wright and Sons Ltd, Bristol

Madden J S and Kenyon, W H (1975). Group counselling of alcoholics by a voluntary agency. *British Journal of Psychiatry* **126,** 289–91

Malcolm, M T, Madden, J S and Williams, A G (1974). Disulfiram implantation critically evaluated. *British Journal of Psychiatry* **125,** 485–9

Miller, P M (1977). *Behavioural Treatment of Alcoholism.* Pergamon Press, London

Nathan, P E and Briddell, D W (1977). Behavioural Assessment and Treatment of Alcoholism. In: *The Biology of Alcoholism Vol 15 Treatment and Rehabilitation of the Chronic Alcoholic* (ed. B Kissin and H Begleiter). Plenum Press, New York

Norris, J L (1978). The role of Alcoholics Anonymous in rehabilitation. In: *Alcoholism Rehabilitation* (ed. V. Groupé). NIAAA–RUCAS Alcoholism Treatment Series, No. 3, New Brunswick, New Jersey

Ogborne, A C (1978). Patient Characteristics as Predictors of Treatment Outcomes for Alcoholics and Drug Abusers. In: *Recent Advances in Alcohol and Drug Problems*, vol. 4 (ed. Y Israel *et al*). New York, Plenum Press

Olbrich, R (1979). Alcohol withdrawal states and the need for treatment. *British Journal of Psychiatry* **134**, 466–9

Orford, J and Edwards, G (1977). *Alcoholism. A Comparison of Treatment and Advice with a Study of the Influence of Marriage.* Institute of Psychiatry Maudsley Monograph 26. Oxford University Press

Orford, J Hawker, A and Nicholls, P (1975). An investigation of an alcoholism rehabilitation halfway house: III Reciprocal staff-resident evaluations. *British Journal of Addiction* **70**, 23–32

Orford, J. Oppenheimer, E, Egert, S, Hensman, C and Guthrie, S (1976). The cohesiveness of alcoholism-complicated marriage and its influence on treatment outcome. *British Journal of Psychiatry* **128**, 318–39

Otto, S and Orford, J (1978). *Not Quite Like Home. Small Hostels for Alcoholics and others.* J Wiley & Sons, Chichester

Pattison, E M (1979). The Selection of Treatment Modalities for the Alcoholic Patient. In *The Diagnosis and Treatment of Alcoholism* (eds Mendelson and Mello), McGraw-Hill, New York

Piorkowski, M and Axtell, L A (1976). Effect of circuit exercise training on physical fitness of alcoholics. *Physical Therapy* **56**, 403–6

Plant, M (1979). *Drinking Careers.* Tavistock Publications. London

Polich, J M, Armor, D J and Braiker, H B (1980). Patterns of alcoholism over four years. *Journal of Studies on Alcohol* **41**, 397–416

Rathod, N H and Thomson, I G (1971). Women alcoholics. *Quarterly Journal of Studies on Alcohol* **32**, 45–52

Rathod, N H, Gregory E, Blows, D and Thomas, G H (1966). A two year follow-up study of alcoholic patients. *British Journal of Psychiatry* **112**, 683–92

Ritson, B and Hassall, C (1970). *The Management of the Alcoholic.* E. and S. Livingstone, Edinburgh

Room, R (1980). Treatment Seeking Populations and Larger Realities. In *Alcoholism Treatment in Transition* (ed. G Edwards and M Grant). Croom Helm, London

Rubington, E (1977). The Role of the Halfway House in the Rehabilitation of Alcoholics *The Biology of Alcoholism Vol 5 Treatment and Rehabilitation of the Chronic Alcoholic* (ed. B Kissin and H Begleiter). Plenum Press, New York

Rubington, E (1979). Halfway houses and treatment outcomes. A relationship between institutional atmosphere and therapeutic effectiveness. *Journal of Studies on Alcohol* **40**, 419–27

Saunders, W (1980). Psychological Aspects of Women and Alcohol. In *Women and Alcohol.* Camberwell Council on Alcoholism. Tavistock Publications, London

Saunders, W and Kershaw, P W (1978). The prevalence of problem drinking and alcoholism in the west of Scotland. *British Journal of Psychiatry* **133**, 493–9

Sclare, A B (1970). The female alcoholic. *British Journal of Addiction* **65**, 99–107

Scottish Council on Alcoholism (1974–5). *Alcoholism and Alcohol Abuse. A Scottish Problem.* 1st Annual Report, Edinburgh

Shaw, S, Cartwright, A, Spratley, T and Harwin, J (1978). *Responding to Drinking Problems.* Croom Helm, London

Sheehan, M and Watson, J (1980). Response and Recognition. In *Women and Alcohol.* Camberwell Council on Alcoholism. Tavistock, London, 133–58

Sobell, M B and Sobell, L C (1973). Alcoholics treated by individualised behaviour therapy: one year treatment outcome. *Behaviour Research and Therapy* **11,** 599–618

Steinglass, P (1977). Family Therapy in Alcoholism. *The Biology of Alcoholism Vol 5 Treatment and Rehabilitation of the Chronic Alcoholic* (ed. B Kissin and H Begleiter). Plenum Press, New York

Stockwell, T, Hodgson, R, Edwards, G and Rankin, H (1979). The development of a questionnaire to measure severity of alcoholic dependence. *British Journal of Addiction* **74,** 79–87

Syme, L (1957). Personality characteristics and the alcoholic. A critique of current studies. *Quarterly Journal of Studies on Alcohol* **18,** 288–301

Tournier, R E (1979). Alcoholics Anonymous as treatment and as ideology. *Journal of Studies on Alcohol* **40,** 230–39

Trotter, T (1812). *An essay medical philosophical and chemical on drunkenness and its effects on the human body.* Longmans and Rees, London

Wallerstein, R S, Chotlos, J W, Friend, M B, Hammersley, D W, Perlswig, E A and Winship, E M (1957). *Hospital Treatment of Alcoholism. A Comparative Experimental Study.* Basic Books, New York

WHO (1952). Technical Report Series No 48. WHO Geneva

Wilkinson, P, Kornaczewski, A, Rankin, J G and Santamaria, J N (1969). Physical disease in alcoholism. Initial survey of 1000 patients. *Medical Journal of Australia* **1,** 1217–23

Willems, P J A, Letemendia, F J J and Arroyave, F A (1973). A two year follow-up study comparing short with long-stay in-patient treatment of alcoholism. *British Journal of Psychiatry* **122,** 637–48

Zimberg, S (1978). Diagnosis and treatment of the elderly alcoholic. *Alcoholism Clinical and Experimental Research* **2(1),** 27–29

10 Misuse of Drugs

Anthony Thorley, MA, MB, MRC Psych
Martin Plant, BSc, MA, PhD

The Background

Psychotropic drug use is virtually universal. The earliest writings allude to the use of alcohol, cannabis and opium, and drugs were almost certainly taken by man long before he became literate. The types of drug favoured by specific social groups have, in the past, largely been determined by botanical and geographical convenience. During the twentieth century 'drug misuse' has become widely acknowledged to be one of society's greatest problems. It is apparent that all over the world various types of drugs are increasingly being taken inappropriately, excessively and often harmfully. At the same time, ease of transport and communications, together with an inventive and prolific drug industry, have made available an altogether unprecedented and often highly effective choice of psychotropic substances (Plant 1981).

The demand for drugs is enormous and their acceptance is extremely widespread. As noted by Thorley (1979):

Acceptable drug taking and dependent behaviour are common features of stable society, but probably all societies have some degree of unacceptable drug taking. In the last hundred years this has been an increasing area of social concern. As medical opinion has been sought by the lawyer, politician and social planner, drug taking behaviour and its social consequences have come into the province of medical and psychiatric illness.

Complex social, legal and moral issues impinge upon the use and misuse of psychotropic drugs. There are huge and perplexing variations between national practices and gross anomalies in the legal status of certain types of drug use which have little or nothing to do with any objective assessment of the relative 'safety' or 'dangers' of any specific substance. These complexities have been cogently described by Edwards (1971):

Sometimes the state would sell the drug and take the profit, sometimes the profit would go to the legally operating entrepreneur, sometimes that role would be played by the man with the mule train who makes his way over the mountain paths. The money at stake is immense and countries might finance their treasuries to a large extent from drug revenues. Conflicts of opinion are violent, the state's response to unpermitted drug use draconian. The situation on which you looked down would, however, seem to be characterised by an unusual degree of confusion: a drug which was permissible yesterday might tomorrow be prohibited, a drug which for one society was of importance in religious sacrament might in another place be preached against. You could conclude that one of the main businesses of the world was to cultivate, manufacture, advertise, legislate on, tax, consume, adulate and decry mind-acting substances. The complexity of the matter is overwhelming, its ramifications endless.

Beyond doubt the vast majority of drug taking in the United Kingdom, as in other industrial countries, is legal and much of this use does not, *per se*, constitute a cause for concern. The health hazards related to tobacco are catastrophic and well known. It is conservatively estimated that tobacco use in Britain annually causes 25 000, possibly 50 000, premature deaths (Royal College of Physicians 1977). The problems associated with alcohol misuse have been indicated in the previous chapter. Even so, there is a huge demand for alcohol and tobacco as well as for a growing range of legally available prescribed drugs. Over 36 000 people are employed in tobacco production and over 100 000 in alcohol production in Britain. Many more work in the pharmaceutical industry. Virtually all types of drug taking appear to be increasing. The only important exceptions are tobacco and barbiturates (Plant 1981).

There is little doubt that more people are adversely affected by the legal drugs than by the illegal ones, simply because the former are much more widely available and in use. It is worth stating that the Home Office currently records *only* 3000 known opiate dependents and that only 13 000 people are convicted annually of offences under the Misuse of Drugs Act 1971. Neither of these figures gives an accurate measure of the extent of illegal drug use, but they are dwarfed by the 18 000 annual hospital admissions for alcoholism, over 226 000 drunkenness convictions, thousands of tobacco-related deaths, and possibly by the unrecorded extent of dependence on prescribed tranquillizers.

The Definition of Drug Misuse

During the past 20 years there has been a major change in the conceptualization of what constitutes drug dependence. A parallel development has occurred in relation to alcohol. In 1950 the World Health Organization (WHO) defined drug addiction as:

> . . . a state of periodic or chronic addiction detrimental to the individual and to the society, produced by the repeated consumption of a drug (natural or synthetic). Characteristics include: (1) an overpowering

desire or need (compulsion) to continue taking the drug and to obtain it by any means; (2) a tendency to increase the dose; (3) psychic (or psychological) and sometimes physical dependence on the effects of the drug; (4) a detrimental effect on the individual and on society.

In 1957 the WHO amended this definition, by changing point (3) to 'generally a physical dependence'. In 1961 the Brain Committee in the United Kingdom (Interdepartmental Committee 1961) defined addiction in a similar way, emphasizing physical dependence and a separate, milder, state of habituation with 'some degree of psychological dependence' and 'detrimental effects, if any, primarily on the individual'. As the use of drug taking spread, including polydrug use, the distinction between addiction and habituation became less tenable. In 1964 the WHO recommended that dependence was a preferable term and should be defined in relation to the specific drugs used. More recent literature has replaced the terms 'addiction' and 'habituation' with the more general term, 'drug abuse':

(1) A drug is any substance that, when taken into the living organism, may modify one or more of its functions.
(2) Drug abuse is persistent or sporadic excessive use of a drug inconsistent with, or unrelated to, acceptable medical practice.
(3) Drug dependence is a state—psychic and sometimes also physical—resulting from the interaction between a living organism and a drug, characterized by behavioural and other responses that always include a compulsion to take the drug on a continuous or periodic basis in order to experience its psychic effects and sometimes to avoid the discomfort of its absence. Tolerance may or may not be present. A person may be dependent on more than one drug. (WHO 1969)

Russell (1976) has suggested that the difficulty of ceasing drug use is more crucial to the concept of dependence than the frequency or continousness of use. He advanced a broader definition that can equally well be applied to non-drug dependency, such as compulsive gambling:

The notion of dependence on a drug, object, role, activity or any other stimulus/source requires the crucial feature of a negative affect experienced in its absence. The degree of dependence can be equated with the amount of this negative affect, which may range from mild discomfort to extreme distress, or it may be equated with the amount of difficulty or effort required to do without the drug, object, etc. . . .

The Implications of Epidemiology for Rehabilitation

A considerable amount of research has been carried out into the incidence and prevalence of various forms of drug use and misuse (e.g. Lindesmith 1968; Goode 1970; Plant 1975). In addition, several longitudinal studies have monitored what becomes of drug takers over time (e.g. Kandel 1978; Thorley 1981a). From this and from other evidence it is clear that parallel to the development of thought about what constitutes alcohol-related problems, drug misuse or abuse is most usefully identified as lying within a continuum of drug-related behaviour much of which is harmless. People with drug problems, like those with alcohol problems, do not conform to a narrow stereotype. They are varied in relation to their personal traits and patterns of use and in relation to the problems that they encounter. In addition, it has been revealed that many people who at some time experience drug problems subsequently overcome these and often do so without recourse to professional help. Again the same is true of problem drinkers. Follow-up studies of physically dependent opiate users have shown that at least 10 per cent are abstinent after one year, 25 per cent after five years and 40 per cent after ten years. In addition two to three per cent of such a sample die of drug-related causes each year (Thorley 1981a). Such figures reflect fairly basic 'treatment' approaches. Rehabilitation should, in consequence, be aimed at significantly improving upon such results. Stimson et al (1978) found, in a seven-year follow-up of 128 British opiate dependents, that relapse was rare after six months abstinence.

In the United States prospective studies of the general population have helped to identify who becomes a drug taker and what factors are related (Kandel 1978). More significantly, two major North American follow-up studies have attempted to evaluate treatment and rehabilitation effectiveness by following up drug takers who had graduated from one of a variety of rehabilitation or treatment approaches: assessment only and no treatment; out-patient detoxification; methadone maintenance; therapeutic community; drug-free out-patients (Bale et al 1977; Sells and Simpson 1980; Simpson et al 1979). These studies can be criticized simply because the samples are not necessarily representative of American problem drug takers in general, and that there was no random allocation of patients into each treatment group (see Maisto and Cooper 1980). Even so, the results from both studies suggest that therapeutic communities, drug-free out-patients and methadone maintenance programmes produce higher rates of abstinence from illegal drugs, employment and reduction in criminality as compared with detoxification or assessment only (Bale et al 1977; Sells and Simpson 1980). Applying the most rigorous criteria of improvement, e.g. totally free of illegal drug use, three years after the Drug Abuse Reporting Program (DARP) treatment had terminated, the percentage abstinent in each category was as follows: methadone maintenance 29·5 per cent; therapeutic community 36·9 per cent; drug-free out-patients 34·4 per cent; detoxification 19·6 per cent; assessment only 21·0 per cent (Sells and Simpson 1980). This suggests that at three years follow-up at least three of the treatment and rehabilitation modalities were more effective than the 25 per cent abstinent at five years associated with a more naturalistic recovery rate. It is still necessary to consider with caution all these follow-up studies which implicate treatment and rehabilitation effects, but there is a weight of evidence emerging which suggests that long-term treatment and re-habilitation strategies are significantly effective as compared with random processes.

While the multiple causation of drug problems has long been acknow-ledged it is important to emphasize that a single solution to the diversity of drug problems seems, at best, impossible. In addition to the many interacting factors such as availability, personality, social deprivation, psychic stress and the chemistry of the substance used, a host of cultural and social forces often foster and perpetuate drug misuse. Not the least of these is the power of the 'drug scene', the sub-culture of hedonism and retreatism in which some people engage in their drug taking and upon which, rather than upon any specific drug, some become dependent (Young 1971). Other factors that have major practical implications are the general unpopularity of drug misusers in many 'treatment' settings; the oft-noted poor motivation of some drug misusers to reduce their drug use and the increasing tendency for drug misusers to abuse not one but several or many types of psychotropic drugs including alcohol, tobacco, halluci-nogens, barbiturates, solvents and glues (Woodside 1973; Thorley 1979; Plant 1981).

The extent of illicit drug taking is unknown. During the past decade, police forces throughout the United Kingdom have established drug squads of officers whose special responsibility is to enforce the drug control laws. In consequence, the increased level of police activity in this field has led to a steady increase in the numbers of drug offenders detected and brought to court. The number of drug seizures has also greatly increased. It must be emphasized that Home Office statistics of drug seizures and offences *do not* in themselves serve as an indication of the extent of drug use in the community. Such figures reflect many other factors including police policies, methods of detection and the conspicuousness, or inepti-tude, of drug users and traffickers. In 1978, 13 444 separate drug seizures were recorded. These vary enormously in size. For example, during 1977 relatively few LSD seizures were recorded, yet the quantity of the drug seized was immense due to 'Operation Julie' in which approximately 15 000 doses were impounded. More recently, in 1979, 'Operation Cyril' suc-ceeded in seizing over four tons of cannabis.

There has been a steady rise in the number of drug offences recorded by the Home Office. In 1978 these totalled 13 394. Approximately 80 per cent of such convictions related to cannabis and the majority certainly do not involve people who are physically drug dependent (unless on tobacco).

Between 1970 and 1978 the total number of recorded narcotic addicts in the United Kingdom rose by 69 per cent, an average increase of six per cent per year. Between 1975 and 1979 there was an increase of approxi-mately 19 per cent per year to a total of 2887. Home Office figures do not measure more than a minority of such drug dependence. There is a flourishing illegal trade in opiates and allied drugs, the extent of which is unclear (Moser 1974; Plant 1981; Thorley 1981b).

A Possible Perspective

It appears that no disease-oriented, dependence-oriented perspective, or any other that attempts to reduce dependence, misuse etc., to a single explanation is adequate. Such narrow models are not consistent with the variety and complexity of the range of drug-related behaviour. In addition, these approaches are singularly unhelpful in multidisciplinary or non-medical settings and are least appropriate in the non-medical non-statutory rehabilitation agencies which predominate in the United Kingdom.

A more useful model is problem (and thereby task or service) oriented. This is exemplified by the Department of Health and Social Security's Advisory Committee on Alcoholism Report on the Pattern and Range of Services (DHSS 1978). This document adopted the implicitly multidisciplinary term of 'problem drinker'. It is thereby suggested that a similar definition of 'problem drug taker' is that which is most helpful in a multidisciplinary or non-medical rehabilitation setting.

A *problem drug taker* is any person who experiences psychological, physical, social or legal problems related to intoxication, and/or excessive consumption, and/or dependence as a consequence of his or her own use of drugs or chemical substances excluding alcohol or tobacco. (Thorley 1980b.)

This wide definition implies psychotropic drug use and would include glue and solvent misuse, and whilst admitting iatrogenic drug problems it would exclude side-effects of drugs prescribed in accepted medical practice.

It has been explained elsewhere (Thorley 1980a) how a problem-oriented model of drug problems aids a rehabilitative and treatment approach. It is evident that antecedent difficulties and numerous causal factors lead to drug-related problems which may then give rise to additional problems which may be directly or indirectly related. It is this sytem of antecedent and consequent problems in medical, social and legal modalities together with the specific pattern of drug taking or drinking which has to be carefully assessed in any history from patient or client, and it follows that it is this system which is open for intervention and change—treatment and rehabilitation. The pattern of problematic drug taking may fall into three interrelated (but mutually exclusive) elements: intoxication, excessive consumption and dependence. Each of these elements produces its own characteristic problems. Drug problems are not interpreted implicitly as diseases, although physical pathology is sometimes present, but as patterns of behaviour leading to a multiplicity of problems in personal and social functioning. The three elements often overlap to form a composite, but in planning rehabilitation it is productive to identify the extent to which each element contributes to the whole. This perspective applies to people exhibiting drug-relating problems with their implicit symptomatologies and outcomes. In addition, emphasis is focused on the range of the individual's difficulties and the implication that several treatment responses may be appropriate.

Distinguishing Rehabilitation from Treatment

In relation to drug misuse, *treatment* may be defined as the response in a specific modality (e.g. psychotherapy, behaviour therapy) to specific symptoms or problem behaviour. In this context the patient is often regarded as suffering from a disease, is expected to adopt an appropriate sick role and is also expected to respond positively to treatment. Classically the patient in the sick role may not be (or feel) accountable for his symptoms or problems. This is true for manic depressive psychosis or schizophrenia, but it is much less so for alcohol or drug problems where clearly there is a powerful volitional element, personal responsibility is implicit, and determinism plays a less prominent role (Robinson 1972). To date, as outlined above, models of drug addiction have stressed illness and disease and this has encouraged patients to embrace strongly the sick role and so avoid, or only obliquely acknowledge, accountability. 'Once a drug addict always a drug addict': the heroin addict may give up heroin, but will transfer his dependence to barbiturates or alcohol or safer tranquillizers and so in essence is still a drug addict. Ideas of fixity in drug takers predominate in spite of evidence to the contrary (Thorley 1978). A further paradox arises in the treatment of drug problems by 'maintenance' prescriptions of opiates or benzodiazepine tranquillizers given by general practitioners, or psychiatrists in drug clinics. In the sick role the patient's expectations of the prescribed drugs is that they will cure his addiction or problem; often, as many observers have noted, they only add to his problem and perpetuate his drug using career. These then are powerful and enduring images of the sick role in drug addiction and they must necessarily be disarmed in any radical re-evaluation of treatment (Thorley 1980a).

Rehabilitation, in contrast to treatment, is a much more active process in which the patient or client is urged to abandon the passive sick role and to assume responsibility for his improved social functioning, including the control or cessation of harmful drug taking. A clear appeal of rehabilitation in relation to drug misuse is that optimum results may be achieved, namely the complete reintegration of the client into society, possibly without some of the residual disabilities evident amongst other patient groups in general psychiatry.

Treatment, as depicted in this chapter, relates to responses that are generally of a short-term nature. Medical responses related to overdoses, bad trips, withdrawal, social work responses to personal crises are all treatment strategies usually applied for only two to three weeks. Rehabilitation implies a longer-term response that is less directed to the amelioration of symptoms than to the development or re-learning of skills and coping mechanisms. Traditionally, the need for rehabilitation presumes that there is some residual personal or social dysfunction (if not handicap) remaining *after* treatment. In response to handicap, or personal and social dysfunction, the traditional sick role with its implied patient compliance and non-accountability is less important than a role and a therapeutic process involving personal responsibility and self-determination. A combination of these responses leading to increased social integration, personal effectiveness and independence is encompassed within the term rehabilitation.

The United Nations Division of Narcotic Drugs (1978), reflecting a view of drug problems more as a chronic handicap than a chronic disease, usefully suggests that for drug takers

> Rehabilitation is the process of helping individuals to establish a state in which they are physically, psychologically and socially capable of coping with situations encountered, thus enabling them to take advantage of the opportunities that are available to other people in the same age group in society.

This definition is equally apt for problem drinkers and it is to be noted how emphasis is placed on the process of social reintegration. Clearly for many disturbed clients this integrative element of rehabilitation is less reintegration than primary integration—*habilitation* rather than rehabilitation.

Most authorities identify two essential elements in the rehabilitation process for drug misusers. There are processes centred on the *individual* and processes concurrently centred on the *environment* in which the individual is learning new skills. One may denote the two basic processes as follows:

(1) To enable drug misusers to utilize personal resources and so modify attitudes, behaviour and skills in order to achieve a stable and fulfilling way of life with minimal or no drug-related problems.

(2) To provide the graded social supports and agencies required to facilitate the development of the individual so as to establish or re-establish drug misusers in the community in roles which they find more stable and fulfilling than those related to their previous drug use.

Clearly if rehabilitation is to succeed, the individual and environmental processes of development must be fostered and reconciled to each other in an active and graded programme through time which increases individual competence and limits problems.

Having outlined some of the essential differences between treatment and rehabilitation in relation to drug problems, it now remains to examine the present and future optimal relationship between these two basic responses. If management is to be seen as the overall co-ordination of treatment and rehabilitation, a change of emphasis appears justified in relation to services for drug misusers.

In the past, and often even today, treatment (e.g. hospital based) has been the predominant helping response. Short-term measures have often only produced limited success and contact with agencies concerned primarily with long-term rehabilitation (e.g. community-based hostels) has been tenuous, with co-ordination fragmentary and disorganized. In some areas there is an element of co-ordination between treatment and rehabilitation. This is particularly so in relation to services for problem drinkers. Even so, medical treatment is usually viewed as the dominant member of such partnerships whenever they do exist. During recent years rehabilitation has been accorded greater prominence and is widely perceived as making a major contribution to recovery. Often, however, rehabilitation is viewed as subsidiary to the main medical (short-term) response.

Drug misuse is much less a short-term treatable entity than a constellation of chronic handicaps and behavioural disorders. Viewed as such, rehabilitation is possibly the most appropriate primary response. Emphasis on rehabilitation is further justified by the time often taken to achieve 'recovery' which may be two to three years. In addition, an illness model does not correspond to the diversity of drug misuse or to the multidisciplinary workers in the field.

Non-statutory ('voluntary') rehabilitation agencies are the fastest expanding type of response in the United Kingdom and this development is enthusiastically fostered by the Government (e.g. DHSS 1978). The United Nations Narcotics Division recognizes a temporal distinction or continuum between, first, treatment leading to rehabilitation, and then social reintegration (UN 1978). In the United States, where most of those working in the drug field are not medical personnel, rehabilitation is almost certainly the predominant approach to managing drug problems. While there is a less marked movement in this direction in the United Kingdom, it is much less developed in relation to drug misuse than in relation to alcohol problems (e.g. FARE 1978). It is logical that rehabilitation should be much more widely developed and should therefore be the primary objective when considering individual assessment and the provision of specific services.

Principles of Assessment and Management

Assessment and management of problem drug takers must necessarily take into account the two basic elements of rehabilitation: the individual's potential response and resources in the environment. As indicated above, it is useful always to have rehabilitation in mind whatever the service setting. Thus good treatment must anticipate and look to rehabilitation, and good rehabilitation must reflect or even actively integrate treatment. For instance, the patient or client who is undergoing withdrawal (treatment) can be actively introduced and encouraged to affiliate to a network of rehabilitation services: in fact withdrawal which is not a prelude to such affiliation is a poor form of treatment. General principles of treatment will not be dwelt upon here; basic accounts have been provided by Madden (1979) and Thorley (1979). The enduring problem of client motivation and specific treatment techniques relevant for alcohol problems have also been explored in detail by Thorley (1980a).

Assessment of the individual is most usefully accomplished thus. A basic history from and discussion with the client will identify the pattern of problems, symptoms and dysfunctions which the client and worker must place in some kind of order or priority and agree to attend to. Rehabilitation, even more than treatment, depends crucially on the negotiation between doctor/worker and patient/client as to the meaning and basis of the problems and the strategy for dealing with them (Scheff 1968). As problems and dysfunctions are often ranged across medical, social and legal areas, it makes sense where a multidisciplinary team is present to allow each member to make his contribution to the assessment of individual dysfunction and potential. Past levels of functioning and stability are as important as current functioning and need to be considered when realistically planning for the future. Many patients entering rehabilitation tend to recall the good times in the past: 'if only I could be like I was ten years ago I would be fine.' In truth, there are caveats in a backward-looking approach because something in that idealized past may have led to the chaos of the present. Rehabilitation should therefore be forward looking.

Concomitant to this general assessment of functioning will be an analysis of the current pattern of drug taking and the way specific problems relate to that pattern. For instance, chronic opiate use may lead to financial problems if not to theft and conflict with the law as well as physical damage. Rehabilitation must take into account the most realistic goals with regard to future drug use. Abstinence may be a first goal in the process of withdrawal, but it may be unrealistic to plan future overall rehabilitation on a totally drug-free setting which has no relationship to the 'real world' which clients will eventually try to re-enter. In spite of the criticism of observers, many drug takers rehabilitate in the context of carefully monitored 'maintenance' or slowly reducing drug prescriptions (Wille 1979) and there is much evidence that many drinkers will slowly achieve stability and harm-free status without total abstinence (Lloyd and Salzberg 1975; Armor *et al* 1976). The distinction between harm-free alcohol or drug use and abstinence as a goal is an important one in planning rehabilitation, and Thorley (1980a) has examined some of the factors relevant to the right choice for problem drinkers. Rehabilitation can occur from both abstinent and harm-free alcohol or drug use bases and there is no place here for dogmatic attitudes. Too many patients have inevitably failed because of unrealistic goals imposed upon them by the doctor or worker instead of mutually agreeing about a realistic goal as a first priority. It is vital therefore to be realistic about goals without being pessimistic. It is also useful to create a structure to the process of rehabilitation by identifying with the client short, mid and long term goals regarding all the problems being tackled. Rehabilitation, like treatment, is valued much more if the patient or client can see the purpose and meaning of it: cognitive elements are always vital in change.

Whilst it is possible for client or patient to have a dramatic flight into abstinent stability or a 'spontaneous' remission, this cannot be relied upon. Accordingly the functional and developmental needs of the individual have to be matched against the provision of local resources. In general, local resources are more useful than distant ones as this allows for easier work with the patient's spouse, family or occupational base. However in some circumstances, moving away from a problematic subculture or disturbed family can be a crucial element in mangement. Hence, a dry hostel or house is not only a residential resource for the non-domiciled drug taker who has shown he can manage abstinence with support, it is also relevant for the inappropriately domiciled: the client who risks almost certain relapse if he returns to spouse or family, but who may benefit immeasurably from a period in a dry house before attempting a return home. Most specialist residential units are in fact dry, but non-specialist agencies often allow a limited degree of drug use and should be utilized when a non-abstinent goal is agreed upon.

In general, environmental facilities should be used in a co-ordinated and graded way: close supervision possibly in a residential setting should lead to less supervision and more independence. Finally, it must be remembered that no one is totally independent of support and that many socially reintegrated clients will need nominal support from social worker or volunteers for many years.

It is clear from all this complexity of the system that management of integrated rehabilitation and treatment requires co-ordination and some kind of identifiable co-ordinating agent or person who will help the patient or client keep his perspective over progress and present and future goals. Initial assessment carried out by a multidisciplinary team must be co-ordinated into a strategy which client and agency clearly understand. If the strategy involves other agencies, the procedures and goals involved must be clearly communicated. Case conferences with all relevant agencies present (including the client!) are just one practical model to use. The guiding agent or co-ordinator is best some person who will not move on but will provide continuity and perspective over the two to three year period of rehabilitation: a probation officer, social worker, general practitioner or a hospital consultant are obvious candidates. At any one time in the programme team members other than the co-ordinator may have a closer or more therapeutic relationship. Management must be flexible and allow for mutual re-negotiation of the goals of rehabilitation. Finally, management should not allow for the concept of absolutely 'hopeless cases'. It is necessary to be absolutely realistic about unmotivated individuals apparently set on self-destructive drug-taking careers and the paucity of overworked resources, but the attitude of the agency worker is half the negotiated contract. Clients are likely to respond as much to workers' nihilism as to enthusiasm and encouragement. Successful rehabilitation requires care, concern for the individual client and considerable commitment.

Services for Problem Drug Takers

Detoxification

Some problem drug takers are physically dependent and for many such individuals detoxification is a crucial precursor of successful rehabilitation. Detoxification alone is unlikely to play a major role in long-term change, but nevertheless is a fairly technical procedure that requires specialist support and services to reduce drug intake (Kleber 1977; Thorley 1979). Many of those requiring help in the United Kingdom are young polydrug takers who, if they are physically dependent, may be on barbiturates rather than opiates (Ghodse 1976). Some drug dependence clinics facilitate detoxification through their in-patient beds or on an out-patient basis, but many are unable to cope with the large numbers of polydrug takers who contact them.

The experimental City Roads Project was established in London during 1978. This has attempted to provide assessment, detoxification and contacts with residential rehabilitative projects for polydrug takers. This venture provides a 24-hour service staffed by nurses and social workers. Referrals come from many sources and some clients refer themselves. The average age of clients is 24 and two-thirds are males. More than half are homeless and clients come from the complete spectrum of social class backgrounds. Eighty per cent are dependent upon barbiturates. More than 50 per cent also use opiates and about 30 per cent inject drugs (Glanz *et al* 1980). After initial referral and assessment the project provides a three-week residential programme which offers detoxification (using a liquid phenobarbitone regime for barbiturate dependence), primary medical care, social work and counselling. The average client stays with the Project for two weeks and 38 per cent of clients are referred for further residential rehabilitation such as that provided by therapeutic communities. It is the intention that this Project provides a 'breathing space' which will equip clients to benefit from the help offered by therapeutic communities. It is proposed that further research will evaluate whether or not this aim is achieved (Glanz *et al* 1980). It is already apparent that the City Roads Project has great merit and that this model, if extended, would be of considerable value in relation to polydrug takers.

Other helping agencies have experimented with the value of electro-acupuncture and stimulation techniques (e.g. 'the black box') as an adjunct to detoxification. Such approaches appear worth while but are unlikely in themselves to compensate for a more general rehabilitation programme involving the co-operation of other agencies (Patterson 1979).

Medical Services

Medical provision for problem drug takers is firmly rooted upon general practice. The general practitioner, in particular, through his long-term contact with patients is in a unique position to contain iatrogenic drug problems, to advise drug takers to reduce their drug use and to overcome their difficulties (Edwards 1977; Bewley 1980). General and psychiatric hospitals can fulfil an important treatment role within a wider rehabilitation framework. The Advisory Council on the Misuse of Drugs has recently drawn attention to the crucial role of hospital accident and emergency departments in identifying drug dependent parasuicides (Ghodse 1976; DHSS 1977).

The Drug Clinic

Since their inception during 1968, the drug clinics have widely, if inaccurately, been regarded as the mainstay of the British response to drug misuse. The emergence of the so-called 'British system' of coping with drug dependence has been reviewed elsewhere (Edwards and Busch 1981; Thorley 1979; Plant 1981). The basis of the drug clinics is the assumption that legal prescribing to addicts notified officially to the Home Office would limit the demand for illegal supplies of opiates. Since 1968 only those holding a special Home Office licence have been legitimately able to prescribe heroin or cocaine to addicts. Most of these practitioners are psychiatrists in drug treatment clinics.

The Misuse of Drugs Act 1971 is the basis of the United Kingdom's current drug control laws. The Act classifies prescribed drugs into three categories according to their harmfulness and specified different maximum penalties for possession, production or sale of drugs in each of these three categories:

Class A includes opium, heroin, methadone, morphine, pethidine, cannabinol (except when contained in cannabis or cannabis resin), cocaine, injectable amphetamines, LSD, mescalin and psilocybin.
Class B includes cannabis and cannabis resin, codeine, pholcodine, amphetamines (Methedrine, Benzedrine, Dinamyl, Dexedrine).

Class C includes methaqualone (Mandrax) and certain amphetamines (Bezphetamine, Chlorphentermine, Mephentermine and six others all of which are considered less dangerous or potent).

The 1971 Act also enabled the Home Secretary to prevent doctors from over-prescribing controlled drugs and to bring new substances under control as the need emerged. In 1977 the definition of 'cannabis' was widened from the flowering and fruiting tops to cover the whole plant, except mature stalk and seed, already separated from it. In 1979 'Angel Dust' (PCP) was made an illegal Class A drug.

There is a recommendation that barbiturates be placed in Class B and that cannabis might be transferred to Class C. The 1973 Notification and Supply to Addicts regulation of the 1971 Act lists 14 opiate drugs and cocaine, and states that any person addicted or supected of addiction (in terms of the Act addiction means 'as a result of repeated administration [the individual] becomes so dependent upon the drug that he has an overpowering desire for the administration to be continued') has to be notified by medical practititioners to the Home Office, although many doctors continue to be unaware of this statutory regulation.

The drug clinic, using out-patient and in-patient facilities and the resource of a multidisciplinary team, is in a strong position to provide a general assessment of the drug taker's problems and provide treatment and rehabilitation (Thorley 1979). Unfortunately, treatment in the past has focused too much on the transaction of the legal opiate prescription to the detriment of other treatment techniques and some clinics have become somewhat isolated from other drug agencies and rehabilitation projects (Stimson and Oppenheimer 1981). The range of prescribing policies, varieties of drug taker patient, and differences between metropolitan and provincial setting make a general assessment of the drug clinic rather elusive. Although enthusiastically advocated by some, there does appear to be a limited role for a non-opiate prescribing clinic, but it cannot adequately deal with all drug problems (Thorley 1979; DHSS 1977). Most clinics continue to prescribe oral, and more uncommonly, injectable methadone to new patients, whilst long-term patients may still receive injectable heroin (Wille 1980). Mitcheson and Hartnoll (1980) have evaluated the advantages of prescribing oral methadone as against injected heroin, and find that whilst oral methadone is more effective than heroin in reducing doses for a majority, a significant minority will increase their criminal activities to finance the purchase of illegal drug supplies.

Most clinics are now overloaded with patients and there is a need to expand this service to cope with the increasing drug problem. In the opinion of some drug agency workers, rehabilitation can only be achieved in a drug-free environment, and therefore opiate prescribing (such as methadone maintenance) is regarded with suspicion. Abstinence may be a desirable prelude for personal change and growth, but many individuals can only make the change within the context of a legal opiate prescription and therapeutic support, possibly during several years in an out-patient setting (Newman and Whitehill 1979; Stimson *et al* 1978; Wille 1979).

The full potential of the drug treatment clinic has yet to be realized. Like alcoholism treatment units (or alcohol problem clinics) drug clinics may have to extend their links with other services and work in close co-ordination with such agencies and not, as too often at present, in isolation from them.

Community Projects and Services

Those deeply involved with the drug scene are often antagonistic to 'officialdom', which includes those working in drug treatment clinics. Drug takers are also extremely unpopular with medical and nursing staff (Plant 1981). Accordingly, there is an important role for less formal helping agencies. At a statutory level, many local education authorities have unattached youth workers who can be a major source of support to some disorganized multi-problem drug takers. Other non-statutory agencies such as Release and Lifeline offer advice, counselling, support and communication with other rehabilitation services. The Hungerford Centre is a detached social work venture for drug takers in the West End of London where there is a high prevalence of homeless young people, many of whom have drug-related problems. In 1979, 86 per cent of this agency's clients had no legal drug supplies. This reflects a thriving illicit drug supply, overloaded drug treatment clinics and the reluctance of many youthful drug takers to use such clinics (Turning Point 1980). Street agencies have a crucial rehabilitative role. They need to be much more fully developed to cope with the still largely unmet demand.

Day Hospitals and Centres

During the 1970s several drug treatment clinics and non-statutory agencies extended their out-patient facilities into day care programmes. Some of these permitted clients to inject drugs on their premises and many offered individual and group counselling and other therapeutic facilities. Few of these projects survived, most being overwhelmed by the countervailing ideologies and inducements of the drug-taking milieu. Experience at Parkwood House Day Hospital in Newcastle has demonstrated that abstinent drug takers with innumerable personal problems can be rehabilitated in a group setting and attached to suitable residential projects if appropriate (Thorley 1981c). The rehabilitation of active drug takers from a day centre or clinic can be more satisfactorily and effectively carried out using behavioural contract techniques in addition to supportive counselling (Boudin 1980), or by community visits and therapeutic work in a family and domiciliary setting (Thorley 1981c). One innovative day centre which has produced a successful formula and avoided drug scene culture contamination through adherence to a strict abstinence rule, is the Lifeline Project in Manchester. Founded in 1971, project workers see their role as identifying and challenging negative attitudes in the client, either through direct confrontation from staff or peer group pressures. The aim is to assist attenders to become aware of their own potential capacity to live without drugs. Access to the day programme is only by being drug free, either through hospitalized detoxification, or daily affiliation to the project's 'shop front' (Lifeline 1980). The programme offers a wide variety of group and individual work and utilizes an internal structure not unlike those found in therapeutic communities. Recognizing the value of assessing and preparing day attenders for the right kind of residential rehabilitation, the project has developed a two-week multifacility induction programme which is proving a significant advantage in placement. Early evidence suggests that clients so prepared are less likely to drop out ('split') and more likely to maintain high achievement rates in a therapeutic community (Lifeline 1980).

Residential Rehabilitation Projects

There are widely differing types of residential rehabilitation projects. The number of such agencies is pitifully inadequate in the United Kingdom and there are none in either Scotland or Wales. Funding for clients presents a major problem. Even so, the role played by non-specialist probation and local authority social services' hostels, in addition to therapeutic communities such as the Richmond Fellowship houses, is significant (Jansen 1980).

More specifically oriented therapeutic communities and 'concept houses' stem largely from ventures such as Synanon, Daytop and Phoenix House which were established in the United States during the 1960s (Glaser 1981). These projects have been widely and not always favourably publicized, but the essential principles of a specialist service have survived and evolved into structured programmes of integrated and co-ordinated rehabilitation (Hinshelwood and Manning 1979). A therapeutic community is essentially a closed system of residents and staff creating a unique culture based on security, hierarchy and structured growth in which a client can make significant changes of personal attitude and behaviour. One of the enduring problems of therapeutic communities has been the reintroduction of clients to the community. So often it has appeared that the client who has 'graduated' from the full programme, often of one to two years' duration, has only been prepared for one role: a drug-free worker in another therapeutic community! (Hart 1972; Wilson 1980). Many communities, now more aware of relevance to the outside world, have more structured re-entry phases with secure outside accommodation from which clients can get out to employment but still have access to the community in the evenings and at weekends: a true 'half-way' house.

It has always been clear to therapeutic community workers what the processes of client rehabilitation are, but only in the last few years has objective evidence of change been presented. A major problem is the high rate of client dropout of up to 80 per cent within three months in many projects. Clearly, to improve a graduation rate of 5–15 per cent many factors could be altered: client selection, degree of obligation (as in Court Orders), induction programmes (see Lifeline above) and the basis and structure of the house programme and re-entry. Many houses have examined these factors and replaced a philosophy of rigid hierarchical achievement through confrontation techniques with a more flexible hierarchy and a wider range of individual and group activities, and so improved 'survival' rates (Ogborne 1978; Phoenix House 1980).

Kennard and Wilson (1979) found that, at the Ley Community in Oxford, clients remaining with the programme for longer than six months tended to become less disturbed and more extraverted. The change from introversion to extraversion may be important since the former was linked in a two-year follow-up with subsequent criminal activity (Wilson and Mandelbrote 1978a). Longer stays were also associated with less criminality and less drug use or injection of drugs (Wilson and Mandelbrote 1978b; Wilson 1978). Comparable American studies have shown that clients who complete their intended stays in therapeutic communities improve most, as compared with other helping agencies, in relation to drug use, crime and employment (Bale *et al* 1977; Sells and Simpson 1980). Other studies have shown that some of those who drop out also improve in these respects, but that they generally have higher rates of psychopathology than those who do not (De Leon *et al* 1973; De Leon 1977; De Leon *et al* 1979; Romond *et al* 1975). Many of these studies did not employ random allocation of clients or control groups, but do, altogether, produce evidence that rehabilitation can be effective.

Detailed information about therapeutic communities and other drug projects in the United Kingdom is published by the Standing Conference on Drug Abuse (SCODA 1980). Broadly, there are several varieties of community project with considerable overlap (Langley 1980).

(1) *Concept Houses* (e.g. Phoenix House, Alpha House, Suffolk House, Inward House). These projects operate on hierarchical and confrontational lines and can be a tough proposition for poorly motivated, ill prepared or very disturbed individuals.
(2) *Religious Houses* (e.g. The Red House, Life for the World, Coke Hole Trust). This heading cannot adequately represent a group of projects whose only common factor is that they place religious faith and activities as a central theme in the rehabilitation process and clearly clients must be selected with care.
(3) *Social Group Work Houses* (e.g. Cranstoun, Elizabeth House). These projects are less hierarchical and depend more upon a flexible

and eclectic group social work approach. They may not suit clients in need of discipline and structure.

Therapeutic communities and drug rehabilitation agencies are becoming more sophisticated and possibly more clearly effective. Projects to enable problem drug takers to re-enter the community are becoming more realistic as such approaches increasingly develop links with other agencies in the community.

Rehabilitation for Offenders

A substantial number of problem drug takers come to the attention of 'official agencies' as a result of their commission of drug offences or offences such as theft which may sometimes clearly be linked with drug misuse. In consequence, many drug takers are handled by the police, courts of law and the probation service. Probation orders for up to three years, served often with a requirement of treatment at a clinic or residence at a rehabilitation house, provide a natural setting for a rehabilitation perspective, and many agencies like Lifeline and City Roads work very closely with the probation service. Services for the drug offender within the prison system are much less developed but a recent advisory document from the Home Office (1980) has made important recommendations with regard to medical treatment in prisons and the provision of wider opportunities of rehabilitation and aftercare.

An Approach to Services for Problem Drug Takers

Rehabilitation of extremely varied problem drug takers demands an equally heterogeneous range of co-ordinated agencies attuned to the longer-term rehabilitation perspective outlined above. Such patterns have been described elsewhere (e.g. Berntsen 1976), but at present nothing comparable exists in the United Kingdom. Even so, the seeds of such a system are already in existence in the form of the relatively few, yet extremely varied agencies already working in the field. Unless drug-related problems for some (unlikely) reason diminish, much needs to be done in future.

References

Armor, D J, Polich, J M and Stambul, H B (1976). *Alcoholism and Treatment*. CA Report R-1739-NIAAA, Rand Corp., Santa Monica
Bale, R N, Van Stone, W W and Zarcone, V P (1977). Two year follow-up results

from a randomised comparison study of methadone maintenance and therapeutic communities. Paper presented to National Drug Abuse Conference, San Francisco

Berntsen, K (1976). Treatment of drug addicts: a six years' experiment. *Bulletin on Narcotics* **28,** i, 9–24

Bewley, T H (1980). Prescribing psychoactive drugs to addicts. *British Medical Journal* **281,** ii, 497–8

Boudin, H M (1980). Contingency Contracting with Drug Abusers in the Natural Environment: Treatment Evaluation. In *Evaluating Alcohol and Drug Abuse Treatment Effectiveness: Recent Advances* (eds L C Sobell, M B Sobell and E Ward). Pergamon, New York

De Leon, G (1977). Therapeutic community dropouts, 5 years later: Preliminary findings on self-reported status. From *Proceedings of Second World Conference of Therapeutic Communities*, at Montreal. ICAA, Lausanne

De Leon, G, Skodol, A and Rosenthal, M S (1973). Phoenix House: Changes in psychopathological signs of resident drug addicts. *Archives of General Psychiatry* **28,** 131–5

De Leon, G, Andrews, M, Wexler, H K, Jaffe, J and Rosenthal, M S (1979). Therapeutic community dropouts: Criminal behaviour five years after treatment. *American Journal of Drug and Alcohol Abuse* **6** (3), 253–71

DHSS (1977). Advisory Council on the Misuse of Drugs. First Interim Report of Treatment and Rehabilitation. DHSS, London

DHSS (1978). Advisory Committee on Alcoholism: The Pattern and Range of Services for Problem Drinkers. DHSS, London

Edwards, G (1971). *Unreason in an Age of Reason*. Edward Stevens Lectures for the Laity. Royal Society of Medicine, London

Edwards, G (1977). Clinical review of dependence. *General Practitioner*, 15 April, 13–28

Edwards, G and Busch, C (1981). *The British Drug Problem and the Responses 1966–1977* (eds G Edwards and C Busch, in press). Academic Press, London

FARE (1978). *Community Services for Alcoholics*. Report of FARE Working Party at the House of Commons April–October 1978. FARE, London

Ghodse, A H (1976). Drug problems dealt with by 62 London casualty departments. *British Journal of Preventative and Social Medicine* **30,** 251–6

Glanz, A, Jamieson, A and MacGregor, S (1980). *City Roads: Interim Evaluation Report*. DHSS, London

Glaser, F B (1981). The origins of the drug-free therapeutic community. *British Journal of Addiction* **76** (1), 13–26

Goode, E (1970). *The Marijuana Smoker*. Basic Books, New York

Hart, L (1972). Milieu management for drug addicts: extended drug subculture or rehabilitation? *British Journal of Addiction* **67,** 291–301

Hinshelwood, R D and Manning, N (1979). *Therapeutic Communities: Reflections and Progress* (eds R D Hinshelwood and N Manning). Routledge Kegan Paul, London

Home Office (1980). *Report on Drug Dependents within the Prison System in England and Wales*. Advisory Council on the Misuse of Drugs. Home Office, London

Interdepartmental Committee on Drug Addiction (1961) (Brain Committee). *Report*. HMSO, London

Jansen, E (1980). *The Therapeutic Community outside the Hospital* (ed. E Jansen). Croom Helm, London

Kandel, D B (1978). *Longitudinal Research on Drug Use: empirical findings and methodological issues.* Halsted Press, New York

Kennard, D and Wilson, S (1979). The modification of personality disturbance in a therapeutic community for drug abusers. *British Journal of Medical Psychology* **52** (3), 215–21

Kleber, H B (1977). Detoxification from methadone maintenance: the state of the art. *International Journal of the Addictions* **12** (7), 807–20

Langley, B (1980). Client and Worker, Options for Drug Rehabilitation Houses in the United Kingdom. Paper presented at NISW course. Bristol, 1980

Lifeline (1980). *Multifacility Induction: the first six months*. Lifeline Project, Manchester

Lindesmith, A R (1968). *Addiction and Opiates*. Aldine Books, Chicago

Lloyd, R W and Salzburg, H C (1975). Controlled social drinking: an alternative to abstinence as a treatment goal for some social drinkers. *Psychological Bulletin* **82** (6), 815–42

Madden, J S (1979). *A Guide to Alcohol and Drug Dependence*. John Wright, Bristol

Maisto, S A and Cooper, A M (1980). A Historical Perspective on Alcohol and Drug Treatment Outcome Research. In *Evaluating Alcohol and Drug Abuse Treatment Effectiveness: Recent Advances* (eds L C Sobell, M B Sobell, and E Ward). Pergamon, New York

Mitcheson, M and Hartnoll, R (1980). Evaluation of heroin maintenance in a controlled trial. *Archives of General Psychiatry* **37,** 877–84

Moser, J (1974). *Problems and Programmes related to Drugs and Drug Dependence in 33 Countries*. WHO, Geneva

Newman, R G and Whitehill, W B (1979). Double-blind comparison of Methadone and placebo maintenance treatments of narcotic addicts in Hong Kong. *Lancet* **ii,** 485–8

Ogborne, A C (1978). Program stability and resident turnover in residential rehabilitation program for alcoholics and drug addicts. *British Journal of Addiction* **73,** 47–50

Patterson, M A (1979). Addiction and neuroelectric therapy. *Nursing Times*, 29 November, 2080–3

Phoenix House (1980). *Phoenix House Annual Report*, London

Plant, M A (1975). *Drugtakers in an English Town*. Tavistock, London

Plant, M A (1981). *Drugs in Perspective*. Hodder and Stoughton, London

Robinson, D (1972). The alcohologist's addiction: some implications of having lost control over the disease concept of alcoholism. *Quarterly Journal of Studies on Alcohol* **33,** 1028–42

Romond, A M, Forrest, C K and Kleber, H D (1975). Follow up of participants in a drug dependence therapeutic community. *Archives of General Psychiatry* **32,** 369–74

Royal College of Physicians (1977). *Smoking* or *Health*. Pitman Medical, London

Russell, M A H (1976). What is Dependence? In *Drugs and Drug Dependence* (eds G Edwards, M A H Russell, D Hawks and M MacCafferty). Saxon House/ Lexington Books, London

Scheff, T (1968). Negotiating reality: notes on power in the assessment of responsibility. *Social Problems* **16**, 3–17

SCODA (1980). *Residential Rehabilitation Projects for Drug Dependents: Referral Guide*. Standing Conference on Drug Abuse, London

Sells, S B and Simpson, D D (1980). The case for drug abuse treatment effectiveness, based on DARP Research Program. *British Journal of Addiction* **75**, 117–32

Simpson, D, Savage, J and Lloyd, M R (1979). Follow up evaluation of treatment of drug abuse during 1969 to 1972. *Archives of General Psychiatry* **36**, 772–8

Stimson, G V, Oppenheimer, E and Thorley, A (1978). Seven year follow up of heroin addicts: drug use and outcome. *British Medical Journal* **i**, 1190–92

Stimson, G V and Oppenheimer, E (1981). A Response to Heroin Addiction: a study of addicts' lives and social policy in Britain. (In press)

Thorley, A (1978). How natural is the natural history of opiate drug dependence? *British Journal of Addiction* **73**, 229–32

Thorley, A (1979). Drug Dependence. In *Essentials of Postgraduate Psychiatry* (eds P Hill, R Murray and A Thorley). Academic Press, London

Thorley, A (1980a). Medical responses to problem drinking. *Medicine* (3rd Series), No. 35, 1816–22

Thorley, A (1980b). *What is Meant by Rehabilitation?* Internal paper presented to treatment and rehabilitation working group of the Advisory Council on the Misuse of Drugs, Home Office, London

Thorley, A (1981a). Longitudinal Studies of Drug Dependence. In *The British Drug Problem and the Responses 1966–1977* (eds G Edwards and C Busch (in press)). Academic Press, London

Thorley, A. (1981b). Drug Problems in the United Kingdom: retrospect and prospect. *Transactions of the Royal Society of Medicine* (in press)

Thorley, A (1981c). *Parkwood House Alcohol and Drug Problem Service: handbook for professional workers*, Newcastle

Turning Point (1980). *Turning Point: The Helping Hand Organisation. Annual Report 1979–1980*. London

United Nations (1978). *Resource Book on Measures to Reduce the Illicit Demand for Drugs*. UN Division of Narcotic Drugs, Geneva

WHO (1950). Report of Expert Committee on Addiction producing Drugs. *WHO Technical Report Series* **21**, 6

WHO (1969). Report of Expert Committee on Addiction producing drugs. *WHO Technical Report Series* **407**, 11

Wille, R (1979). Case Studies I. Natural Processes of Recovery. In *Drug Dependence in Socio-cultural Context* (eds G Edwards and G Arif). WHO, Geneva

Wille, R (1980). Ten year follow-up of a representative sample of London heroin addicts: clinical attendance, abstinence and mortality (in press)

Wilson, D (1978). The effect of treatment in a therapeutic community on intravenous drug abuse. *British Journal of Addiction* **73**, 407–11

Wilson, D (1980). Addiction therapist: a transient status passage in drug rehabilitation. *International Journal of the Addictions* **15** (6), 927–30

Wilson, D and Mandelbrote, B (1978a). Drug rehabilitation and criminality: factors related to conviction after treatment in a therapeutic community. *British Journal of Criminology* **18** (4), 381–6

Wilson, D and Mandelbrote, B (1978b). The relationship between duration of treatment in a therapeutic community for drug abusers and subsequent criminality. *British Journal of Psychiatry* **132,** 487–91

Woodside, M (1973). The first 100 referrals to a Scottish Drug Treatment Centre. *British Journal of Addiction* **68** (3), 231–41

Young, J (1971). *The Drug Takers: The Social Meaning of Drug Use.* Paladin, London

Part 4 Forensic Psychiatry

11 The Adult Offender

Michael Lee-Evans, BA, MSc

Forensic psychiatry has been defined as: 'The application of the principles of general psychiatry to that part of the population that comes into contact with the crimimal law' (Gunn 1975). This covers a wide variety of functions including assessment before trial and sentencing, advising on disposal, treatment and rehabilitation and assisting with decisions concerning release. It also includes a range of possible clients, from children to the elderly. This chapter is restricted to an account of the work of psychiatrists and psychologists in the rehabilitation of adult 'offenders',[1] but excludes the problems of addiction. (These, together with the general area of child psychiatry are considered elsewhere in this book.) The focus is exclusively on those special services provided in the United Kingdom, their problems and limitations.

The development of forensic psychiatry in England has been traced by Walker and McCabe (1973) and with special reference to the Prison Service by Gunn *et al* (1978). Fundamental to this development is the legal concept of 'responsibility' which, based on a doctrine of 'free-will', assumes that man normally has control over his actions and intends their consequences. Therefore, the 'legally responsible' or 'normal' offender is considered to be properly dealt with by a penal system, punishment being intended to act as a deterrent to the offender and (by example) to others (Wootton 1978). However, criminal law recognizes the need to identify a group of offenders who on account of 'mental disorder' cannot be considered liable to punishment. On the premise that one should not be punished for being ill, such 'mentally abnormal' offenders have previously been considered properly treated by hospital services outside the penal system. The Mental Health Act 1959[2] defines mental disorder as: 'mental

---

1 The special facilities for offenders in the Health Service are usually shared by compulsory patients who may present similar management problems and in some instances may have committed similar offensive acts but without having been charged or convicted.

2 This Act applies only to England and Wales. There is different legislation for both Scotland and Northern Ireland and some variation in the categorization of mental disorder and also in the provision for review. However, for the purpose of this discussion the requirements of the different Acts are essentially similar. The main provisions of the Mental Health Act 1959 for dealing with offenders are summarized in *A Human Condition*, vol. 2 (Gostin 1977), table 1, page 10. Recommendations for alterations to this Act are made in *The Review of the Mental Health Act 1959*; (DHSS 1978), though these have not yet been legislated.

illness, arrested or incomplete development of mind, psychopathic disorder and any other disorder or disability of mind'. This terminology reflects the prevailing psychiatric emphasis upon 'medical models'[3] of deviant behaviour which assume that this is the product of mental disease or illness. If considered dangerous, mentally abnormal offenders are liable to compulsory and indefinite detention in hospital. Release is dependent upon the doctor's decision that a patient is no longer dangerous and also, where a restriction order has been applied, on the Home Secretary's approval. As Wootton (1978) remarks: 'Law breakers are thus divided into two distinct classes, the criminally responsible goats and the medically irresponsible sheep—or the wicked and the sick'. It is to psychiatry that the Law looks to discriminate these two classes of offenders and to assume responsibility for the treatment of the 'sick'.

Whilst the psychiatrist's treatment role may have been intended originally for mentally abnormal offenders outside the prison system, it has become extended increasingly to include 'legally normal' offenders within it. Gunn *et al* (1978) note that, consistent with the punishment/deterrence role of imprisonment, prison doctors had previously been concerned to transfer those in need of psychiatric treatment to asylums or hospitals outside the prison system. However, a gradual change in this policy took place as psychiatry developed to include psychological as well as biological explanations of abnormal behaviour. Most influential in this respect was the development of psychoanalytic theories which offered far more comprehensive explanations of behaviour and which in contrast to biological theories emphasized the continuity between normal and deviant behaviour. This made it more difficult and arbitrary to draw the sharp distinctions between the 'mad' and the 'bad' assumed in law. One consequence was the recognition that there remained within the prisons many inmates who would not satisfy the criteria for mental abnormality that would justify transfer to hospital, but who might none the less benefit from psychiatric treatment. A major step towards confirming the legitimacy of psychiatric treatment within prisons was taken with the publication of the East–Hubert report in 1939. This recommended the provision of a special establishment for psychiatric treatment within the prison system itself. Gunn *et al* (1978) emphasize the significance of this particular event:

> The East–Hubert report, although its recommendations were not implemented for about 25 years, marks a turning point in the history of British Prison Psychiatry. In the first place, it shows the prison medical authority anxious to take on, rather than to shed, the task of treating the mentally abnormal prisoner. Secondly, it defines the objective of the

---

3 This term is used loosely to describe both those models which assume that the determinants of abnormal behaviour are organic and those that postulate some intra-psychic disease or psychodynamic determinants. Such models have in common the assumption that abnormal behaviour is symptomatic of some underlying disturbance.

treatment, not as a medical objective but as a behavioural one: 'The main object of psychotherapy in criminal work is to prevent crime being committed and repeated by the individual' (Para. 58). By explicitly defining the main purpose of prison psychiatry as the prevention of recidivism, the authors assured that the prison authorities would, in their search for ways of making prisons reformative, henceforward pay increasing attention to the views of psychiatrists.

Consequently, psychiatry has been seen as giving considerable impetus to what has been described as the 'rehabilitative ideal' within penology (Bean 1976). This has gathered momentum since the original recommendation of the Gladstone Committee in 1895, to the effect that the prison service should extend its role beyond simple punishment and deterrence to one of 'reformation'. Basic to the 'rehabilitative ideal' are what can be described as those theories based on 'personal inadequacy' models of crime which share a common assumption that crime reflects some personal deficit or inadequacy within the offender, which requires 'treatment' to prevent recidivism. Psychiatry has been perhaps the most influential example of this kind of explanation and involves the assumption that, in certain cases, criminal behaviour may be a direct reflection of mental disorder. What has remained uncertain is the proportion of offenders for which psychiatric treatment might be appropriate. There has previously been a tendency to assume a special relationship between crime and mental illness which has given rise to unrealistic expectations concerning the 'reformative' value of psychiatric treatment. However, as Gunn (1979) is concerned to emphasize, any assumption of a general relationship between crime and psychiatric disorder is misleading on 'a priori' grounds: 'Mental illness, even psychiatric abnormality is a biological concept. Criminal behaviour is a social concept, it is arbitrarily determined by legislation . . .' Whilst Bowden (1978a) describes a 'retrenchment' from treatment and rehabilitative ideals (at least amongst psychiatrists) and Gunn et al (1978) deplore expectations that psychiatry may hold a panacea for crime, there is a general consensus that a substantial proportion of prisoners are in need of treatment. Estimates of this proportion vary quite widely (Gunn 1977). In the most recent study, involving a survey of 811 men, Gunn et al (1978) found that approximately 20 per cent had had psychiatric treatment previously and that approximately one third could be considered in need of treatment. Psychiatric treatment within the Prison Service is intended for those who do not present the degree of mental disorder that would justify compulsory admission to hospital under mental health legislation. However, the extreme reluctance of ordinary hospitals to admit mentally abnormal offenders suggests that many of these may enter prisons (Orr 1978; Bowden 1978a).

A second area of uncertainty has been the extent to which psychiatric treatment should be expected to reduce antisocial behaviour. A corollary to the premise that there is no necessary relationship between crime and psychiatric disorder is that it is only in those cases where a relationship can be assumed that it is reasonable to expect successful treatment to reduce recidivism. However, implicit in the practice of both imposing and removing compulsory status for patients on the grounds of presumed dangerousness, must be the expectation that successful treatment will reduce the probability of future antisocial behaviour. Moreover a particularly common form of psychiatric diagnosis for offenders is one involving 'personality', 'behaviour' or 'habit' disorders (e.g. Gunn 1977; Bowden 1978a). As Walker (1965) suggests, the antisocial behaviour is often itself the essence of such diagnoses and consequently the repetition of offensive behaviour is a valid measure of treatment results.

The outcome of such developments is that, whilst there remains a legal distinction between mentally normal and abnormal offenders which relate to two very different systems of management, i.e. Health Service and Prison Service, both these systems offer psychiatric treatment to clients that are compulsorily detained. Moreover, in both systems there is some expectation that successful treatment should be instrumental in preventing further antisocial behaviour. Also, the indefinite detention of the 'mentally abnormal' offender is considered necessary to avoid restricting treatment procedures, and for similar reasons judges have previously been advised to avoid short sentences for 'mentally normal' offenders (Home Office 1979).

Treatment and Rehabilitation

Within psychiatry any clear distinction between rehabilitation and treatment presupposes a 'medical model' of deviant behaviour. Under such a model, treatment is concerned primarily with the underlying pathology, whether an identifiable or assumed organic process or a more nebulous psychic disturbance. Rehabilitation is directed towards helping the patient overcome any residual disabilities or social handicaps. In this manner rehabilitation has become associated with 'social treatments' (Bennett 1978) and with attempts to mitigate the effects of both illness and institutionalization in chronic patients (Royal College of Psychiatrists 1980a). It is now customary to emphasize that the two procedures, whilst distinct, may need to be linked and interdependent (e.g. Wing 1978). However, the distinction has as its legacy the assumption that valid gains in treatment may be made before rehabilitation is considered or started and often also the separation of treatment and rehabilitative agencies (Wing 1978).

Any distinction between treatment and rehabilitation becomes far more tenuous under a 'behavioural model' of deviant behaviour which in the absence of demonstrable and relevant organic disorder requires no assumption of underlying 'psychic' disturbance. Instead the behavioural model emphasizes the role of the patient's learning history and situational influences in determining the presentation of deviant behaviour (Kazdin 1978). Under this model 'treatment' itself is concerned with encouraging the patient to learn and perform appropriate behaviours and to inhibit inappropriate behaviours. Therefore, it is not surprising that one can trace common principles underlying both the behavioural literature on treatment (e.g. Agras 1972) and the non-behavioural literature on rehabilitation (e.g. Bennett 1978). Both of these emphasize the importance of the interaction between the patient and the treatment environment and include an emphasis on the following basic requirements.

(1) Assessment and goal-setting: Relevant treatment goals and progress towards these should be identified by assessing the patient's abilities and performance in relationship to the various demands of the social situation to which he must adjust.

(2) Prompting and reinforcing appropriate behaviour: Where competence deficits are identified the patient should be taught more appropriate behaviour within the constraints of any relevant organic disorder, and where possible, making special allowances for this. Treatment environments should be as 'natural' as possible to ensure that appropriate behaviours can be acquired and practised. Unnecessarily artificial environments should be avoided as these might encourage the loss of previous skills and the development of inappropriate behaviours.

(3) Generalization and maintenance: In order to ensure that appropriate behaviour is maintained, there should be a gradual and controlled transition from the treatment situation to the environment to which the patient is to return.

These basic principles will later provide a framework with which to identify the limitations of the present facilities for treating offenders. Subsequently, the relevance and implications of a more comprehensive behavioural approach to treatment will be considered.

The Present Facilities and Approach to Rehabilitation

The Prison Service

In Scotland and Northern Ireland the Prison Services have no separate psychiatric and psychological services but draw instead on 'outside' staff, particularly from within the National Health Service. Whilst the Prison Service in England and Wales also draws upon National Health Service staff (particularly psychiatrists), it also has its own Prison Medical and Psychological Services. With the exception of a few joint and 'honorary appointments', these are essentially independent of services in the NHS.

Whilst there are a number of psychiatric units within the Prison Service, the largest and probably the most significant treatment facility is Grendon Underwood Psychiatric Prison. (Opened in 1962, this was the eventual response to the East–Hubert recommendation for a special psychiatric prison). Treatment at Grendon Underwood is based on therapeutic community principles and has been very fully described and studied by Gunn *et al* (1978). Those authors monitored the adjustment of a single year's intake of 107 inmates using a range of structured assessment techniques applied at regular intervals throughout each inmate's stay. Grendon Underwood admits inmates only on a voluntary basis and will not accept those who are psychotic or subnormal. The cohort studied comprised relatively young men (average age: 27 years) with substantial criminal and prison records. They tended to resent authority, exhibit neurotic disturbance and have difficulties involving personal relationships. Treatment involved a relatively informal and non-authoritarian regime with frequent group meetings and an emphasis upon accepting responsibility and understanding personal relationships. This was found to result in a highly significant reduction of neurotic symptoms following treatment, combined with improvements in social confidence and self-esteem. In contrasting this treatment offered at Grendon Underwood with the more traditional psychotherapy given at Wormwood Scrubs (within a 'normal' prison regime), Gunn *et al* suggest that group treatment, particularly within a therapeutic community, may be more beneficial. They note that staff at either prison were unable to offer a follow-up service or long-term care in the community. Their own follow-up study of a small sample of Grendon Underwood men showed that 70 per cent were reconvicted within a period of approximately two years.

Laycock (1979) has described the recent applications of 'behavioural' treatment procedures by Prison Psychologists. These include relaxation training, social skills training, and various procedures for modifying sexual orientation in male sex offenders. Much of this work has not been fully reported either because it is still in progress or because of practical difficulties arising in connection with methodology. However, Matthews (1980) has reported the results of a combination of aversion therapy and orgasmic reconditioning treatments for 10 male sex offenders, who were not considered to be deficient in social skills. 'Self-report' and penile response measures indicated the desired change in sexual interest at the end of treatment, for nine patients. Follow-up showed that none of these patients had been convicted for a sexual offence within two years after release. One had been charged for a sexual offence, but not convicted.

Priestley and McGuire (1977) have described a very comprehensive 'pre-release' course for prisoners (in general), one that concentrates specifically on teaching those skills relevant to solving problems likely to be encountered after release. Their own survey indicated that most common amongst these are problems involving work, accommodation, money, personal rights, family relationships and friendships. Whilst they deliberately adopt a 'learning' or 'teaching' approach, they draw upon a very wide range of procedures including direct teaching and educational methods, counselling and group-work techniques of various kinds and 'behavioural' social skills training methods including roleplay, modelling and rehearsal. [4] Noting the uncertainty experienced by prison officers concerning their own role in rehabilitation, Priestley and McGuire set out specifically to involve prison officers in an active training role. Whilst this does appear to be a highly relevant approach and one which has apparently met with a favourable response from both prisoners and officers, detailed outcome and follow-up results have yet to be reported.

The Special Hospitals[5]

These are provided for compulsory patients who require conditions of special security because of their 'dangerous, violent or criminal propensities' (MHA 1959). These hospitals provide 'maximum security' conditions involving considerable emphasis upon both physical security arrangements and close supervision of patients. They are administered directly by the Secretary of State and serve national catchment areas. Consequently, their professional staff have no formal links with local psychiatric services. The patient populations tend to vary between these hospitals though together they provide for a wide range of subnormal and mentally ill patients including a high proportion of 'personality disorders' (Gostin 1977; Tennent et al 1980).

Until recently accounts of rehabilitation programmes within these hospitals have been restricted to general descriptions of the hospital regimes rather than to details of specific programmes. The general 'flavour' of these regimes has been described as involving:

> Careful, patient training towards social conformity, with a complex system of rewards, both social and monetary, and an equivalent range of disincentives to unacceptable behaviour, by loss of privilege and amenities and a return to a more strictly structured and closely observed stratum of the hospital society (McGrath 1966)

More recent inquiries have been explicit in their criticisms of unnecessary regimentation in such hospitals and the need for more and better co-ordinated rehabilitation programmes (Gostin 1977; DHSS 1980). The adverse publicity that has attached to such inquiries detracts from those rehabilitative efforts that are made in these hospitals, which usually offer a range of occupational, educational and recreational opportunities and, in

4 Priestley et al (1978) have subsequently described their assessment and training procedures in more detail.

5 There are four Special Hospitals in England (Broadmoor, Rampton, Moss Side and Park Lane) and one in Scotland (the State Hospital, Carstairs). A recent description of the former is available in A Human Condition, vol. 2 (Gostin 1977).

some cases, courses intended to prepare patients for return to the community (Hepworth—personal communication; Pratt—personal communication). However there have been extremely few reported studies of treatment in Special Hospitals and consequently the value of those programmes that do exist is difficult to assess. None the less Bennett (1977, 1980) has described the special curriculum that has been developed to meet the particular educational needs of patients at Rampton Hospital. This is based on Gunzburg's analysis of basic social competence skills (Gunzburg 1973), and is currently being evaluated.

An exception to the relative dearth of studies of treatment in the Special Hospitals is to be found in the recent work of David Crawford and his colleagues at Broadmoor Hospital. This work exemplifies the increasing involvement of psychologists in behavioural treatments particularly of sex offenders, within the Special Hospitals. Crawford (1979) emphasizes that it is too simple to view sexual deviance as a problem of deviant interest alone. He stresses the need for a far more comprehensive approach, including attention to a wide range of possible related problems such as sexual dysfunction, anxiety, deficient social skills, inadequate sexual knowledge and poor self-control. Crawford and his colleagues report the use of social skills training and sex education programmes for inadequate sex offenders (Crawford and Allen 1979; Crawford and Howells 1978). Whilst this work has involved the systematic demonstration of the immediate beneficial effects of these programmes, follow-up work has yet to be reported. Howells (1976) has also reported the extension of social skills training to teach more appropriate assertive behaviours in violent offenders at Broadmoor.

A number of follow-up studies of Special Hospital patients have been undertaken, but these are typically unrelated to any specific rehabilitation programmes. These studies are reviewed in detail by Bowden (1981). Although their diversity allows few firm conclusions, a fairly consistent finding is that approximately 20 per cent of those leaving Special Hospitals are subsequently returned. Reconviction rates vary widely according to diagnosis, manner of discharge and follow-up period. However, Bowden summarizes these by suggesting that up to 50 per cent may receive a subsequent conviction but only 10 per cent may become involved in serious acts of violence.

Special Units in the National Health Service

There have been a number of units within the NHS which have provided special services for psychopathic patients. Probably the best known of these is the Henderson Hospital which is organized as a therapeutic community (Taylor 1966). Whiteley (1970) reports a follow-up study of 122 consecutive departures from the Henderson Hospital and found that 40 per cent of these had no subsequent criminal or hospital record after two years.

Most of the published studies concerning units for psychopaths have involved the general description and evaluation of different regimes, rather than more specific programmes. Comparisons of 'self-governing' regimes with more traditional authoritarian regimes have been reported by Miles (1969), Craft *et al* (1964) and Craft (1966; 1968). The diversity of these studies allows few firm conclusions other than the general and perhaps obvious one that neither regime is better for all patients. Whiteley (1970) has suggested that inadequate and 'acting out' psychopaths may do better in a structured regime and Craft (1966) has tentatively reached similar conclusions concerning young psychopaths of dull intelligence.

The need for more secure facilities within the NHS, particularly to bridge the gap between the 'maximum security' conditions of the Special Hospitals and the 'open door' conditions of the local hospitals, has been urged consistently over the last 20 years. Most recently the Butler Committee published an interim report urgently recommending the provision of secure units in each Regional Health Authority Area, for both offender and non-offender patients (Butler Committee 1974). Despite allocation of specific funds by central government there has been considerable resistance to the establishment of such 'regional secure units' (Bluglass 1978a). However, a recent review by the Royal College of Psychiatrists (1980b) suggests that some progress towards providing special facilities is being made, albeit very slowly. Nevertheless, several 'interim' secure units have been established and short descriptions of these have been reported (e.g. Faulk 1979; Higgins 1979).

A full account of rehabilitation programmes in an interim secure unit is given by Reid and Lea (1980) in their description of Elton Ward at Prestwich Hospital. Forty-four patients had been admitted to this unit in the three and a half years that it had beeen open. Most of these were recidivists and had a previous institutional history. The most frequent primary diagnoses were schizophrenia (23) and personality disorder (14). The aims of the unit are clearly stated in terms of preparing patients to live as independently as possible by teaching patients skills in which they are deficient and substituting socially appropriate for previously inappropriate behaviours. There are a wide range of activities including work, education and recreation as well as training in self-help skills, social skills training, social activities and outings into the community. Patients are gradually introduced to the community before discharge, for example by attending educational or training courses or by 'working out' whilst 'living in' the ward. Contacts between the ward staff and patients' relatives and after-care services are encouraged. Whilst a proper follow-up study has not been possible yet, initial outcome data seem promising. Of the 27 patients who had left the unit (and after follow-up periods ranging between three and thirty-two months) only five had committed further offences and been sent to Special Hospitals or a Remand Centre (Reid and Lea 1980).

Apart from certain 'psychopathic' and interim secure units there are other specialized units and services. These include a secure unit for mentally ill patients (Carney and Nolan 1978) and a short-term sociopathic ward in Edinburgh (Woodside *et al* 1976). The treatment programmes in both these units are described in only very general terms but share an emphasis upon group meetings, occupational therapy and recreational activities.

The Eastdale unit at Balderton Hospital is unique in specializing in the rehabilitation of Special Hospital patients. Hunter (personal communication) has described the first 100 admissions to this unit since it opened in 1974. All had a history of seriously disturbed behaviour, and had been in a Special Hospital for between one and twenty-two years before transfer to Eastdale. Only 12 were legally classified as Mentally Ill, the rest falling into the Psychopathic Disorder and Subnormality categories. The unit's rehabilitation programmes emphasize educational and vocational training, as well as the development of leisure interests and frequent visits to the outside community. Social skills training and sex education are also considered particularly important. At the time of the study 13 (of the total 100) patients were still in Eastdale, 17 had been returned to a Special Hospital, 17 had progressed to alternative NHS facilities and 51 were living in the community (2 had gone AWOL). The subsequent adjustment of patients leaving Eastdale was compared with a group discharged by the Mental Health Review Tribunal from the Special Hospitals straight into the community. Both groups were discharged over a similar period and the maximum follow-up period was two years. A significantly greater proportion of those discharged directly by the MHRT had been either sent to prison or returned to Special Hospitals. As the two discharged groups were not matched (indeed almost by 'definition' they could not be) one must be cautious about this finding. Hunter himself suggests that this seems to attest to the success of Eastdale since those patients discharged directly by the MHRT are likely to be considered better adjusted than those in need of transfer to Eastdale as a first step. Hunter (personal communication) has since described the first 100 discharges from Eastdale, followed up over a period ranging from one and a half to five and a half years. Of these 72 had had no convictions at all and only 12 had received convictions for indictable offences.

The preceding account has been focused deliberately on those special services that provide for the treatment of offenders. It is important to emphasize that offenders are also frequently treated in ordinary NHS facilities, including out-patient clinics. Whilst NHS services have been unwilling to accept patients that might present management problems, many mentally abnormal offenders present very few management difficulties and can be managed quite adequately within ordinary facilities (Royal College of Psychiatrists 1980b). Special out-patient services also exist. Wardrop (1975) has described the Douglas Inch Centre for Forensic Psychiatry which offers a special out-patient treatment service to delinquents in Glasgow where treatment has been based on different forms of 'group-work'. Bluglass (1975) describes the Midland Centre for Forensic Psychiatry at Birmingham which provides out-patient treatment for offenders over the age of 15 years. He refers to the fact that this kind of service can provide continuity of contact with therapists for prisoners after release and also long-term after-care.

Commentary

It is clear that published work describing actual rehabilitation programmes for adult offenders in the United Kingdom is scant. Moreover, some of the reports that are available do no more than describe a service or facility. Apart from the few more specific activities described, a recurring theme in accounts of 'rehabilitation', particularly within custodial institutions, is an emphasis upon structured routine and work and to a lesser extent recreation and education. Of course such activities can and no doubt do have value. However, one is occasionally confused at the extent to which they are intended to be rehabilitative or may be intended to be (or have otherwise become) more simply diversional. Walker and McCabe (1973) summarize this uncertainty aptly in their comments on occupational activities:

> . . . the activity which must take up most patient-hours in any type of mental hospital (apart from sleep) is occupational therapy, and . . . very much the same could be said of prisons, although the term used in their case is 'work' . . . What is interesting to the detached observer is the intense criticism to which prison work is subjected and the comparative rarity of any critical examination of the nature of occupational therapy.

Those studies that do make any attempt at evaluation typically fall far short of meeting the various minimal requirements for such research.[6] (In these terms the study by Gunn *et al* (1978) is certainly by far the most rigorous.) This lack of satisfactory evaluative research is probably due to the relatively small number of those actively involved with the rehabilitation of offenders on any large scale. No doubt it may also reflect a reluctance of some who are working in this area to examine their work critically. However, there are quite considerable problems facing the research worker and it is noteworthy that in her review of prison psychologists' work Laycock (1979) revealed that much of the work that is undertaken falls short of publication standards because of difficulties with control groups, assessing change and follow-up after release or discharge. One such

6 Logan (1972) lists several minimal requirements for evaluative research with offenders. These are (1) a clear definition of the programme; (2) programme should be replicable; (3) the use of matched controls; (4) the essential treatment is received by treatment group only; (5) before and after measurement; (6) reliable criteria of success and (7) follow-up into the community.

problem is exemplified by Gunn *et al* (1978) who attempted to identify a matched control group of inmates who had not received psychiatric treatment, to compare with a sample released from Grendon Underwood. Although they had access to detailed records on some 4000 men eligible for parole and were able to select a matched control group on the basis of at least seven key variables, which resulted in matching on several secondary variables, the two groups were still found to differ in ways that could invalidate the comparisons between them.

Whilst the lack of more adequate information makes it impossible to evaluate present services on empirical grounds, one can still ask more basic questions concerning the 'face validity' of these services. One such question might be: Can present services meet the basic requirements for effective rehabilitation to make it reasonable to expect success? This leads us to consider the practical difficulties that may arise.

Practical Problems

The fact that a patient has committed an offence does not in itself require that his particular treatment needs should differ substantially from those of one who has not. However, there are three factors which can arise to make the rehabilitation of offenders more problematic than that of non-offenders. These are (1) the involuntary or compulsory status of the 'client', (2) the conflict between therapeutic and custodial needs and in particular the artificial and restrictive environments of secure institutions and (3) the interdependence and yet poor co-ordination of existing services. The practical difficulties that these can cause for each of the three basic requirements for rehabilitation or behavioural treatment are now considered.

Assessment and goal-setting

There are three general kinds of assessment: (i) Self-report measures (including interviews, check-lists, questionnaires, etc.); (ii) observational measures based on direct observation of the client's behaviour in either (*a*) the natural environment or (*b*) a contrived or analogue situation and (iii) psychophysiological measures. Since the different types of response-measure frequently do not inter-correlate highly, a comprehensive behavioural assessment should include data from at least two, if not all three sources (Ciminero 1977).

With self-report measures one can be confronted by the problem that detained offenders may feel constrained to behave in a manner that they consider will best expedite their release. Consequently their motivation for change may be only temporary and they may tend to exaggerate progress. Alternatively they may simply deny or minimize difficulties. This may be prompted by their fear of punitive consequences or their scepticism concerning what help may be available or their own capacity for change. Alternatively, once cloistered in the artificial environment of a custodial institution, in which he is sheltered from certain temptations and difficulties, the offender may simply become less aware of his former problems (Matthews 1980). These various considerations, often combined with the fact that the offender may be of dull intelligence or have been psychotic and may, therefore, be poor at verbalizing events, suggest particular difficulties for self-report measures.

Direct observations of an offender's behaviour in an institutional or restrictive setting may give misleading or irrelevant information about his rehabilitation needs. Problems that the patient has experienced in the outside community may no longer arise in the institution. Alternatively, problems that do arise within the institution may be specific to that situation and not reliably indicate problems that the offender will experience on his return to the community:

> The dictates of security mean that we cannot generally expose the patient to his problem situation or to problem stimuli. Patients are not allowed alcohol so one has no way of knowing whether patients with a history of excessive drinking have changed . . . Contact with female patients is only under controlled and supervised conditions so that we cannot assess whether sex offenders have learned to exercise self-control . . . As these examples illustrate the secure environment at Broadmoor, whilst minimizing problems within the institution, does make it difficult to assess problems and change in the very areas where it is most crucial. Conversely there may be some behaviour problems which are precipitated by the hospital but which disappear once the patient is released. Problems such as institutionalization, reaction against authority, some forms of aggression and sexual frustration, may be caused by the unnatural and artificial nature of the secure environment. There is a danger that such behaviour will be misinterpreted as evidence of the unsuitability of the patient for discharge (Crawford 1980a).

In the same manner Ross and McKay (1976) found that institutional behaviour of delinquent girls bore little relationship to behaviour after release.

It is because of the limitations of alternative measures that the use of 'analogue' and also psychophysiological measures is being explored increasingly. Analogue measures involve observing the client's response to a simulated situation. Amongst their various measures of social skills Crawford and Allen (1979) used two kinds of analogue measure. The first involved having a patient respond to audio-taped sequences in which a scene was described and followed by someone speaking to him. The patient's responses were themselves tape-recorded for analysis.[7] A second analogue measure involved video-taping the patient as he made conversation with a 'stooge' in an imaginary party situation. Crawford and Allen found that both these measures reflected changes in behaviour following social skills training. The main psychophysiological assessment procedure to have been used for clinical purposes with male sex offenders is penile plethysmography (e.g. Hinton *et al* 1976; Matthews 1980). This procedure involves the continuous monitoring of penile volume or diameter changes whilst the patient views possible erotic stimuli. Crawford (1980b) has reviewed the value of this particular procedure not simply in helping distinguish sexual preferences but also in enabling the clinician to identify which particular aspects of a situation might stimulate deviant arousal. Whilst the use of analogue and psychophysiological measures certainly appears promising, they still require further development and validation.

Arising directly from problems of assessment, and in particular from the fact that institutional behaviour may have no direct bearing upon community adjustment, is the risk of selecting inappropriate treatment goals. Both Feldman (1977) and Blackburn (1980a) have commented on the extent to which programmes for offenders frequently concentrate on 'convenience' behaviours, i.e. behaviours which appear significant within an institution but which can be more closely related to the smooth running of the institution than to the rehabilitation of the patient. Of course some attention to reducing seriously disruptive or damaging behaviour can be justified, but conformity within the institution should not be emphasized to the neglect of more relevant goals and to the point of simply increasing institutionalization. Similarly there is a danger that certain goals which do have some validity become exaggerated to the neglect of others, simply because these are easier to attain within an institution. In this respect Feldman (1977) criticizes behavioural treatments of offenders for concentrating too much on goals that may be only indirectly related to the offenders' problems:

> They imply the same (usually unspoken) assumption as does the psychodynamic approach, namely that criminal behaviour relates to some personal deficit in the offender, the typical area of emphasis being on a lack of educational skill. The implication is that if only he was fluent at reading, arithmetic or had command of some job skill, he would not 'need' to offend . . . What rarely has happened is a direct attempt to change the behaviour, outside the institution, which led to a conviction.

This criticism is not intended to deny the value of educational or vocational training programmes, but to suggest that this may be exaggerated so that

---

7 Crawford and Allen (1979) describe an example of a sequence: 'You are at a dance when someone you don't know comes over to you and says: "Hello, don't I know you from somewhere?" '

little attention is paid directly to problems far more relevant to the patient's offences, e.g. aggression, sexual behaviour, etc.

Prompting and Reinforcing Appropriate Behaviour

A number of practical problems arise in connection with ensuring that appropriate behaviours are acquired and reinforced within institutions, particularly custodial institutions. The first is the simple fact that the possibility of certain adaptive behaviours being learned or practised may be precluded, mixing freely in female company being the most common (and often the most relevant) example. McGrath (1966; 1968) has commented perceptively on the manner in which security requirements in a Special Hospital restrict patients' independence and activities and also staff–patient relationships. Laycock (1979) has described a different kind of restriction, that created by overcrowding and prison design. Many prisons in England and Wales were built before or during the nineteenth century and designed to reflect the penal philosophy of 'separation' at that time. These buildings, now seriously overcrowded, place severe restrictions on the extent to which rehabilitation facilities and activities can be properly accommodated.

The danger of staff valuing goals that may be more consistent with institutionalization has already been noted. There is also a danger that staff expectations and selective attention may actually encourage disturbed behaviour (e.g. Weaver *et al* 1978). However, even more serious is the influence that inmates may exert on each other. The prison inmate sub-culture has been identified as being generally anti-authoritarian and having a particularly powerful influence over its members (Bean 1976). Buehler *et al* (1966) have shown that the inmates of a Borstal not only reinforced deviant behaviour but also exercised more effective control over each other, than did the staff. Indeed Grendon Underwood was modelled on therapeutic community principles specifically in an attempt to avoid the development of such anti-therapeutic peer-group influences (Gray 1973).

Generalization and Maintenance

As noted before, rehabilitation should be conducted in as natural an environment as possible, the most 'natural' being the community itself. Where rehabilitation must take place in an institutional or other artificial setting, then it is important to encourage behaviour changes that are likely to be reinforced in the outside community settings and the transition from the treatment to the 'outside community' should be as gradual as possible (Ayllon and Milan 1979). Thus an effective rehabilitation programme will require an understanding of the situation to which an offender will return and the ability to plan and control his transition to this. One recurring theme in British studies is the lack of follow-up and the need for more effective 'aftercare'. However, the present 'systems of care' in the United Kingdom place certain constraints on the more effective planning of generalization and maintenance. One such 'obstacle' is the fact that offenders can be released precipitously as a result of discharge decisions being taken on purely legal rather than clinical grounds. For example compulsory patients who are not subjects of a restriction order have the right of appeal against detention to a Mental Health Review Tribunal. This must discharge a patient if it is satisfied that he is no longer suffering from mental disorder or does not represent a substantial risk to himself or others. (The MHRT initiates approximately 10 per cent of discharges from the Special Hospitals—Bowden 1981.) Once the decision to release is taken by the MHRT it has immediate effect and consequently allows no time at all for aftercare arrangements. The expectation that such precipitate release would be detrimental to maintenance receives some support from a review of follow-up studies of Special Hospital patients (Bowden 1981). This showed that poor outcome does tend to be associated with MHRT discharge. In recognition of this problem both the Butler Committee (1975) and the Review of the Mental Health Act 1959 (DHSS 1978) have suggested that Tribunals should be able to delay the effect of their discharge order for up to three months. West (1980) refers to a similar problem in the penal system with regard to parole decisions which tend to make release unpredictable and unrelated to treatment considerations.

A second problem is the reluctance of custodial institutions to consider any substantial relaxation in security even when the offender is approaching release. For example Gostin (1977) notes the observations of a report on Broadmoor which describes staff attitudes to rehabilitation:

> It is a fact that Broadmoor staff in general view rehabilitation with some suspicion. They equate it with certain practices which are welcome in an open hospital, but which are unacceptable with Broadmoor.

This attitude, that rehabilitation is not the responsibility of the Special Hospital was encouraged by the Aarvold Committee (1973) which recommended that patients leaving Special Hospitals should normally be transferred first to an ordinary hospital, rather than released directly. The fact that Special Hospitals serve a National Catchment Area and are often isolated, both geographically and professionally, from the ordinary hospitals to which patients must return, militates against the co-operation and co-ordination between professional staff that would be required for effective rehabilitation in this manner.[8] Dell (1980) reported that two-thirds of patients leaving Special Hospitals do so on transfer to an ordinary hospital. She noted the exceptional reluctance of ordinary hospitals to

---

8 As Prins (1980) observes, the National catchment areas of the Special Hospitals also make for difficulties in assessing the patients' home circumstances and in ensuring that contact with relatives is adequately maintained.

accept Special Hospital patients and that a third of those ready for transfer had been waiting for a bed for more than two years, some for up to eight years. (Quite apart from the nonsense this makes of any attempts to plan and co-ordinate rehabilitative efforts, such delays raise serious questions concerning civil rights.) Significantly, Dell found that transfers were likely to take place far more rapidly if close communication took place between staff from the different hospitals, for example by having ordinary hospital staff visit the Special Hospitals themselves and see the patient there. Dell suggests that Special Hospitals should make more use of direct discharges. Whilst this would undoubtedly avoid some unnecessary delays, it still begs the question of how effectively treatment started in Special Hospitals can be gradually extended into the outside community in a controlled manner.

Professional Problems

To such practical problems can be added two kinds of 'professional' difficulty, the first concerning the nature of the 'client–therapist' relation-ships, and in particular the latter's obligations and the second concerning the maintenance of appropriate professional standards.

The psychiatrist's or psychologist's professional obligations are usually relatively uncomplicated. Whilst he has obligations to society in general, these rarely come into direct conflict with those to his 'client'. However, this is certainly not always the case when the client is compulsorily detained and may feel constrained to seek treatment, and is aware that the therapist's opinions may influence his prospects for release.

> Whereas traditionally the function of the doctor has been to attend to the medical needs of his patient, we now suddenly find a bunch of the medical profession acting as an agent of the state and making decisions about the patient that do not have the patient's approval (Bean 1976).

In the case of the offender who genuinely wishes successful treatment and fears release without it, i.e. whose values coincide with those of society, the therapist need not be placed in serious conflict. However, in many other cases conflict can arise and whilst some therapists may like to pretend that their primary obligation is to the client, there can be little doubt that this is to society (Bowden 1978b). Thus McGrath (1968) acknowledges that the awareness of society's needs for protection probably makes clinicians excessively cautious in recommending release. Feldman (1977) has sug-gested that clinicians working with offenders are reluctant to recognize their roles as 'agents of society', instead of the traditional role as 'agents of the patient'. This reluctance prompts them to define their role in terms of relieving the patient's distress or teaching new skills rather than in terms of dealing more directly with the patient's 'offensive' behaviour. Bancroft (1979) has discussed how the therapist working with offenders is inevitably cast as 'an extension of the arm of the law'. This makes the

'adult–adult' type of therapeutic relationship involving active client participation and co-operation, normally required in contemporary behavioural
treatments, difficult to achieve.

The maintenance of professional standards for those working in custodial institutions is difficult for various reasons. First, staff may be employed
and work in relative professional isolation. Small independent services
dealing with offenders alone (e.g. the Special Hospitals and the Prison
Service) can have difficulty in recruiting and maintaining well-qualified
staff (Bowden 1978b; DHSS 1980). Given the constraints that custodial
institutions impose on rehabilitation and the relative lack of research and
'corrective-feedback' from outcome studies, staff can all too easily confuse
experience for expertise. (Logically one should expect limits to the expertise developed by any staff whose rehabilitative efforts are confined to
custodial institutions alone.) Further, the inward-looking mentality that
has been associated with total institutions can all too easily make staff
'disinclined to hazard their comfortable prejudices and vulnerable self-
esteem in the hurly burly of the wider community' (McKeith 1978).

Finally, having previously considered the effects of an institution's
reinforcement contingencies on patients, one must recognize their effects
on the professional worker himself.

> There is still the evident danger that the forensic psychiatrist may too
> easily fall in with the system in which he works . . . It is not always the
> psychiatrist, the psychologist or the social worker who changes the
> institution it is sometimes the institution that changes the professional
> (WHO 1977).

This process of falling in with the system can involve accommodating
rehabilitative programmes to the constraints of the institution. This may
reach the point of providing little more than a façade of treatment that may
even serve to disguise the institution's limitations (Bean 1976). In this
respect it is ironic that the enthusiasm and diligence of a naïve clinician
might lead to accusations of compromise or even collusion.

Disillusionment with the 'Rehabilitative Ideal'

Misgivings about the psychiatric treatment of offenders and the 'rehabilitative ideal' in general have been steadily growing (e.g. Bean 1976). Walker
(1976) has contrasted the 'right to treatment' protest in the United States,
with the 'right to punishment' protest in Scandinavia. The former implies
that compulsory patients do not receive proper treatment programmes,
whilst the latter implies that offenders should not be detained for unjust
periods in pursuit of treatment goals. Other misgivings include concern at
the constraints imposed on offenders to seek or to consent to treatment
and the inhumanity and degradation of particular treatment procedures.

However, a particularly common criticism is the presumed ineffectiveness of treatment programmes, which gains most strength from reviews of different management strategies within the penal system. Most influential in this respect has been a review by Martinson (1974) of American studies, in which he examines 231 reports of psychological, psychiatric, educational and social treatment programmes published between 1945 and 1967. Martinson's summary is as unequivocal as it was widely-publicized: 'With few and isolated exceptions the rehabilitative efforts that have been reported so far, have had no appreciable effect on recidivism.' A similarly pessimistic conclusion is reached in a review of outcome studies for offenders, reported in *A Review of Criminal Justice Policy* (Home Office 1976):

> Longer sentences seem no more effective than short ones, different types of institutions appear to work about equally as well and rehabilitative programmes, whether involving psychiatric treatment, counselling, case-work or intensive contact and special attention, in custodial or non-custodial settings—appear overall to have no certain beneficial effects.

This indictment of psychiatric treatments (amongst others) within penal settings tends to be generalized to the treatment of abnormal offenders within the Health Services, helped no doubt by the general lack of evaluative research in this field and also doubts as to the effectiveness of psychotherapy generally (Walker 1976). Equally relevant to the discrediting of treatment for mentally abnormal offenders have been the recent criticisms of Special Hospitals (Gostin 1977; DHSS 1980).

In view of such doubts about the effectiveness of treatment one of the most telling criticisms of treatment has been of its association with longer sentences and indeterminate detention. Gostin (1977) has described how abnormal offenders in hospitals are detained for substantially longer periods than ordinary offenders who have similar criminal records and re-conviction rates. Of direct relevance to the issue of prolonged detention is the therapist's role in assessing dangerousness, for it is the presumed dangerousness of compulsory patients that prevents their release. The clinical prediction of dangerousness has been widely criticized on a number of grounds. These include the fact that dangerousness is typically grossly over-predicted (Steadman 1979), the typically highly subjective nature and conceptual inadequacy of the clinical decision-making procedure (e.g. Pfohl 1979) and the fact that such decisions should in any case be more properly considered matters of legal and public, rather than clinical concern (Shah 1975). Quinsey and Ambtman (1979) report a study which casts doubt on the particular expertise of forensic psychiatrists in assessing dangerousness and also the relevance of psychiatric assessment data. They demonstrated that psychiatrists' assessments did not differ significantly from those of laymen (teachers) and that neither groups' assessments were substantially altered by the addition of psychiatric data to basic background information.

Given the presumed ineffectiveness of treatment programmes and the difficulties of assessing dangerousness it is understandable that prolonged detention, even in a hospital setting, is being regarded increasingly as unjust. Prins (1980) underlines the irony of the situation that has resulted from the original legal premise that the mentally ill should be excused the normal rigours of a penal system:

> It is merely necessary at this stage to point to the curious paradox by which a man may be found 'not guilty by reason of insanity', yet can be ordered to be detained without limit of time in a Special Hospital under conditions which may appear to him and his family to be hardly different from those of imprisonment. Other offender/patients may be detained in hospital, ostensibly in their 'best interests', for periods of time far beyond those for which their depredations would normally be punished by fixed sentences of imprisonment. In effect, we seem to be saying that because a man may be deemed to be mad, he may be doubly punished.

It is in response to such misgivings that there has recently occurred a gradual 'withdrawal' of psychiatry from the treatment of offenders. This has been most marked in Scandinavian countries where the dislike of the indeterminate sentence has been associated with a marked reduction in psychiatric services to offenders (WHO 1977). Whilst far less striking, some evidence for a retreat from the rehabilitative ideal can also be found in the United Kingdom. Within the Health Service there is increasing caution in recommending hospital treatment for offenders. For example Woodside (1980) describes how, despite the fact that a substantial number of offenders referred by the Edinburgh Courts for assessments are considered mentally disturbed, treatment recommendations are made only in those carefully selected cases where this is expected to have some benefit. In response to the increasing scepticism concerning the response of 'psychopaths' to treatment, the *Review of the 1959 Mental Health Act* (DHSS 1978) suggests that such offenders should be admitted to hospital only where there is a likelihood of response to treatment. Similarly, it recommends that sexual deviancy, alcohol and drug-dependence in themselves are not to be regarded as mental disorder. Therefore offenders with such 'behaviour disorders' will presumably be liable to imprisonment. If the suggested trends continue and such recommendations become law, then one may expect an increasing number of offenders, previously considered in need of hospital treatment, to become imprisoned instead.

Within the Prison System itself the aims of psychiatry would seem to have become far more modest and even further from pretending to be a panacea for crime. The case for continuing to offer psychiatric treatment is more often argued in terms of improving the mental health and well-being of offenders rather than in terms of any direct reduction in recidivism. Even in those cases where a specific relationship between mental disorder and criminal behaviour must be assumed, the 'reformative' value of treatment is doubted if this must be restricted to a penal setting and no control can be exercised over subsequent powerful situational influences (Gunn *et al* 1978). Similarly, and particularly in view of the considerable problems involving staffing and overcrowding in the prison service, the Home Office has recently called for far more modest and realistic aspirations (Home Office 1979). Criminologists call for a radical reappraisal of penal policy following the loss of faith in the 'rehabilitative ideal' (e.g. Bottomley 1979).

However, whilst the resulting situation is one of considerable uncertainty and confusion, it is clear there is a reluctance to abandon totally all former aspirations to treat and 'reform'. At the very least it is recognized that there can be no such thing as 'neutral detention' and that there must always be the responsibility both to mitigate the adverse effects of detention and also to make available to offenders the same clinical services as are available to non-offenders (e.g. Crawford 1980c). Beyond this is also the recognition that a penal system alone is inadequate for the task of reducing crime and that alternative 'rehabilitative' procedures should be sought. For example, the Butler committee (1975) in accepting evidence that psychopathic offenders are not susceptible to medical treatment, urge that alternative 'social' methods of treatment should be explored in experimental units within the prison service, a recommendation which the Home Office appears reluctant to accept (Home Office 1979). Walker (1976) clearly refutes any suggestion that treatment should be abandoned, as both impractical and undesirable.

> What is valuable, however, is scepticism about treatment if it makes us ask the right question. Is what we are doing really treatment or smooth management? If it is treatment, what evidence is there for its efficacy? If it is effective, at what cost in terms of services and suffering? So long as these questions are asked and answered we shall not abandon all efforts to devise effective forms of treatment.

More recent reviews of American studies of general prison populations do in any case give more grounds for optimism concerning rehabilitative efforts, than does that of Martinson. In a less publicized review Palmer (1978) re-examined the same studies considered by Martinson. Palmer suggests that Martinson's conclusion was misleading in its pessimism since Martinson had reached conclusions about the overall effectiveness of each particular treatment approach by generalizing from a number of different studies representative of that approach. When he considered each study separately, Palmer found that 45 per cent of these had in fact reported positive results in terms of reduced recidivism rates. Similarly, the *Review of Criminal Justice Policy* (Home Office 1976) suggests that highly specific treatment effects do occur but are not remarkable when the overall rates of large samples of offenders are compared. More recently Blackburn (1980a) has reviewed 40 studies involving the treatment of 'normal' offenders, published between 1973 and 1978. Of the 21 of those that reported results in terms of recidivism 11 (i.e. 52 per cent) reported positive results. Moreover, all 5 of those that met basic methodological requirements for evaluative research, including a two-year follow-up period, reported success in reducing recidivism, though the overall effects are slight.

Rather than completely abandon the rehabilitative ideal one might first question how treatment programmes might be improved. Martinson (1974) suggests that a possible reason why programmes may fail is that they are uncritical in their application of 'personal inadequacy' models and thereby neglect the sociological explanations that criminal behaviour may represent a normal adaptation to social conditions. This suggestion indicates the need for a more comprehensive theory of criminal behaviour than one based on 'personal inadequacy' models alone and the need to be far more selective in identifying those in need of treatment. However, as Blackburn (1980a) has suggested personal inadequacy models should not be totally rejected in view not only of the incidence of mental disorder in criminal populations but also the fact that studies of delinquents commonly do indicate deficits in education and social skills as well as emotional difficulties. Blackburn himself suggests that no particular treatment approach may be more effective, though he does present tentative suggestions that those programmes which deal with teaching offenders practical skills may be more effective than those dealing with 'convenience behaviours' or 'covert processes' such as attitudes and self-concept, etc. However, Martinson's second explanation for the ineffectiveness of rehabilitation programmes is that these simply may not be good enough or may not be appropriately applied in custodial settings. The preceding account of practical problems and pitfalls concerning rehabilitation programmes for offenders in custodial settings makes it particularly plausible to assume that the more relevant the 'learning' as opposed to the 'medical' component of treatment, the more likely is treatment to fail unless such problems are overcome. The fact that no valid distinction between treatment and rehabilitation is possible under a 'learning model', suggests that treatment of those disorders for which this kind of explanation is appropriate, is likely to be particularly handicapped. Therefore, some consideration of the relevance and implications of such a model is now required.

A More Comprehensive Approach

A detailed critique of some of the assumptions underlying current mental health legislation has been made by the British Psychological Society (Black *et al* 1973) in its evidence to the Butler Committee and also by the

Special Hospital Clinical Psychologists (1973) in an additional memorandum of evidence. This includes criticism of the over-generalization of the medical model in accounting for offending behaviour at the cost of recognition of the relevance and implications of a 'learning' model. Particularly relevant to this is the lack of any logical necessity for assuming that a disease process must underlie serious, repugnant or repetitive anti-social acts and the unsatisfactory circular reasoning by which mental disorder is frequently inferred from those anti-social acts it seeks to explain. (Similar arguments are found in Wootton (1978).) Add to this the fact that psychiatric illness is itself seldom a sufficient, let alone a necessary explanation for offending or dangerous behaviour, then the relevance of a learning model in accounting for this in mentally abnormal offenders must be considered. (At a slightly more pragmatic level one might also note the relatively minor role of medicine in the treatment of the bulk of mentally abnormal offenders classified as psychopathic, subnormal or severely subnormal, where the main emphasis is typically on 'social retraining'.) It is argued that 'medical' and 'learning' models should be combined to explain the range of disorders found in abnormal offenders, and that in few cases can an exclusively medical approach be considered appropriate but that a learning model can be applied to many 'mentally abnormal' offenders, as well as to 'normal' criminals (Black *et al* 1973).

The 'learning model' advocated by the BPS is akin to the 'behavioural model'. As does the psychodynamic approach, the behavioural approach[9] assumes a continuity between normal and abnormal behaviour. However, it departs from the psychodynamic approach in rejecting any assumptions of 'intra-psychic conflict'. Behavioural treatments focus more directly on the problem behaviours and the current determinants of these. They will typically place far greater emphasis on the importance of environmental influences in effecting behaviour change and on the relevance of prompting performance as well as attitude changes (Kazdin 1978). In this respect behavioural treatments make more demands on the total treatment environment than do medical or psychodynamic approaches. They make it more necessary to recognize the inadequacies of custodial institutions and even less plausible to avoid this by attempting to separate treatment from rehabilitation.

Despite their relevance, behavioural treatment programmes for adult offenders have been reported only rarely in the United Kingdom, though some examples are found in the preceding review (e.g. Laycock 1979; Crawford and Allen 1979; Howells 1976; Matthews 1980). None the less,

---

9 Whilst a traditional emphasis in the behavioural approach has been upon modifying overt behaviours alone, increasing attention has been paid more recently to intervening cognitive variables. This serves to blur former distinctions between behavioural treatments and psychotherapies (Blackburn 1980b), though the former still retain the distinguishing characteristics suggested, including a greater emphasis on experimentation and evaluation (Kazdin 1978).

behavioural treatments have been used extensively with offenders in North America and have been reviewed comprehensively by Feldman (1977) and Nietzel (1979). Both these authors suggest that behavioural treatments with offenders have been less adequate conceptually and less successful than those for non-offenders. They have typically 'foundered' on the kinds of problems described above. The implications of a more comprehensive approach that takes further account of the relevance of behavioural treatments can be considered at two levels: (1) Procedural and (2) organizational.

Procedural Implications

There has been a tendency to contrast traditional 'authoritarian' regimes with those that are more permissive and usually influenced by therapeutic community principles. The precise rationale and operation of a therapeutic community remains unclear, although Jansen (1980) has described it in general terms as drawing upon principles from social psychiatry, group psychoanalysis and humanitarian ideals.[10] Advocates of a behavioural approach would no doubt applaud much that characterizes the therapeutic community and in particular its emphasis on the patient's total environment and on the need to arrange this to prompt 'healthy' rather than 'sick' behaviour. However, they might dispute particular procedures arising from a psychodynamic model and question the relevance and efficiency of certain procedures in effecting behaviour changes. Feldman (1977) has suggested that a psychodynamic approach may lead to an unrealistically permissive regime, one that may be inefficient in encouraging appropriate, and in discouraging inappropriate behaviour. Whilst he recommends a general ethos of care and concern for the individual, he advocates a closer adherence to learning principles in structuring a regime conducive to behaviour change.[11] The use of the token economy to structure general 'treatment' regimes in American custodial institutions is reviewed by Ayllon and Milan (1979) and Nietzel (1979). However in the United Kingdom there have been no published reports of such an approach for adult offenders, though Hoghughi (1979) has used a token economy programme with delinquents and Ostapiuk and Reid (1980) have described

10 Cumming (1969) distinguishes between 'therapeutic community' approaches (intended to promote insight) and 'milieu therapy' approaches (intended to prompt appropriate behavioural skills). However, she acknowledges that these two aims are not always separated and that there can be much overlap, if not confusion, between the two approaches.

11 Paul and Lentz (1977) have compared the effects of a milieu therapy approach incorporating therapeutic community principles, with a behavioural social learning approach which included a token economy. Comparisons of these approaches in rehabilitating chronic psychotic patients consistently favoured the superiority of the behavioural approach.

an excellent example of a comprehensive 'behavioural' regime in a hostel for adolescent offenders.

Both Feldman (1977) and Nietzel (1979) have outlined ways in which behavioural treatment programmes for offenders might be improved. The starting point is the selection of more relevant treatment goals. The dangers of pursuing irrelevant or only partially relevant goals have already been laboured. Whilst it remains true that certain problems cannot be directly assessed within custodial institutions (e.g. child molestation), one should at least attempt to identify goals closely related to such behaviour (e.g. social inadequacy, deviant sexual orientation, deficient self-controlling skills, etc.). A second important general principle is the need to concentrate on the development of appropriate alternative behaviours to the offending behaviour rather than to concentrate exclusively on the removal of the latter alone. For example Crawford (1980a) has shown how, in his approach to the treatment of sex offenders, he first directs treatment towards encouraging acceptable sexual interests and behaviour before he addresses the problem of removing inappropriate interests or behaviours, if indeed such problems still persist. Thirdly, it is particularly important that the actual procedures for inhibiting offending behaviours and for enhancing alternative behaviours should be based as closely as possible on psychological principles of learning (these are considered in detail by Feldman (1977, pp. 265–6)). Amongst the principles relevant to enhancing appropriate behaviours are 'modelling', 'behaviour rehearsal and feedback', 'shaping' and 'systematic reinforcement'. Feldman suggests that it may not be possible to avoid completely the use of negative consequences but emphasizes the dangers and potentially counter-productive effects of the poorly controlled use of punishment. A final important principle, and one which would appear to have been totally neglected in rehabilitation programmes in the United Kingdom, is the deliberate training of self-control and self-approval which is an important prerequisite for ensuring that treatment effects will generalize and be maintained.

Organizational Implications

It has been noted that rehabilitation requires as 'natural' a treatment environment as possible. In this connection the recent development of out-patient and community forensic services appears promising and there seems a general consensus that this is a direction in which forensic services should develop (e.g. Bluglass 1975). Similarly Bowden (1978c) has described a psychiatric clinic in a probation office which is considered a useful step towards increasing liaison between psychiatrists and probation officers. Bluglass (1980) has emphasized the need to explore more fully alternative non-custodial forms of management for both normal and abnormal offenders. However, whilst desirable, it should not be assumed that community-based intervention is necessarily less problematic or more successful than intervention in institutions. Blackburn (1980a) found that programmes based in the community were no more successful than those based in institutions and often failed because of their inability to control the influences of relatives or peer groups.

Whilst more community-orientated services are necessary, it would be quite unrealistic to expect that custodial treatment should or could be done away with totally. Two kinds of changes need to be considered to the services provided within custodial institutions. First, there is ample scope for radically reducing the restrictiveness of such environments without abandoning the need for security, where this is necessary. Some custodial institutions, for example the Special Hospitals, already operate a system whereby some relaxation in security takes place as the patient progresses so that, before departure, he may be on a far more relaxed ward, be permitted 'ground parole', usually within the secure perimeter, and have visits to the outside community. There is ample scope for extending this practice, in particular for introducing far more self-management and personal responsibility into patients' lives, for creating far more frequent and appropriate opportunities for mixing with the opposite sex and for having more contact with the outside community. Custodial institutions could vastly improve their rehabilitation programmes if they adopted a far more flexible use of security, one which involves a gradual (and eventually total) relaxation of this as a 'patient' progresses. This would allow far more adequate opportunities for assessing treatment needs and for prompting relevant behavioural changes. Special Hospitals have previously not simply resisted any suggestion that they should be involved in rehabilitation but also have rejected the notion of having hostels with them, on the grounds that these would meet with marked resistance by local communities and also create a further 'stigma' for patients sent to them (e.g. McGrath 1968). Whilst community resistance is a problem that has plagued the establishment of special units in the NHS, the apparent success of the Eastdale Unit (which specializes in the rehabilitation of Special Hospital patients) in overcoming such difficulties suggests that this may be an unduly pessimistic view. However, the second major change required to make custodial institutions more effective is to arrange for more carefully planned release and far more effective aftercare. This itself suggests two requirements: (1) the need for custodial institutions to have relatively small catchment areas (in sharp contrast to the present national catchment areas of the Special Hospitals), so that their staff can either arrange aftercare themselves or liaise very closely with those concerned with this; (2) the need for far closer and more effective co-ordination of staff involved in aftercare services. Within the Health Service such co-ordination could be facilitated by joint appointments between Special Forensic, National Health Service and University Clinics. (Such appointments would probably have the additional advantages of improving the calibre, expertise and morale of staff working within institutions.)

Conclusion

As Walker (1976) has suggested, the current scepticism concerning the treatment of offenders can be constructive providing it raises the right kinds of questions. Whilst one should not suggest that all offenders require, or are susceptible to treatment, there is a need to recognize that many do present a wide range of psychiatric disorders, though common amongst these are the so-called 'habit' or behaviour disorders. The preceding account suggests the inevitable conclusion that 'learning' and 'medical' models need to be combined to understand and treat more adequately the range of disorders found in offenders who might require treatment. It is clear that the more relevant the learning model, the less reasonable it is to expect treatment to have any substantial or lasting effects unless the problems that can arise, particularly within custodial institutions, are confronted more openly.

Within the NHS there is growing dissatisfaction with the lack of adequate treatment facilities for offenders that might present particular management problems and the consequent inappropriate retention of abnormal offenders in prisons and Special Hospitals (e.g. Noble 1981). Hope for the resolution of such difficulties has been placed in the proposed development of Regional Secure Units. However, as the Royal College of Psychiatrists (1980b) emphasizes, these would solve existing problems only if they are complemented by a comprehensive range of services at sub-regional, district and hospital levels. These services could be arranged to meet many of the organizational changes required for improved rehabilitation, including local catchment areas, a more flexible range of security conditions and continuity in treatment and aftercare. Certainly, the programme reported by Reid and Lea (1980) at an interim secure unit appears promising in these respects. However, a major question confronting the Health Service is the future role of the Special Hospitals which are presently faced by most, if not all of the obstacles to more effective treatment. Unless these Hospitals are both inclined and encouraged to effect radical organizational changes, their limitations are likely to become increasingly highlighted. There is a danger that such institutions could become relegated to a limited 'asylum' role for those patients with exceptionally poor prognoses, whom regional services will be inclined to reject.

Within the Prison Service there seem to be even fewer grounds for optimism, in view of the prevailing disenchantment with the 'rehabilitative ideal' in general and the serious overcrowding and limited resources that make it difficult to contemplate innovation, but which in fact might eventually necessitate this. Bluglass (1980) has expressed pessimism concerning the influence of psychiatry and clinical psychology within the Prison Service. He notes the rejection of recommendations for the integration of the Prison Medical Service with the NHS, a move which has been consistently recommended in the interests of improved co-ordination of services. The few joint appointments that have been made between the Prison Service and the NHS have not been considered successful (Bluglass 1978b).

The development of psychiatry within the Prison Service has served previously to erode the essential differences between the philosophies of punishment for the 'normal', and treatment for the 'abnormal' offender. In recognition of the treatment needs of many prisoners it has been urged that there should be far closer co-ordination between and far more flexible use of Health Service and Prison Service treatment facilities (e.g. Prins 1980). However, recent trends suggest a reluctance to consider such developments and if anything there would appear to be a reassertion of the essential differences between the two systems. This is mirrored in the reasoning underlying the *Review of the Mental Health Act*'s recommendations that offenders who present social or habit disorders should be sent to hospitals only if they also show evidence of mental disorder. (This contrasts with the Butler Committee's recommendation that they should have access to hospital treatment.) This suggests a clear intention to preserve the distinction between the 'sick' and the 'wicked' which is based in law on a restricted medical model of disorder that prevents full recognition of the treatment needs of those prisoners for whom a 'learning' model is more appropriate.

The reluctance to consider a more comprehensive model to account for the various treatment needs of offenders reflects the basic conflict between the philosophy of 'free will' that underlies the legal concept of responsibility and the scientific philosophy of determinism. Feldman (1977) has pointed to the illogicality by which the law is prepared to accept only a limited form of determinism involving medical explanations, but is concerned to reject any extension of the determinist principle that results from a more comprehensive model of abnormal behaviour.[12] Such an extension would cause the further erosion of the legal concept of responsibility and the blurring of the distinction between the 'sick' and 'wicked'. Yet the shift within psychiatry from biological models of behaviour (which do imply different explanations for normal and abnormal behaviour) to psychological models (which imply a continuity of explanation) does make it increasingly difficult and arbitrary to make the distinctions assumed in law. Wootton (1978; 1980) has argued for the abandonment of the legal concept of responsibility and the associated distinction between penal and treatment disposals, in favour of a more flexible system of disposal based on the treatment needs of offenders:

We end with the hope that in the fullness of time the present distinction

12 The logical implications of an extension of the determinist principle have been considered in detail by Black *et al* (1973) and Feldman (1977). Wootton (1978; 1980) questions the assumptions underlying the legal concept of responsibility and the psychiatrist's role in assessing this.

between the wicked and the sick will be regarded as largely irrelevant to the classification of antisocial behaviour: That the boundary between penal and medical territory will be obliterated, along with the consequent distinction between the punitive and the remedial institution . . . once that is accomplished we could look to every offender's future, not to his past record, concentrating on the search for whatever method (medical or other) of dealing with each individual case looks most promising. Places of detention would cease to be labelled as hospitals or prisons but would combine the best features of both; nor would their inmates be classified as wicked or as sick. (Wootton 1980)

A total rejection of the legal concept of responsibility tends not to be favoured by forensic psychiatrists (e.g. Gunn, 1979; Bluglass, 1980) and may perhaps previously have seemed unnecessary in view of the former emphasis upon treatment within the Prison Service. However, any reassertion of the essential differences between the philosophies of the two systems of disposal, particularly one that denies prisoners access to treatment through adherence to a restricted medical model, will make far more urgent the critical re-appraisal of the Law's basic premises.

References

Aarvold Committee (1973). *Report on the Review of Procedures for Discharge and Supervision of Psychiatric Patients subject to Special Restrictions*. Cmnd 5191, HMSO, London

Agras, W S (1972). *Behaviour Modification: Principles and Clinical Applications*. Little, Brown and Co., Boston

Ayllon, T and Milan, M A (1979). *Correctional Rehabilitation and Management*. John Wiley and Sons, New York

Bancroft, J (1979). The nature of the patient–therapist relationship. *British Journal of Criminology* **19**, 416–19

Bean, P (1976). *Rehabilitation and Deviance*. Routledge and Kegan Paul, London

Bennett, B (1977). A method for structuring a basic education course at Rampton. *Adult Education* **50** (1), 22–8

Bennett, B (1980). An evaluation of the Rampton basic studies course. *Adult Education* **52** (6), 378–85

Bennett, D (1978). Social Forms of Psychiatric Treatment. In *Schizophrenia: Towards a New Synthesis* (ed. J. K. Wing). Academic Press, London

Black, D A, Blackburn, R, Blackler, C D and Haward, L R C (1973). Memorandum of evidence to the Butler Committee on the law relating to the mentally abnormal offender. *Bulletin of the British Psychological Society* **26**, 331–42

Blackburn, R (1980a). Still not working? A look at recent outcomes in offender rehabilitation. Paper presented at the Scottish Branch of the British Psychological Society Conference on Deviance, University of Stirling

Blackburn, R (1980b). Behaviour change versus attitude change: implications for psychotherapy. Open Lecture in the series 'Themes and Issues in Psychotherapy'. Department of Mental Health, University of Aberdeen

Bluglass, R (1975). Forensic Psychiatric Services in the Community. *Journal of the Irish Medical Association* **68** (18), 454–9

Bluglass, R (1978a). Regional secure units and interim security for psychiatric patients. *British Medical Journal* **1**, 489–93

Bluglass, R (1978b). Medical Services for Offenders: Strengths and Weaknesses of the Joint Appointment Consultant Post. In *Medical Services for Prisoners*. King's Fund Centre, London

Bluglass, R (1980). *Psychiatry, the Law and the Offender—present dilemmas and future prospects*. The Seventh Denis Carroll Memorial Lecture. Institute for the Study and Treatment of Delinquency, Croydon.

Bottomley, A K (1979). *Criminology in Focus: Past Trends and Future Prospects*. Martin Robertson, Oxford

Bowden, P (1978a). The Nine Hundred. *Prison Medical Journal* **19**, 3–6

Bowden, P (1978b). Ethical aspects of the role of the medical officers in prison. In *Medical Services for Prisoners*. King's Fund Centre, London

Bowden, P (1978c). A psychiatric clinic in a probation office. *British Journal of Psychiatry* **133**, 448–51

Bowden, P (1981). What happens to patients released from the Special Hospitals? *British Journal of Psychiatry* **138**, 340–5

Buehler, R E, Patterson, C R and Furniss, J M (1966). The reinforcement of behaviour in institutional settings. *Behaviour Research and Therapy* **4**, 157

Butler Committee (1974). *Interim Report of the Committee on Mentally Abnormal Offenders*, Cmnd 5698, HMSO, London

Butler Committee (1975). *Report of the Committee on Mentally Abnormal Offenders*. Cmnd 6244, HMSO, London

Carney, M W P and Nolan, P A (1978). Area Security Unit in a Psychiatric Hospital. *British Medical Journal* **1**, 27–8

Ciminero, A R (1977). Behavioural Assessment: An Overview. In *Handbook of Behavioural Assessment* (eds A R Ciminero, K S Calhoun and H E Adams). John Wiley & Sons, New York

Craft, M (1966) (ed). *Psychopathic Disorder*. Pergamon Press, Oxford

Craft, M (1968). Psychopathic disorder: a second trial of treatment. *British Journal of Psychiatry* **114**, 813–20

Craft, M, Stephenson, E and Granger, C (1964). A controlled trial of authoritarian and self-governing regimes with adolescent psychopaths. *American Journal of Orthopsychiatry* **34**, 543–54

Crawford, D (1979). Modification of deviant sexual behaviour: the need for a comprehensive approach. *British Journal of Medical Psychology* **52**, 151–6

Crawford, D (1980a). Problems for the assessment and treatment of sexual offenders in closed institutions: and some solutions. Paper presented to the British Psychological Society Conference, London

Crawford, D (1980b). Applications of penile response monitoring to the assessment of sexual offenders. In *Sex Offenders in the Criminal Justice System* (ed D J West). Cropwood Publications, Cambridge

Crawford, D (1980c). Deviant Behaviour: Problems and Issues. Paper presented at the British Association for Behavioural Psychotherapy Annual Conference, Sheffield

Crawford, D and Allen, J V (1979). A Social Skills Training Programme with Sex Offenders. In *Love and Attraction* (eds M Cook and G Wilson). Pergamon Press, Oxford

Crawford, D and Howells, K (1978). The Effect of Sex Education on violent offenders. Unpublished paper. Department of Psychology, Broadmoor Hospital, Crowthorne, Berkshire

Cumming, E (1969). 'Therapeutic Community' and 'Milieu Therapy' Strategies can be distinguished. *International Journal of Psychiatry* **7,** 204–8.

Dell, S (1980). Transfer of Special Hospital patients to the NHS. *British Journal of Psychiatry* **136,** 222–34

DHSS (1978). *Review of the Mental Health Act 1959.* Cmnd 7320. HMSO, London

DHSS (1980). *Report of the Review of Rampton Hospital.* Cmnd 8073. HMSO, London

Faulk, M (1979). The Lyndhurst Unit at Knowle Hospital, Fareham. *Bulletin of the Royal College of Psychiatrists.* March, 44–6

Feldman, M P (1977). *Criminal Behaviour: A Psychological Analysis.* John Wiley and Sons, London

Gostin, L O (1977). *A Human Condition.* Vol. 2, *Mind.* (National Association for Mental Health), London.

Gray, W J (1973). The English Prison Medical Service. In *The Medical Care of Prisoners and Detainees.* Ciba. Elsevier, Amsterdam

Gunn, J (1975). Forensic Psychiatry and Psychopathic Patients. In *Contemporary Psychiatry: selected reviews from the British Journal of Hospital Medicine* (eds T Silverstone and B Barraclough). Headley Brothers, Kent

Gunn, J (1977). Criminal behaviour and mental disorder. *British Journal of Psychiatry* **130,** 317–29.

Gunn, J (1979). Forensic Psychiatry, In: *Recent Advances in Clinical Psychiatry* No. 3 (ed. K Granville-Grossman). Churchill Livingstone, London and New York

Gunn, J, Robertson, G, Dell, S and Way, C (1978). *Psychiatric Aspects of Imprisonment.* Academic Press, London

Gunzburg, H C (1973). *Social Competence and Mental Handicap.* Baillière, Tindall, London

Higgins, J (1979). Rainford Ward, Rainhill Hospital, Merseyside. *Bulletin of the Royal College of Psychiatrists.* March, 43–4

Hinton, J, O'Neill, M and Wooldridge, J (1976). Psychophysiological Assessment of Sex Offenders. In *Sex Offenders—A Symposium* (ed. J Gunn). Special Hospitals Research Report. Special Hospitals Research Unit, London.

Hoghughi, M (1979). The Aycliffe Token Economy. *British Journal of Criminology* **19,** 384–99.

Home Office (1976). *A Review of Criminal Justice Policy.* Home Office Working Paper. HMSO, London

Home Office (1979). *Inquiry into the United Kingdom Prison Services.* Evidence by the Home Office, the Scottish Home and Health Department and the Northern Ireland Office. Vol. 2. HMSO, London

Howells, K (1976). Interpersonal Aggression. *International Journal of Criminology and Penology* **4,** 319–30

Jansen, E (1980). *The Therapeutic Community.* Croom Helm, London

Kazdin, A E (1978). *History of Behaviour Modification.* University Park Press, Baltimore

Laycock, G (1979). Behaviour Modification in Prisons. *British Journal of Criminology* **19,** 400–15

Logan, C H (1972). Evaluation Research in Crime and Deliquency: A Reappraisal. *Journal of Criminal Law, Criminology and Police Science* **63,** 378–87

McGrath, P (1966). The English Special Hospital System. In: *Psychopathic Disorders* (ed. M Craft). Pergamon Press, Oxford

McGrath, P (1968). Custody and Release of Dangerous Offenders. In: *The Mentally Abnormal Offender* (eds A V S de Reuck and R Porter) Ciba Foundation. J and A Churchill Limited, London

McKeith, J A C (1978). Practical Constraints of the Work of the Prison Medical Officer. In *Medical Services for Prisoners*. Kings Fund, London.

Martinson, R (1974). What Works? Questions and answers about prison reform. *The Public Interest* **35**, 22–54

Matthews, R (1980). Assessment of Sexual Offenders at Wormwood Scrubs. In *Sex Offenders in the Criminal Justice System* (ed. D J West) Cropwood Publications, Cambridge

Miles, A E (1969). The effects of a therapeutic community on the interpersonal relationships of a group of psychopaths. *British Journal of Criminology* **9**, 23–38

Nietzel, M T (1979). *Crime and its Modification. A Social Learning Perspective.* Pergamon Press, New York

Noble, P (1981). Mental Health Service and legislation—an historical review. *Medicine Science and the Law* **21**, 16–24

Orr, J H (1978). The imprisonment of mentally disordered offenders. *British Journal of Psychiatry* **133**, 194–9

Ostapiuk, E B and Reid, I D (1981). Rehabilitation Offenders in the Community: Implication for Penal Policy and Professional Practice. In *Reconstructing Psychological Practice* (eds I McPherson and A Sutton). Croom Helm, London

Palmer, T (1978). *Correctional Intervention and Research.* D C Heath & Co., Lexington

Paul, E L and Lentz, R J (1977). *Psychosocial Treatment of Chronic Mental Patients.* Harvard University Press, Cambridge, Massachusetts and London

Pfohl, S J (1979). From whom will we be protected? Comparative approaches to the assessment of dangerousness. *International Journal of Law and Psychiatry* **2**, 55–78

Priestley, P and McGuire, J (1977). Preparing Prisoners for Release. Discussion paper presented at the 'State of the Prisons' Conference sponsored by the Howard League for Penal Reform, Canterbury

Priestley, P, McGuire, J, Flegg, D, Hemsley, V and Welham, D (1978). *Social Skills and Personal Problem Solving: A Handbook of Methods.* Tavistock Publications, London

Prins, H (1980). *Offenders, Deviants or Patients? An Introduction to the Study of Socio-Forensic Problems.* Tavistock Publications, London

Quinsey, V L and Ambtman, R (1979). Variables affecting psychiatrists' and teachers' assessments of the dangerousness of mentally ill offenders. *Journal of Consulting and Clinical Psychology* **47**, 353–62

Reid, A M and Lea, J (1980). Rehabilitation in Elton Ward, An Interim Regional Secure Unit. Paper presented to the Annual Conference of the British Association for Behavioural Psychotherapy, Sheffield

Ross, R R and McKay, H B (1976). A study of institutional treatment programmes. *International Journal of Offender Therapy and Comparative Criminology* **20**, 165–73

Royal College of Psychiatrists (1980a). *Psychiatric Rehabilitation in the 1980s.*

Report of the Working Party on Rehabilitation of the Social and Community Psychiatry Section

Royal College of Psychiatrists (1980b) *Secure Facilities for Psychiatric Patients: A Comprehensive Policy*

Shah, S A (1975). Dangerousness and civil commitment of the mentally ill: some public policy considerations. *American Journal of Psychiatry* **132**, 501–5

Special Hospitals Clinical Psychologists (1973). *Memorandum of Supplementary Evidence to the Butler Committee Reviewing the Law Affecting the Mentallly Abnormal Offender.* Psychology Department, Broadmoor Hospital, Crowthorne, Berkshire

Steadman, H J (1979). Attempting to protect patients' rights under a medical model. *International Journal of Law and Psychiatry* **2**, 185–197

Taylor, F H (1966). The Henderson Therapeutic Community. In *Psychopathic Disorders* (ed. M Craft). Pergamon Press, London

Tennent G, Parker E, McGrath P and Street, D (1980). Male Admissions to the English Special Hospitals 1961–1965: a demographic survey. *British Journal of Psychiatry* **136**, 181–90

Walker, N (1965). *Crime and Punishment in Britain*. The University Press, Edinburgh

Walker, N (1976). *Treatment and Justice in Penology and Psychiatry*. The Sandoz Lecture 1976. The University Press, Edinburgh

Walker, N and McCabe, S (1973). *Crime and Insanity in England* Vol. 2. The University Press, Edinburgh

Wardrop, K R H (1975). The Douglas Inch Centre for Forensic Psychiatry. *International Journal of Offender Therapy and Comparative Criminology* **19**, 219–27.

Weaver, S M, Broome, A K and Kat, B J B (1978). Some patterns of disturbed behaviour in a closed ward environment. *Journal of Advanced Nursing* **3**, 251–63

West, D J (1980). Treatment in Theory and Practice. In *Sex offenders in the Criminal Justice System* (ed. D J West). Cropwood Publications, Cambridge

Whiteley, J S (1970). The response of psychopaths to a therapeutic community. *British Journal of Psychiatry* **116**, 517–29

WHO (1977). *Forensic Psychiatry*. Report on a Working Group. Regional Office for Europe. WHO, Copenhagen

Wing, J K (1978). *Reasoning about Madness*. Oxford University Press, Oxford

Woodside, M (1980). Forensic Psychiatry and a Scottish Court. *Journal of the Law Society of Scotland* **25**, 405–6

Woodside, M, Harrow, A, Basson, J V and Affleck, J W (1976). Experiment in managing sociopathic behaviour disorders. *British Medical Journal* **2**, 1056–9

Wootton, B (1978). *Crime and Penal Policy: Reflections on Fifty Years' Experience*. George Allen and Unwin, London

Wootton, B (1980). Psychiatry, ethics and the criminal law. *British Journal of Psychiatry* **136**, 525–32

Part 5 Child Psychiatry

12 Chronically Disabled Children and Their Families

D James, MB, ChB, Dip Ed, DCH, DPM, MRC Psych

Rehabilitation of the adult aims to approximate his abilities to the pre-morbid level. The situation is different in childhood where individuals are for ever moving forward on the escalator of development. Development occurs in three main areas simultaneously, the first being physical growth with increase in height, weight and sexual maturity. The second concerns gain in cognitive skills depending on innate brain power as well as environmental opportunities. The third area concerns emotional development which affects feelings, relationships, ability to cope with frustration, anger and guilt. Much pathology presenting to the child psychiatrist can be seen in terms of faulty emotional development and the cause is frequently due to inappropriate parent/child relationships. Almost any disability in a child, either inborn or acquired, will increase the risk of harmful attitudes occurring in other family members. The aim in rehabilitating a child is not merely to get him to his pre-morbid state, but to replace him on the moving developmental stair so that he can continue to mature in these three areas in the best possible way, bearing in mind the inevitable limits of the disorder.

Many child psychiatric disorders have a multi-factorial aetiology. The latest classification (Rutter *et al* 1975) enables codings to be made simultaneously on five axes. The first axis is the International Classification of Disease (ICD) psychiatric diagnosis. The second axis gives a list of developmental delays including speech and motor development. The third axis rates intelligence and the fourth axis enables biological components to be included, e.g. asthma, epilepsy, renal failure. The fifth axis is a carefully thought-out list of psychosocial factors ranging from psychiatric disorder in another family member and inadequate social stimulation to social transplantation. Quite frequently a disorder needs to be rated in two or three of these categories simultaneously. Often one of these areas is particularly difficult to treat or modify which impairs the overall rate of progress. A depressed school phobic child may be suffering from a neurosis which usually carries a reasonable prognosis. The fifth axis may show up long-standing psychiatric disorder in the mother who grossly over-protects and finds difficulty in changing her behaviour patterns. This may necessitate the child having perhaps a year off school and attending a psychiatric unit, hence his return to ordinary school will require an exercise in

215

rehabilitation. Another example may be a child with hyperkinesis and associated specific developmental delays. Even if the family and social factors are optimal, this kind of dysfunction may require years of special schooling and then rehabilitation to return the child to the normal educational system. A third example would be a child with chronic renal failure on thrice-weekly haemodialysis where the father had died and the mother had personality and mental health problems. The restrictions of special diet, low haemoglobin and the need to be in hospital for three days a week would necessitate the renal unit team being well aware of the psychosocial difficulties which produce a situation where years of skill and attention will be needed to effect a satisfactory adjustment.

Psychological Aspects of Rehabilitation in Chronic Illness

Liaison in child psychiatry is becoming more important to child psychiatrists, especially those working in specialist children's hospitals. Technical advances enable increasing numbers of children to be kept alive where chronic or relapsing illnesses can now be managed by modern treatments. These situations may cause months or years of physical and emotional stress. There is now literature about the psychosocial aspects of renal dialysis and transplantation, both in adults and in children (Abram 1970; Bernstein 1971; Korsch et al 1971; Chantler et al 1980; Wass et al 1977). There is an increasing child psychiatric involvement in oncology, haematology, diabetic clinics and other areas of stress in children's hospitals. Children with brain pathology are very prone to maladjustment. On the Isle of Wight one third of children with a neuro-epileptic disorder were found to be psychiatrically disturbed (Rutter et al 1970a; Rutter et al 1970b). Interestingly the psychiatric symptoms are not always a direct neurological sequela of the illness. Psychological aspects of chronic illness have been described by Steinhauer et al (1974) and these problems have been reviewed with regard to paediatric haemodialysis patients by James (1978). Both these writers show that a stressful chronic illness can cause decompensation in an already vulnerable family. Disruption of life experiences also causes risk to the cognitive and emotional development of the child. Robertson's work (1958) on the admission of young children into hospital describes an initial stage of protest when the child demands the parents who do not always appear. This is followed by the stage of despair with withdrawal and loss of interest in the environment. Detachment follows when the relationship with the parent is probably jeopardized and repeated separations of this kind cause the damage to be more permanent. The effects of restriction and isolation may impair a child's relationships with medical and nursing staff as well as with the parents and gives rise to excessive anxiety, fantasy and sometimes withdrawal. Increased dependency on parents and nursing staff may become a pattern with secondary gain so that self-confidence, initiative and other moves towards age-appropriate independence and maturity may be blocked. A young child may perceive pain and clinical procedures as punishment and become distressed or angry when repeated traumatic experiences are not properly explained, or if they are done by staff who are out of rapport with the child.

There are additional concerns where the illness may be terminal. The young child does not understand that death is irreversible (Yudkin 1967) and views dying as sleep, separation or punishment. Parents may have greater anxieties than the child about his prognosis so that they may be unable to show appropriate supportive responses as they have already commenced a bereavement reaction. The child may view their depression as being his fault, resulting in a further deterioration in what should be at that time in the illness, a supportive contact.

Responses Occurring in the Family

We see the following responses within the family which may interfere with treatment or impair the chronically ill child's development:

Denial. This occurs where the loss of function and prognosis has not been accepted. The parent may be unable to see the need to keep to dietary regimes or for the taking of essential medications. This response may also put pressure on the child to be normal and hence deprive him of the support and comfort needed when feeling unwell. It can sometimes be seen in professional caring people who have a large emotional investment in the outcome of their patients.

Anger. When the permanent loss of function is accepted there is often a rebound of anger as if someone needs to be blamed. Sometimes the family doctor takes the brunt of criticism but often parents will be over-concerned about nursing procedures and administration of treatment. Intelligence is not a barrier and one has to keep reassuring medical and nursing colleagues not to take anger personally, otherwise confrontations occur. Clinicians hide behind their authority and communications become poorer and more strained while the tension rises around the child's bedside.

Guilt. Some of the anger is nearly always turned inward so that much soul-searching goes on. Parents feel they should have insisted on the hospital consultation earlier or they may keep troubling staff with apparently trivial conversation which, if listened to, indicates a need for reassurance. They may feel that something they had done or omitted to do at the onset of the illness was its cause. If guilt is not coped with, or if the loss is particularly severe to the parents, the mourning may develop depressive symptoms with sleep disturbance, appetite loss, poor concentration and irritability. The child tunes in with the parents' unhelpful morbid concern with an overall worsening of the situation.

Marital Stresses. Frequently the mother derives support from the hospital; indeed many mothers are admitted for periods of time with their children. The father may be equally distressed and is not only pushed out, but his own emotional and physical needs may be neglected. Husbands opt out into less supportive patterns of behaviour, for example working excessive hours or calling in at the local pub. Neither parent has enough spare psychological space to support the other, and a vulnerable marriage may become even more stressed with deterioration in morale of other family members including the patient.

Siblings. A sick child may derive extra time and support from the parents. The siblings are hardly able to voice their displeasure because their brother or sister is unwell. I have known one child express regret when told that her urinary infection needed antibiotics and not years of dialysis like her sister.

Abnormal Parental Attitudes. Some parents reject the chronically ill child. This may be overt or may be subtle; for example the patient may be dressed in less fashionable clothes than the siblings. There may be repeated unnecessary requests for readmission to hospital and sometimes the treatment regimes are almost purposely ignored. Other parents initially give the impression of appearing to care, but they are adopting the role of martyr and saying 'Look what good parents we are; doing all this for him and still he will not be well.' Patterns of excessive anxiety and over-protection are also common.

Responses Occurring in the Child

Denial. Denial seems to be adaptive if it shields a child from giving up hope. A careful explanation of the disorder and its management usually improves the child's relationships with staff and helps him to cope. By no means does this destroy healthy denial, because even if a disorder is known to be serious, the child will probably still feel to be one of the lucky ones. Occasionally denial may cause the child to be detached and inconsistent about the demands of treatment, for example, refusing to measure urine or keep to a diet which may improve the prognosis.

Reaction Formation. Children who feel vulnerable may try to be tough and dominate friends or family. When a relationship is built up with such a child he usually emerges as anxious and brittle. One boy was blasé about his insulin and insisted on being the fastest runner in his school. He eventually disclosed being told that he would die after a hundred hypo-glycaemic attacks. He was noting each attack as it occurred and adding this to the total which was approaching treble figures.

Regression. Children under stress may become dependent and infantile. If the illness is long this pattern has to be gradually interrupted to allow normal emotional development to proceed. This is best done by helping the child to feel safe and to trust those who are treating him, rather than by making demands and setting authoritarian limits.

Obsessions. Patients sometimes indulge in magical thinking and superstitions before dialysis or other repeated treatment situations.

Fantasy. Younger children shut out the unpleasant reality world by becoming lost in make-believe. Sometimes fantasies can be horrific and are fed by inadequate information. One child thought he had to enter the storage cupboard of his dialysis machine and sit in it to have a blood wash.

These are coping mechanisms which are often useful in keeping a child in adequate mental health to cope with the day-to-day stresses of a treatment situation. Sometimes the child's reactions become more frankly maladaptive and in the hospital setting we see three particularly difficult situations. The first is a massive withdrawal with lack of co-operation in a passive kind of way. Children sometimes curl up and turn away from drip lines, needles and medications, becoming non-communicative and wanting to die. The second reaction is a display of marked anxiety which may flood the child with tension, making him unable to relax and cope with treatment. The third problem is depression and psychogenic pain may coexist with discomfort from the symptoms or treatment. There is anorexia, sleep disturbance, poor concentration and morbid guilty thoughts that seem out of proportion to the situation. Depressed children are sometimes clingy with parents and resist attempts of nursing and other ward staff to cheer them up. It is often a surprise for nurses to learn that a child is better helped by quiet empathy than by forcing him to be overtly cheerful.

Physicians and other hospital staff may react unhelpfully to the emotional stresses produced by their patient, especially where the illness is not responding well to treatment. Feelings of impotence may cause the doctor to pass by the patient who is most wanting to voice his anxieties and derive support. Doctors may take the parent's anger personally. They become involved in confrontations and then withdraw, leaving junior staff or nurses to deal with the dissatisfied relatives.

The Principles of the Successful Rehabilitation of Children With Chronic Disease

Parents must be given a clear diagnosis and prognosis at the beginning of the illness so that they can work towards a realistic acceptance of the situation as soon as possible. One consultation is insufficient and they should be given opportunities to come back to the same doctor or someone in the team who can answer questions. The parents' attitudes should be assessed, particularly about how they are coping with denial. It is better to see both parents together during these initial consultations, otherwise distortions of communication can occur between all concerned.

The child patient should be encouraged to talk out his anxieties and fantasies about his illness and treatment. Nurses should avoid being too busy with treatment to listen to children's questions. Modified play therapy techniques are to be encouraged and young children can often subject their teddy bears or dolls to the same kind of procedures that they themselves are receiving. How teddy feels about his 'jags' can help the nurse to empathize with the child.

Perhaps the greatest hazard to successful rehabilitation is the problem of time missed from school. Difficulty in catching up is increased when the child feels unwell and his concentration is impaired by the residual effects of his illness or medications. The hospital ward teacher should be prepared to liaise with the local school so that the child can continue with his usual work.

Nursing staff must be careful not to appear as rivals of the parents and where possible should give the parents an active part in the child's treatment. Handing over the child to a nurse can be a very undermining and threatening experience for the parent who feels that her child needs her more than ever at these times of pain and anxiety. A rivalry situation can cause antagonism and tension between parents and nursing staff. The child is caught in the middle. The need to bear hostility has already been made and this applies to all grades of staff in the paediatric ward. Confusion can occur about limit setting when kindliness is wrongly thought to be the same as permissiveness. Children with serious physical illness often require limits to be set about their diet, medications and treatment times. It is seldom helpful to bend the rules because all except babies and toddlers know that, at the end of the day, it is caring for limits to be enforced. A neutral term like 'not coping' can be applied when a child has a temper tantrum and in that way the relationship between child and nurse is preserved without angry confrontation.

Some specialist units are adopting the team approach, using guidance and advice from psychiatrists, social workers and psychologists. Teachers, occupational therapists, play leaders and nursing staff are all involved in the treatment programme. This approach has much to commend it as long as team working is accepted by all participants. They should meet regularly to discuss patients and to share their own feelings. Communications with patients and parents should be passed on so that there is little scope for different members of staff confusing the parents with contradictory information. Where liaison psychiatry has been successful in a particular part of the hospital, one finds that the psychosocial advisers spend less time sorting out problems of management. The necessary skills have become acquired by other staff. Instead time is increasingly spent on staff support and participation in group discussions, reviews and long-term decisions about patients.

Rehabilitation with Reference to Certain Specific Disorders

Head Injury

The psychological sequelae of severe head injury are well known. Once the acute injury and concussion have settled down there may be deficits in general intelligence with forgetfulness, poor concentration, disturbances of reason, subtle judgement and deductive and creative thinking. The deterioration may impair the individual's ability to adjust to new situations or adversely affect tasks which were adequately performed before the injury.

Personality changes occur with poor control of emotional expression, euphoria, superficiality, lack of seriousness, over-talkativeness and loss of tact and manners. The patient is disinhibited and appears excessively cheerful and friendly. Irritability and aggressive outbursts can persist for months to years, if not indefinitely. Mood swings, apathy and inertia are common. The disinhibiting effect of alcohol and many psychotropic drugs, including minor tranquillizers, makes the prescription of medications unreliable.

The following case material illustrates some of these features in young people:

Freddie, a teenager, was seen in the orthopaedic ward having recovered from several hours of unconsciousness. A gastrectomy was done because of intra-gastric bleeding, and a fractured femur had been set. The nursing staff found that he was attempting to undo his abdominal operation wound with a knife in the hope of bleeding to death. He felt guilty because he had been unable to prevent his brother's death during a recent solvent abuse episode. Episodic depressive bouts, with weeping and suicidal ideas followed and these varied with periods of cheerfulness interspersed with periods of being negative and irritable. For example, he would put his hands through the spokes of his wheelchair and refuse to be moved from one place to another. The social circumstances were poor. The father was away and mother drank heavily. Freddie was eventually transferred to the child psychiatric ward where his labile mood could be better controlled. He became over-sensitive about his hemi-paresis and developed minor left-sided seizures which ameliorated with the readjustment of his anti-convulsants. His intelligence was presumably in the normal range before the road accident. Although co-operation was poor a psychological assessment was performed three months after the accident. It showed some diffuse impairment of intellectual and memory functions and some impairment of verbal learning abilities. His speech was still dysarthric but there was no expressive or receptive language difficulties. The verbal IQ was 82 and the non-verbal 74.

Testing almost a year later showed a WISC verbal score of 94 and a performance score of 77. Speech was almost back to normal and he was coping quite well at his ordinary school although he was mildly euphoric. Some months later he developed pneumonia and entered an epileptic twilight state with visual hallucinations which lasted three or four days despite the careful use of anti-convulsants and the use of the least epileptogenic of the phenothiazines. He was seen again some four to five years after the original admission when he was in trouble because of a knifing incident. There seemed little doubt that the impulsive loss of control was still a symptom of his head injury.

A young teenage girl suffered some intellectual deterioration and loss of emotional control following a head injury. Her parents were unsettled but the marital problems were never mentioned before the accident. The post-injury personality changes caused the girl to be less inhibited and much more openly challenging to her father. During the first interview with the family the girl remained quiet and composed for about forty minutes, then a mildly provocative comment from her father caused her to jump up and push her mother against the wall of the consulting room. Rude comments were directed at her father as she fled from the room, only to be found weeping some way down the corridor. Insight into her loss of control made her feel miserable and unworthy. The home difficulties were compensated for by an excellent school record, but after the accident the girl was unable to keep in the top rank of the class. Her distractability and learning problems decreased motivation and caused her self-opinion to deteriorate so that there was more satisfaction from joining a delinquent sub-group. Anti-convulsants were stopped one year after the accident and she is now back to normal some three years after the accident. A period of residential schooling was necessary as an interim measure.

One girl sustained a skull fracture after an accident while playing at home. She had epileptic fits and a marked expressive language problem, which interfered with her schooling and peer-group relationships. Her mother had enormous difficulty coping with the guilt feelings about her child's loss of function. The neurotic bond between mother and girl was a significant part of the overall pathology. This girl needed the full resources of the child psychiatric team with regular social work contact with the mother for several months; psychiatric advice was also needed for the mother's depression. One of the unit teachers worked closely with the team psychologist to devise a rehabilitation programme. The nursing contribution was central in helping the child to gain her self-confidence with her age mates.

Similar problems are occasionally referred from the oncology department. The child has a malignant CNS lesion, leukaemic deposits or a suspected intracranial bleed. It is difficult to predict which patients will need the skills of a multi-disciplinary child psychiatric team to help with rehabilitation.

Shaffer et al (1975) described almost 100 cases of injury where there had been skull penetration and showed that there was no associatioon between the length of unconsciousness and the final psychosocial adjustment. The same study showed that nearly two-thirds of the head injury children showed psychiatric disturbance. Less than 10 per cent had demonstrable neurological impairment. It is likely that young children who receive head injuries are from families where supervision is poor. Shaffer's paper noted that disturbed marriages were relatively common amongst the parents of his head injury group.

Neuro-epileptic Disorders

Pond (1961) was one of the first to show that the adjustment of children with epilepsy and brain damage was as much associated with the child's social and environmental circumstances as the degree of damage itself. The Isle of Wight survey (Rutter *et al* 1970a; Rutter *et al* 1970b) assessed all school-age children on the island known to have epilepsy or unequivocal brain damage. This group were referred to as the neuro-epileptic disorders. Children with chronic physical disease not affecting the central nervous system were also studied. All children aged nine to eleven years on the island were assessed from the point of view of physical health, psychiatric disorder, educational attainments and intelligence. The incidence of psychiatric disorder in the latter group was almost seven per cent. This figure doubled in the children with non-CNS chronic disease, but increased five times in children with a neuro-epileptic disorder. Although family and social factors appeared to make a big difference to the outcome, the type of lesion had very little prognostic effect. Shaffer's (1975) series of traumatically brain-damaged children showed a high rate of psychiatric disorder, which was even higher where social problems co-existed. Both the injury and background factors contribute to the problems that arise. The Isle of Wight survey showed that the psychiatric problems were varied and by no means all organically determined. The relationship between brain damage and psychiatric disorder is therefore more complex than the cause and effect of change in neurological status. Possible mechanisms for this are discussed by Shaffer (1977) who postulates the following aetiological factors: (1) social and family disadvantage; (2) the social stigma and handicap; (3) intellectual and educational handicap; (4) temperament; (5) transactional effect. It is important to understand these mechanisms in order to plan rehabilitation for a child with a brain disorder. Both the Isle of Wight survey and Gruenberg and Pond (1957) found that broken homes, emotional upset in the mother and social disadvantage were all more common in disturbed brain-injured children, than in brain-injured children without psychiatric problems. Shaffer refers to a publication (Office of Health Economics 1971) where 32 per cent of the public stated they would not knowingly allow their child to play with an epileptic friend. Peer-group rejection and social isolation may cause depression and withdrawal and, in some cases, reaction formation with aggressive or conduct disorder behaviour. Examples of intellectual and educational handicap have been cited in the case histories above. Specific learning difficulties are relatively common amongst children with a neuro-epileptic disorder. On the Isle of Wight, 18 per cent of epileptic children were more than two years behind their mental age in reading attainment. Forty per cent of children with structural brain lesions were similarly affected. Shaffer's (1975) study showed that almost one third of his head injury series were similarly retarded in reading. Phenytoin and phenobarbitone may inhibit learning, but periods away from school with parental over-concern and poor expectations of the child may also contribute. The child who fails educationally soon develops a poor self-opinion which can lead to opting-out behaviour. Problems of temperament are often expected in brain-damaged children although there is little systematic information about it. A transactional effect, where the affected child adversely influences his environment which further increases his problems, is sometimes seen. The previous example with the depressed mother illustrates this situation.

Minimal Cerebral Dysfunction

An excellent review of this topic appears in a neuro-psychiatric study in childhood (Rutter *et al* 1970a). Child psychiatrists frequently see children with specific learning difficulties and poor motor skills and hyper-active children. The hyper-kinetic syndrome, with poor concentration, distractability, labile mood, impulsivity and motor restlessness (Laufer and Denhoff 1957; Werry 1968) is a much more popular diagnosis in the United States than in this country. The term 'minimal brain damage' used to be in vogue (Strauss and Lehtinen, 1947) but Shaffer *et al* (1974) and Rutter *et al* (1970a), reviewing the literature, showed that in many instances there is very little direct evidence that actual brain damage is present in these children. More often than expected there are adverse factors which have occurred ante-natally, at the time of birth or post-natally. Anomalies of the EEG are more common amongst 'cerebral dysfunction' children but by no means diagnostic. Neurological examination or appropriate psychometric assessment of motor skills, e.g. the Stott (1966) or the Oseretsky test (Rutter *et al* 1970a) may or may not reveal evidence of soft neurological signs. On occasions the practising clinician discovers similar developmental delays in the family history. For practical purposes the point to be made is that some children with hyper-activity, learning difficulties or poor motor skills seem to behave in this way because of inherent biological reasons. Management, therefore, has to be tailor-made to help the child develop optimally and remedial help or change in the classroom environment may be necessary. Parents must bear in mind the limitations imposed by the disorder, and try not to insist on standards that the child cannot meet. If the child keeps getting told off, both by the teacher and at home, for having a specific problem in writing he will believe that he is bad and lazy. He is upset and symptoms of neurosis appear with sleep problems, weepiness, clinginess and depression. In a family where verbal communication about feelings is not encouraged the child may act out his feelings of distress. He may tear up his books in frustration or, when older, opt into the delinquent sub-culture where he can gain a certain amount of prestige.

Many of the psychiatric sequelae are not a direct effect of the brain dysfunction and the child psychiatry team approach may have much to offer in rehabilitation. Time should be spent with the family and the child to help them come to terms with the nature of the problem. Specific learning and cognitive difficulties need to be isolated and remedial programmes made out. This will involve psychologists within the hospital and educational psychologists who have access to the schools. A decision will need to be made whether the child's needs are best met by a special school with a high staff ratio. If the child stays in ordinary school remedial sessions either at school, in the local child guidance clinic or, in some cases, at the hospital may be very helpful. If anti-convulsants or other psychotropic drugs are needed, a regular out-patient check should be kept to make sure that the dose is effective and signs of toxicity are noted at an early stage. Stimulants like methyl-phenidate (Ritalin) may be helpful for hyperkinesis but again the child should be closely watched for depression, growth retardation, insomnia and other side-effects. One has seen children with epilepsy where the dose of phenytoin has got much too high, sometimes because the 50 mg and 100 mg capsules resemble each other so closely. The resulting symptoms have been mistaken for the original disorder or else a neurotic overlay.

Overactivity in children may be caused by anxiety, emotional deprivation and lack of stimulation. The child's social adjustment needs to be monitored. Psychotherapy is helpful if the child is getting anxious, depressed or having relationship problems. Entry to a therapy group will sometimes help peer relationships and can raise a child's self-opinion. As the child becomes older there is change, hopefully towards amelioration of his disorder. Unfortunately academic pressures and social pressures sometimes increase at a rate which outpaces the resolution of the neurological or developmental problem. The position should be under constant review and hospital day placement or in-patient admission for reassessment of social, physical, cognitive, and emotional factors can often highlight new problems. One is often surprised by the degree of recovery of brain damage in children. The younger the child, the more plastic is the brain. The babe in utero and the neonate have a vulnerable brain, so that early insults may be generalized rather than localized. There seems little doubt that viral and traumatic upsets during pregnancy, at delivery or shortly after can cause non-localized damage. Anoxia, prolonged fits, meningitis and metabolic upsets are all threatening to the developing brain. Perhaps it is little wonder that a definite diagnosis of brain damage is so elusive when several years pass between the assumed brain insult and the child presenting to the clinic.

Conduct Disorder

There is confusion between the diagnostic term conduct disorder and the label of delinquency. Both refer to aggressive and anti-social behaviour and the symptoms alone may not differentiate clearly between the two groups. The delinquent has become entrapped by the legal system or, in Scotland, by the Children's Panel system. Conduct disorder may show itself as disturbed behaviour, perhaps just in the family situation, which escapes detection by the law. Children who are too young to be convicted can therefore not be delinquent. To qualify for conduct disorder, a child should probably fulfil the general criteria for a psychiatric disturbance, i.e. a disorder of emotion, behaviour or relationships, of such a severity to cause distress to the child, his family or others in the community. The International Classification of Diseases subdivides conduct disorder and possibly the most important distinction is whether it is socialized or unsocialized. Socialized conduct disorder is usually of a delinquent kind and occurs in groups, often in gangs, and in areas of social deprivation. Unsocialized conduct disorder is more likely to have a neurotic component, e.g. the depressed child who steals to act out his guilt feelings.

Even if delinquents are excluded conduct disorder represents the largest group of child psychiatric problems. In order to understand rehabilitation the aetiology should be considered. The behaviourist would point out that anything that interferes with consistency of reward and punishment may endanger the child's training about what is right and wrong. The psychotherapist, on the other hand, emphasizes the importance of a consistent, warm, caring parental figure who acts as a model for the child to use to work through the negativism of the toddler stage. If all goes well he will emerge with his own super-ego taking over where the long-suffering parent left off. Anything that interferes with consistency or relationships, especially throughout the vulnerable pre-school period, may predispose to conduct disorder. Barker (1972) looks at causative factors under headings of disturbance in the family, in the child and in the wider social and school environment. Disturbances in the home include parents who are dull or those with personality disorder. Marital tensions, alcoholism and social difficulties can also lead to inconsistent child care. The effects of early rejection and frequent changes of caring figures lead to emotional deprivation. Deprived children find difficulty in forming trusting relationships and their poorly developed social conscience predisposes them to conduct disorder. Some conduct disordered behaviour has a depressive component. Occasionally there is a gross brain damage or minimal cerebral dysfunction present. The effects of medication, especially phenobarbitone, on some epileptic children have already been mentioned in this chapter. Temporal lobe epilepsy in children is particularly associated with psychiatric problems, often of the conduct disorder type (Lindsay *et al* 1979). Difficulties in the wider environment include the quality of the school. Rutter *et al* (1979) indicate how the ethos of the child's school can affect his social functioning. The Isle of Wight survey (Rutter *et al* 1970b) shows that approximately one third of children with conduct disorder are retarded in reading more than two years behind their mental age. There is some evidence that the educational retardation may precede the disturbed behaviour. The conduct disorder may represent frustration when discouraging messages are received from teachers who do not understand the basic problem. Some of the most aggressive behaviour is seen in children who present overwhelming anxiety about parental violence and threats of being abandoned. In some instances children are already in care and have 'tested out' children's homes, other institutions or possibly foster parents, only to become rejected and even more anxious about the next caring relationship.

Wolff (1977) mentions other antecedents of conduct disorder. Although it is more common in males, aggressive behaviour is normal in the pre-school child, declines during the early school years and rises again in adolescence. Teachers' views of the behaviour of lower social class children may well reinforce their learning difficulties and also their antisocial behaviour. Maternal behaviour varies across the social class spectrum, the higher social class mothers being less intrusive and less physically punitive towards their offspring. Children from broken homes tend to be more aggressive and have educational problems. Where there is marital discord, especially involving physical violence by the father, the child may mould his own behaviour on this. The effect of children's interaction with each other and the effect of the mass media are also likely to be relevant.

The outlook for conduct disorder is not as good as generally expected. Robins (1966) found that one-third of boys attending a child guidance clinic with anti-social behaviour were sociopathic as adults. Many of the children had been referred by legal agencies, so there was some pre-selection. The same author (Robins 1970) concluded that pre-school aggressive behaviour was not predictive of later delinquency, but aggressive behaviour in early and middle school years, especially when combined with educational failure, was associated with delinquent behaviour later on. In a survey of social problem families it was shown that delinquent children differed from psychiatrically disturbed children with regard to a number of family background factors (Tonge *et al* 1975). The mental health of fathers and intelligence of children and their mothers were more normal among the delinquent group. This has marked implications for management and rehabilitation of a family with a conduct-disordered child. One needs to ask if the anti-social behaviour is mainly a culturally determined delinquency or if it is a conduct disorder in the psychiatric illness sense of the term.

Wolff (1977) points out that there is little evidence that psychotherapy or social casework techniques make much difference to the outcome of anti-social behaviour in children. It is often the social worker who provides the mainstay of supervision, which may not be effective. Rehabilitation of a conduct-disordered child may therefore need to be done in a residential school, but an attempt should be made in parallel to produce a more caring and more consistent attitude in the parents. Some work has been done helping parents to follow behaviour therapy principles (Johnson and Katz 1973) but parents of conduct-disordered children are often poorly motivated and find involvement in therapy programmes difficult.

Although truancy is a symptom of conduct disorder, most children attend school. Good pupil behaviour is strongly associated with the teacher's style of discipline (Rutter *et al* 1979). The teacher's expectations similarly influence the pupil's academic progress and the importance of the teacher as a model for behaviour is emphasized. It is helpful to focus on good behaviour (Becker *et al* 1967). Teachers who conduct successful lessons are able to deal with disruptions as soon as they arise with minimal upset (Brophy and Evertson 1976). More emphasis should be placed on teacher training, and schools should be ready to take up the challenge of helping the conduct-disordered child towards a better adjustment.

Neurosis

Most neurotic disorders of childhood can be resolved with the usual child psychiatric out-patient or in-patient methods. Neurosis is the second most common diagnostic group of child psychiatric disorders, found in approximately 2 per cent of children on the Isle of Wight (Rutter *et al* 1970b). There are school-phobic children who take a year or more to get over their symptoms and they have usually been in-patients in a child psychiatry unit. Although the psychogenic pain, acute separation anxiety or even suicidal risk phase is over they are still unable to get back into ordinary school. Often the difficulty is because of an unresolved neurosis or attitude of over-protection in one of the parents, usually the mother. If the child is discharged back home, he again becomes enmeshed in the mother's symptoms. Depressed and anxious mothers almost impose symptoms on their children, especially separation fears which are made apparent by verbal and non-verbal means. The child in therapy may worry that he has upset his mother because of his behaviour or has caused her anxiety with his symptoms. Mothers frequently do threaten to leave home or even to harm themselves when depressed. The child feels a need to return home to make sure that the parent is still there and that she is all right. If the mother's mental state or attitudes cannot be modified, the child will almost certainly require to attend a maladjusted day centre or residential school, until he gains resilience. A spell of several months extra help enables the mother or, in some cases, the father to resolve their difficulties while the child receives extra support.

Autism and Communication Disorders

Infantile autism was first described by Kanner (1943). It is a rare disorder with an overall prevalence of about 4·5 in 10 000. Males outnumber females by four to one and some writers agree with Kanner's findings that there is a preponderance of families from social classes one and two (Wing 1976). Possibly social class one and two parents may seek a diagnosis other than mental deficiency. An intellectual environment may partially make up for deficits that might place the child in the globally retarded category. These theories about social class bias are not supported by available data.

Difficulties are always recognized in the first two or three years. The child is not cuddly, or is excessively irritable. At other times he is exceptionally good and makes little demands as he lies in his cot. There is failure to establish social relationships. The child prefers objects to people and may form abnormal attachments to odds and ends which attract light, balance or spin; there is little eye-to-eye contact. Invariably there is a language problem with impaired comprehension and late onset of speech, which if and when it develops is usually echolalic. Ritualistic and compulsive phenomena are seen as the child needs to preserve sameness in his environment. Sometimes if minor things in the child's routine are changed, for example taking a different route to the day unit, there may be a 'catastrophic' reaction. Children may arrange things in sequence, perhaps bricks in a long line, and be unable to cope if an object gets in the way. There is a lack of the usual exploratory behaviour and a tendency to stereotyped, repetitive movements like hand-clapping and aimless wandering.

The aetiology is not clear. An increased incidence of pre- and peri-natal complications have been reported (Kolvin *et al* 1971d). Autistic children may show minor neurological signs (Rutter 1968). Creak and Pampiglione (1969) showed that over half of the children have unusual encephalograms; phenylketonuria and congenital rubella can also be associated with autistic symptoms (Chess 1971). What is more clear is that these disorders are not related to schizophrenia as the term infantile psychosis may have suggested (Kolvin *et al* 1971a–e). The treatment of autism and language problems is mainly educational. Rutter and Bartack (1973) studied the progress of autistic children in three special units over a three and a half to four year period. They concluded that large amounts of specific teaching in a well controlled classroom are likely to bring the greatest benefits in terms of scholastic progress. Teachers working with psychologists and psychiatrists often prove most satisfactory while occupational therapists, speech therapists and other interested workers have a big contribution to make. Each child requires careful psychological assessment and every effort must be made to develop input by routes which are least damaged. Emphasis can be placed on improving non-verbal communication and social skills sometimes with behaviour therapy techniques. Parents need sympathetic support and practical advice. After years of trying to feel warmth for a child who does not reciprocate even eye-to-eye contact their feelings of guilt, helplessness or rejection need to be shared. Often the mother has been blamed for the child's disorder, but frequently mothers have other normal children in the family. Their ability to offer consistent care and limits are by no means always in question. Drugs are in the main unhelpful but sometimes tranquillizers like haloperidol can be used to modify restlessness, anxiety and rage reaction. The response to any particular drug is unpredictable. Autistic children require considerable rehabilitation, sometimes for years. Several basic questions about rehabilitation needs are reviewed by Rutter and Bartack (1973). For example the pros and cons of mixing autistic with non-autistic children and the advantages and disadvantages of smaller units against larger units with more resources covering a wider catchment area. Sometimes special units are situated in child psychiatric departments and sometimes they are run by educational psychologists under local authority care. Severely handicapped children may find their way into the Rudolph Steiner schools. If progress is reasonable, return to a normal educational setting has to be carefully considered. Approximately one-third of autistic children are able to make a reasonable adjustment, but remain erratic, 'shut in' personalities. They relate slightly inappropriately to others and lack social perception. One-third need dependence on the family or an institution and the remaining third usually require long-term placement in mental deficiency hospitals or other institutions. The Maudsley Study (Rutter 1970) showed that 28 per cent of their autistic children developed fits during adolescence, especially those with low IQ. Those with a measured IQ below 50 all have a poor outcome. Reasonable intelligence and the development of speech by the age of five are good prognostic factors.

The similarities and the differences between autism and receptive language disorder have been compared (Bartack *et al* 1975; Cox *et al* 1975). The autistic group of children studied had the more severe language impairment, especially comprehension. There were few differences in non-linguistic skills. No difference was found between parental warmth, mental health or on early stresses of the child. This supports the view that a severe language disability is necessary for the development of autistic behaviour. Children with receptive aphasia are unable to decode what they hear into meaning. Perhaps they feel like someone getting off an aeroplane in a foreign country. It is little wonder that the child with receptive aphasia is in danger of becoming withdrawn and opts out of social behaviour. Much of learning depends on the use of language as a tool. As academic demands increase the child with a communication disorder becomes increasingly disadvantaged.

Most communication disorders are not of the receptive type but are expressive or mixed with central and expressive components. Expressive speech disorders are often accompanied by behaviour problems because the child can understand and formulate ideas, but suffers from the frustration of not making his wishes readily understood. It is not known if communication disorders and autism share a similar aetiology or whether both conditions can be due to cerebral insult and/or developmental delay.

Rehabilitation Resources

Child Psychiatric Units and Adolescent Units

About a half of the in-patients and day patients attending child psychiatric units are there for several months and it is not uncommon for some patients to stay for more than one year. A rehabilitation function cannot be detached from what is usually meant as treatment. Barker (1974) has shown that a number of children in hospital units require further help in maladjusted day centres, residential schools, or other long-term resources. Often there is difficulty in finding or waiting for an appropriate place. The assessment or early treatment all too often turns into early rehabilitation within the psychiatric unit. Children in this category may be school phobic or sometimes show mixed conduct and neurotic symptoms. Those with organic pathology, e.g. the younger hyperactive child, may need several weeks of hospital training, while autistic children and children with severe communication disorders sometimes have their own long-term programme. These groups may attend on a part-time basis and involve teachers, nurses, social workers, psychologists, speech therapists and occupational therapists. Other illnesses like anorexia nervosa may similarly pass from treatment phase into rehabilitation phase as a bridge between concentrated treatment regimes and going back to school. Many child psychiatry units combine in-patients and day-patients in the same milieu. This flexibility is helpful to the individual patient and his family. At first the attendance may be for one or two days per week and then sessions are increased to five days per week before the child becomes an in-patient. More frequently the reverse situation occurs. Children admitted as in-patients go through a day patient stage before they are well enough to be discharged. The multi-disciplinary out-patient style of working, which is now common practice in child psychiatry, extends into the unit. A child and his family may see a psychiatrist as well as a social worker specializing in child psychiatry who is seconded on a permanent career basis to the department. Clinical and sometimes educational psychologists are available not only for diagnostic work but to plan behaviour therapy treatment regimes, to help teachers plan programmes for children with specific learning difficulties and to offer psychotherapy. Nursing staff are usually trained in either psychiatric or paediatric nursing, or sometimes both. In addition to senior staff, nursery nurses, nurses in training and auxiliary nurses make a valuable contribution. Child psychiatric units either have integral schoolrooms or else an adjacent school building. Teachers who work with child psychiatric teams develop sophisticated methods of teaching and of coping with conduct disorder, withdrawal and other behaviour problems. The occupational therapist provides activities which boost the child's self-opinion. The ward milieu enables children to develop relationships while engaged in day-to-day living, recreation and practical activities. Where the unit is part of a general or paediatric hospital, the availability of paediatric expertise, neurology and laboratory investigations is of considerable advantage.

Some units, especially adolescent units, have developed in psychiatric hospitals. These units are often spacious and readily geared to the special and unusual needs and tolerances of young psychiatric patients.

The pattern of weekly attendance, going home on Friday night and back on Monday morning, provides an excellent first stage of rehabilitation almost irrespective of diagnosis. The interaction between those at home and the child can be monitored and discussed weekly with the social worker or psychiatrist or other team member involved. Weekend progress is important in deciding whether to change to day attendance, or in some cases it helps to decide that a residential school will be required in the future.

There are recent experiments in admitting whole families into residential units (Ounsted *et al* 1974). These units have been used for non-accidental injury situations, where family interactions require correction. In-patient child psychiatric units are usually relatively small, seldom totalling more than 25 beds and in many instances the groups are split into at least two, with more immature younger children being separated from the adolescent group. Not all child psychiatric services have beds; many support a day hospital and have the use of a paediatric ward when admission is necessary. Some of the larger units run their day programme separately from the in-patient ward. Much of their work overlaps with in-patient services but the day unit is especially suitable for rehabilitation of pre-school children with disorders that necessitate parental involvement on a part-time basis. Programmes for children with disorders of communication have already been mentioned; also the needs of handicapped children and those with mother–child relationship difficulties can be met.

Day Centres for the Maladjusted

These centres are usually run by the education authority with an input from educational psychology. They cater for a wide variety of diagnostic groups and tend to have a high proportion of children with mixed conduct and neurotic disorders. The youngsters are prone to outbursts of anti-social behaviour and yet they do not exhibit the social delinquency which predestines them for the social work List D school system. Often there is an element of deprivation in the broadest sense of the word, with frequent testing out of limits. Reading retardation (Rutter *et al* 1970b) and other educational difficulties are frequently present.

These units do not cater for physically handicapped children or children with partial sight or deafness, nor do they cater for children in the ESN range. Although there is access to educational psychology and sometimes a visiting psychiatrist, the environment is more educational in nature than a hospital and is usually run along the lines of a school. Some of the junior units have special play provision, and the staff ratio is high with a great deal of flexibility of approach to meet the individual needs of each child. The atmosphere is predominantly friendly and there is liaison with home via the unit's social worker or in some cases the parents already have a contact with the social work department. Some of the children may be on statutory supervision, but this is usually but one aspect of the difficulty.

Residential Schools for Maladjusted Children

The category of maladjusted children was brought into being by the Minister of Education in 1945. Schools were opened to deal with children classified as such before a rationale of management had been worked out. There had been previous work in America and Europe, and independent schools in the private sector of the British Isles began to document their activities (Wills 1941, 1945). The philosophy of their task came largely from psychoanalytical theory, with much emphasis on the warm caring environment and problems of shared group responsibility. The educational curriculum was not emphasized, although art as a form of therapy became more fashionable. Specialization from school to school centred round the philosophy of the head teacher.

Mulberry Bush School specialized in 'emotionally frozen' children. A more educational bias for children with reading problems is seen at Bodenham Manor School in Hertfordshire. Lendrick Muir School in Scotland offers a more academically orientated education. Laslett (1975) has reviewed change in the education of maladjusted children and comments that the charisma of the early pioneers may have produced certain restrictions on the development of other methods. Many of the independent schools did, and still do revolve round the personality of the head teacher. During the last fifteen years groups of staff in maladjusted residential schools have begun to participate in exchanges of feelings and attitudes with a resulting increased awareness of group relationships (Bion 1961).

Behaviour modification was not in vogue in the early days of maladjusted schools. This technique has been adapted to improve the social behaviour of children who have been previously exposed to poor modelling figures (Bandura and Walters 1963). The use of these methods raises doubts about the ethics of controlling behaviour in disturbed people. Nevertheless, there is much evidence that these techniques are useful. Most of these schools use a team-work approach, the main focus of rehabilitation being the milieu or group. Considerable importance is given to selection of children so that they will be compatible with those already in the school. Most schools require a psychological, social work and psychiatric report which, although tedious to those putting the child forward, is perhaps well justified. It is an important decision to take a child from his family into such a specialized resource for an unspecified period of time, which sometimes runs into years. Many children require close relationships with residential child-care staff to make good the effects of inappropriate or inconsistent care in the earlier stages of their development. Most maladjusted schools employ or have the use of their own social worker who acts as an important bridge between family and school. Many of these children come from families where personality difficulties and social problems are entrenched, so that change is slow. Maladjusted schools have access to their own educational or, in some cases, clinical psychologist, and most have the services of a visiting psychiatrist. The role of the psychiatrist varies from school to school. There is usually an element of staff support and a need to be present at case discussions. Some consultants see individual children to clarify aetiological factors in the diagnosis and at other times help decide on the most appropriate method of management. As mentioned, schools vary in the emphasis they put on education. The majority of children are retarded in basic skills like reading. Often their conduct and anxieties are such that concentration is poor, and the small classroom group is an essential part of the overall treatment. Many schools show much imagination in engaging children in out-of-school activities. There is often opportunity for camping, hiking and sporting activities, which can help a child to relax and improve his or her self-opinion. Most of the schools are largely filled by boys, but a number of schools take girls as well. This seems to be helpful to social training and causes little in the way of the sort of problems that might be anticipated.

Maladjusted schools should not be confused with community homes or List D schools, formerly called approved schools, which grew up from the old reformatories for delinquent children. In England, children who come through the juvenile courts and need residential school are usually sent to one of the main classifying centres where a sophisticated assessment is performed. The child's physical health, psychological and cognitive status are reviewed and a psychiatric opinion is available if necessary. Behaviour in the classroom and in the living area is observed and for adolescents vocational aptitude tests are performed. A comprehensive report is prepared so that the child can then be recommended to whichever community home or residential school is considered to be most suitable. The early centres like Kingswood in Bristol and Aycliffe School in Durham have collected copious research data. These schools (Gittins 1952) contain their own long-stay residential units, and Aycliffe has recently focused on behaviour therapy techniques. Kingswood in Bristol has in addition to the classifying school a main school with special expertise in coping with emotionally disturbed children. There is also a secure unit in the same grounds. In Scotland the List D or approved schools now come under the social work umbrella but some are still independently run. The headmasters now have the right to accept or refuse referrals, so there is a greater degree of specialization. Most have access to psychiatrists and psychologists and all the children have their own social worker before coming to the school. Most of the pupils will have been before a children's panel and some will have spent a short period in an assessment centre before entering. The List D schools still retain an emphasis on consistent limit setting, but there is now considerable overlap between some of the more therapeutically orientated List D schools or community homes and some of the maladjusted schools that accept conduct disordered children. A detailed look at rehabilitation of delinquent children cannot be attempted in this chapter.

The Rudolf Steiner schools like Camphill at Aberdeen accept a number of maladjusted children. By attention to community living and sensory training they succeed in helping difficult groups of children who may be autistic, language disordered, hyperactive, brain damaged, mentally defective or borderline psychotic. Steiner felt that maladjustment must be seen as a disharmony between the inner spiritual being of the child and his own physical organization. His treatments were homeopathically orientated with an emphasis on the child finding his own individual destiny in life. Acquaintance with nature and working on the land is important and the Steiner schools nearly always go at least some way to being self-supportive from their own farms and gardens.

Residential Hostels for Maladjusted Children

Most residential schools for maladjusted children close for periods of school holiday and this makes them unsatisfactory for a number of children who are already in local authority care. Such children would then have their own home base, the children's home and the residential school. Each competes for the key role which is particularly confusing for those who have experienced deprivation and inconsistent parenting in the past. Frequently this type of maladjustment produces children whose behaviour difficulties can be managed in the ordinary educational setting, with the option of remedial help. These young people are well managed in hostels where care and attention to emotional needs can be met. Barnardo's now run hostels of this kind which perform a valuable rehabilitation service.

Maladjusted Pupils in Ordinary Schools

The rate of psychiatric disorder in school children in the United Kingdom is somewhere between 6 and 18 per cent (Garside *et al* 1973; Rutter *et al* 1970b; Jones 1975) and about two-thirds are likely to benefit from help. Chazan (1978) showed that in 1955 there were 32 residential and three non-residential maladjusted schools and by 1976 Department of Education and Science figures showed that there were about 100 residential as well as 74 day schools. Even with this increase, it is clear that these special resources can only cope with the minority of disturbed children in school. The Newcastle School Based Action Project (Kolvin *et al* 1976; Baldwin 1977) used social workers, psychologists and psychiatrists to work in 12 schools in ways which helped the teachers to assist their disturbed pupils as well as setting up the activities which follow.

Pupils aged seven to eight years were identified as at risk on the basis of sociometric ratings, reading retardation, teacher rating scales and absenteeism. First-year secondary children were screened by sociometry, teacher ratings and scores on a personality questionnaire. The parents of selected children were interviewed. Four treatment strategies were used:

(1) Parent counselling and teacher consultation in both primary and secondary schools.
(2) Group counselling of children in both age ranges.
(3) Behaviour modification in the older children.
(4) Nurture work using teacher's aides in the younger children.

In England and Wales, part of the Schools Council Project (Evans *et al* 1978) evaluates the work of special classes and units set up in ordinary schools. A rapid growth of this provision has occurred since 1968 and a wide range of difficulties is being coped with. Ease of admission from and return to the main school is an asset and children can attend on a part-time basis. The scheme is relatively cheap to run and the setting up of such units often causes staff in the rest of the school to become more aware of the emotional needs of children. Those at risk in the feeder schools may be helped and admission to the special unit averted. The need for support from the headmaster of the main school as well as from visiting psychiatrists and psychologists is made clear by Jones' (1977) account of the stresses which can accrue from working with maladjusted children in a comprehensive school.

The Warnock Report (Department of Education and Science 1978) encourages special education in ordinary schools with school-based resource centres. One of the three main recommendations was improved teacher training. An expansion in the advice and support services available for teachers providing special education is also envisaged.

Perhaps the term 'educational treatment' will increase in popularity. The successful teacher/therapist forms accepting relationships with his disturbed pupils but routine, discipline and 'strong and infectious interests' are all important (Baldwin 1977). Perhaps the myths that control must be punitive and warm acceptance has to be permissive can be ended. It is likely that many maladjusted children can be helped within the ordinary school setting by improved teaching methods and the availability of special adjustment units.

References

Abram, H S (1970). Survival by machine: The psychological stress of chronic haemodialysis. *Psychiatric Medicine* **1** (1), 37–51

Baldwin, S (1977). Research into maladjustment: I. Schools Council Project II. Newcastle Project. *Therapeutic Education* **5,** no. 2, 30–40

Bandura, A and Walters R H (1963). *Social Learning and Personality Development*. Holt, Rinehart and Winston, London

Barker, P (1972). Antisocial behaviour. *British Medical Journal* **3,** 34–6

Barker, P (1974). The Results of In-patient Care. In *The Residential Psychiatric Treatment of Children* (ed. P Barker). Crosby, Lockwood, Staples, London

Bartack, L, Rutter, M and Cox, A (1975). A comparative study of infantile autism and specific development receptive language disorder: I. The Children. *British Journal of Psychiatry* **126,** 127–45

Becker, W C, Madsen, C H, Arnold C R and Thomas, D R (1967). The contingent use of teacher attention and praise in reducing classroom behaviour problems. *Journal of Special Education* **1,** 287–307

Bernstein, D M (1971). After transplantation. The child's emotional reactions. *American Journal of Psychiatry* **127,** 1189–93

Bion, W R (1961). *Experience in Groups*. Tavistock, London

Brophy, J E and Evertson, C M (1976). *Learning from Teaching*. Allyn and Bacon, Boston

Chantler, C, Carter, J E, Bewick, M, Counahan, R, Cameron, J S, Ogg, C S, Williams, D G and Winder, E (1980). 10 years experience with regular haemodialysis and renal transplantation. *Archives of Disease in Childhood* **55,** 435–45

Chazan, M (1978). School based treatment of maladjusted children. *Therapeutic Education* **6** (1), 3–12

Chess, S (1971). Autism in children with congenital rubella. *Journal of Autism and Childhood Schizophrenia* **1,** 33–47

Cox, A, Rutter, M and Bartack, L (1975). A comparative study of infantile autism and specific development receptive language disorder: II. Parental characteristics. *British Journal of Psychiatry* **126,** 146–59

Creak, M and Pampiglione, G (1969). Clinical and EEG studies on a group of 35 psychotic children. *Developmental Medicine and Child Neurology* **11,** 218–27

Department of Education and Science (1978). *Special Educational Needs: Report of the Committee of Enquiry into the Education of Handicapped Children and Young People* (Chairman Mrs H M Warnock). Cmnd 7212, HMSO, London

Evans, M, Wilson, M D, Dawson, R L and Kiek, J S (1978). Schools Council Project: The education of disturbed pupils in England and Wales. The work of special classes and units. *The Journal of the Association of Workers for Maladjusted Children* **6** (1), 17–26

Garside, R F, Hulbert, C M, Kolvin, I, Van Der Spuy, H I J, Wolstenholme, F and Wrate, R M (1973). Evaluation of Psychiatric Services for children in England and Wales. In *Roots of Evaluation* (eds J K Wing and H Hafner). University Press, Oxford, for Nuffield Provincial Hospitals Trust

Gittins, J (1952). *Approved School Boys*. HMSO, London

Gruenberg, F and Pond, D A (1957). Conduct disorders in epileptic children. *Journal of Neurology, Neurosurgery and Psychiatry* **20,** 65–8

James, D S (1978). Psychological Problems of the Paediatric Haemodialysis Patient. In *Living with Renal Failure* (eds J L Anderton, F M Parsons and D E Jones). MTP, Lancaster

Johnson, C A and Katz, R C (1973). Using parents as change agents for their children. *Journal of Child Psychology and Psychiatry* **14**, 181–200

Jones, N J (1975). Emotionally disturbed children in ordinary schools: Concepts prevalence and management. *British Journal of Guidance and Counselling* **3**, 2

Jones, N J (1977). Special maladjustment units in comprehensive schools. *Therapeutic Education* **5**, no. 2, 12–19

Kanner, L (1943). Autistic disturbances of affective contact. *Nervous Child* **2**, 217–50

Kolvin, I (1971). Studies in the childhood psychoses. I. Diagnostic criteria and classification. *British Journal of Psychiatry* **118**, 381–4

Kolvin, I, Ounsted, C, Humphrey, M and McNay, A (1971a). Studies in the childhood psychoses, II. The phenomenology of childhood psychoses. *British Journal of Psychiatry* **118**, 385–95

Kolvin, I, Ounsted, C, Richardson, L M and Garside, R F (1971b). Studies in the childhood psychoses, III. The family and social background in childhood psychoses. *British Journal of Psychiatry* **118**, 396–402

Kolvin, I, Garside, R F and Kidd, J S H (1971c). Studies in the childhood psychoses, IV. Parental personality and attitudes and childhood psychoses. *British Journal of Psychiatry* **118**, 403–6

Kolvin, I, Ounsted, C and Roth, M (1971d). Studies in the childhood psychoses, V. Cerebral dysfunction and childhood psychoses. *British Journal of Psychiatry* **118**, 407–14

Kolvin, I, Humphrey, M and McNay, A (1971e). Studies in the childhood psychoses, VI. Cognitive factors in childhood psychoses. *British Journal of Psychiatry* **118**, 415–19

Kolvin, I, Garside, R F, Nicol, A R, MacMillan, A and Wolstenholme, F (1976). Maladjusted pupils in ordinary schools. *Special Education* **3**, no. 3

Korsch, B M, Fine, R N, Grushkin, C M and Negrete, V F (1971). Experiences with children and their families during extended haemodialysis and kidney transplantation. *Paediatric Clinics of North America* **18**, 625–37

Laslett, R (1975). Aspects of change in the education of maladjusted children. *The Journal of the Association of Workers for Maladjusted Children* **3** (1), 13–19

Laufer, M and Denhoff, E (1957). Hyperkinetic behaviour syndrome in children. *Journal of Paediatrics* **50**, 463–74

Lindsay, J, Ounsted, C and Richards, P (1979). Long-term outcome in children with temporal lobe seizures, III. Psychiatric aspects in childhood and adult life. *Developmental Medicine and Child Neurology* **21**, 630–6

Office of Health Economics (1971). *Epilepsy in Society*. OHE, London

Ounsted, C, Oppenheimer, R and Lindsay, J (1974). Aspects of bonding failure. The psychopathology and psychotherapeutic treatment of families of battered children. *Developmental Medicine and Child Neurology* **16**, 447–56

Pond, D A (1961). Psychiatric aspects of epileptic and brain-damaged children. *British Medical Journal* **2**, 1377–88, 1454–9

Robertson, J (1958). *Young Children in Hospital*. Tavistock, London

Robins, L N (1966). *Deviant Children Grown Up*. Williams and Wilkins, Baltimore

Robins, L N (1970). Follow up Studies Investigating Childhood Disorders. In *Psychiatric Epidemiology* (eds E H Hare and J K Wing). Oxford University Press, London

Rutter, M (1968). Concepts of autism. A review of research. *Journal of Child Psychology and Psychiatry* **9**, 1–25

Rutter, M (1970). Autistic children; infancy to adulthood. *Seminars in Psychiatry* **2**, 435–50

Rutter, M and Bartack, L (1973). Special educational treatment of autistic children. A comparative study, II. Follow up findings and implications for services. *Journal of Child Psychology and Psychiatry* **14**, 241–70

Rutter, M, Graham, P and Yule, W (1970a). *A Neuropsychiatric Study in Childhood*. Spastics International Medical Publications, London

Rutter, M, Tizard, J and Whitmore, K (1970b). *Education, Health and Behaviour*. Longman, London

Rutter, M, Maughan, B, Mortimore, P and Ouston, J (1979). *Fifteen Thousand Hours. Secondary Schools and Their Effect on Children*. Open Books, London

Rutter, M, Shaffer, D and Shepherd, M (1975). *A Multi-axial Classification of Child Psychiatric Disorders*. WHO, Geneva

Shaffer, D (1977). Brain Injury. In *Child Psychiatry Modern Approaches* (eds M Rutter and L Hersov). Blackwell, Oxford

Shaffer, D, McNamara, N and Pincus, J H (1974). Controlled observations on patterns of activity, attention and impulsivity in brain damaged and psychiatrically disturbed boys. *Psychological Medicine* **4**, 4–18

Shaffer, D, Chadwick, O and Rutter, M (1975). Psychiatric outcome of localised head injury in children. In *Outcome of Severe Damage to the Central Nervous System* (eds R Porter and D W Fitzsimons). CIBA Foundation Symposium no 34, Amsterdam; Elsevier, Excerpta Medica, North Holland

Steinhauer, P D, Mushin, D N and Rae-Grant, Q (1974). Psychological aspects of chronic illness. *Paediatric Clinics of North America* **21**, 825–40

Stott, D H (1966). A general test of motor impairment for children. *Developmental Medicine and Child Neurology* **8**, 523

Strauss, A and Lehtinen, L (1947). *Psychopathology and Education of the Brain-injured Child*. Grune and Stratton, New York

Tonge, W L, James D S and Hillam, S M (1975). *Families without Hope. A controlled study of 33 problem families*. British Journal of Psychiatry, Special Publication no. 11, Headley Brothers, Ashford

Wass, V J, Barratt, T M, Howarth, R V, Marshall, W A, Chantler, C, Ogg, C S, Cameron, J S, Baillod, R A and Moorhead, J F (1977). Home haemodialysis in children. *Lancet* **i,** 242–6

Werry, J (1968). Developmental hyperactivity. *Paediatric Clinics of North America* **15**, 581–99

Wills, W D (1941). *The Hawkspur Experiment*. Allen and Unwin, London

Wills, W D (1945). *The Barns Experiment*. Allen and Unwin, London

Wing, L (1976). *Early Childhood Autism. Clinical, Educational and Social Aspects* (ed. L Wing). Pergamon, Oxford

Wolff, S (1977). Nondelinquent Disturbances of Conduct. In *Child Psychiatry Modern Approaches* (eds M Rutter and L Hersov). Blackwell, Oxford

Yudkin, S (1967). Children and death. *Lancet* **i,** 37–41

Part 6 **Mental Handicap**

13 Proper Settings for the Mentally Handicapped

William I Fraser, MD, FRC Psych, DPM

Changing Concepts

There has been in the past two decades a rapid growth in expertise in rehabilitating mentally handicapped people, but the disparity between existing services and the scope and scale now expected by society has also generally increased. It is illuminating to compare the range and use of facilities available in two Western countries, Scotland and Sweden (Table 13.1). The latter not only makes more provision outside the parental home but makes more provision in the community. Estimates of the number of people that could leave immediately mental handicap hospitals vary but a compromise figure of around 50 per cent is commonly quoted.

In the United Kingdom the 1970s have seen a transition from a 'medical-hospital' model of care to a 'learning difficulty-community' model of care of the mentally handicapped. We have also moved from a view of medicine as being the principal profession involved to a realization that mental handicap is very much a multi-professional business. There is no profession which provides the ideal comprehensive training for work with the mentally handicapped.

Table 13.1 Where the retarded live

Living condition	Sweden %	NE Scotland %
Parental home	31·0	54·0
Own residence	7·2	6·0
Fostering/guardianship	3·0	2·81
Group hostels	53·0	1·4
Boarding schools	—	1·7
Hospital (Special)	6·2	25·0
Mental Illness hospital	—	7·5

SHHD Study No. 38 and Social Styrlesen estimates.

The change in attitudes stems from experiments of twenty years ago, in particular the Brooklands Experiments (Lyle 1960), which demonstrated that institutions damage speech and language development of mentally handicapped children and from the efforts of John F. Kennedy (who had himself a mentally handicapped relative) which resulted in the Presidential Committee promoting a new set of standards, focusing on the retarded person's care, and emphasizing the family group. The larger public institutions at the same time were experiencing a decline in quality of staff, in funds and in morale. Decent services for the mentally handicapped became a civil rights issue in North America, and in Sweden in 1968 Bergt Nirge, the Secretary General of the Swedish Parents Association, enunciated the normalization philosophy which entails minimizing as much as is possible the mentally handicapped person's deficits and differences from ordinary people, maximizing his similarities to ordinary people and ensuring that he lives in homelike circumstances, enjoys non-standardized care, has access to risks, choices, hazards, lives in a world of both sexes, has the dignity of work, and has a normal rhythm of day/week/year cycle. This principle also incorporates the principle of the small group which states that many of the features that we thought in the past as being peculiar to the mentally handicapped are simply due to their being gathered together in large numbers where they cannot learn or practise sociability. The 'stigmata' are maladaptive ways of coping. This normalization philosophy is now widely accepted as a humanitarian and legal principle throughout the Western world, but there are few nations that have yet fully implemented the exhortations of the United Nations Charter for the Mentally Handicapped. In socialist countries public institutions tend to proclaim their deficiencies and inadequacies. In capitalist countries private institutions do not, so there is more complaining for instance in the United Kingdom by institutions than there is in the United States.

In the 1970s the American Association of Retarded Citizens strongly pressurized authorities to 'mainstream' the mentally handicapped. This meant that the mentally handicapped child should exert his right to opt for 'ordinary' facilities rather than 'special' nurses or doctors or teachers and also that he should enter ordinary schools. It was however soon realized on placing the more severely handicapped toddlers into ordinary school playgrounds at the age of five years that ordinary schoolchildren had not read the principles of normalization. The handicapped child readily became the butt of ordinary children. In Christian societies, helping a mentally handicapped child seldom aids the normal child to achieve the state of grace which a Muslim child receives by so doing. What usually happens in schools is that special classes are now incorporated on ordinary school campuses, but have separate lunch and play-times, and avoidance of labelling is best assisted by returning the more mildly mentally handicapped to ordinary schools for the last year or term prior to school-leaving. It seems realistic in the present economic climate, faced with 'start-up' costs and initial 'double costing' (keeping both institutions and hostels funded concurrently) of community care, to expect that we will have to live with a kenspeckled array of facilities dating from different philosophical epochs, with differing degrees of suitability and in more or less convenient locations. Making do with existing buildings rather than custom-built buildings can however have advantages. In the most developed community care system presently known—the Eastern Nebraska Community Office for the Retarded (ENCOR)—even the most difficult mentally handicapped are accommodated outside hospitals in the community, in alternative living units, which are satellite ordinary houses supported by a 'core unit', (a larger ordinary house), with more intensive care facilities available. In Oregon and Washington State also, ordinary housing stock has led to more integration than specialized community houses (Butler and Bjaanes 1978).

In most societies, there is likely in the foreseeable future to be a need for hospital care for some mentally handicapped adults, albeit on a much reduced scale from previously; and as regards children prolonged hospital care except for the profoundly handicapped mentally deteriorating child is no longer needed.

A good guide to individual environmental need is the American Association of Retarded Citizens' view that the mentally handicapped should live in the *least restrictive setting*. This for many people is in the community but for a few profoundly behaviourally or psychiatrically disturbed would be in a hospital.

Individuals should be on their guard against the classical ploy of nations and governments to provide a few 'centres of excellence' in the public service. These are usually showpieces which may deprive other areas of ordinary services rather than act as areas to emulate, in any case an impossibility because of their lavishness.

Numbers and Definition Games

Reasons that governments have for ducking the problem of mental handicap used to include that they did not have any clear idea of numbers. This is no longer true. Table 13.2 provides an approximate aggregated prevalence rate which should serve for most planning purposes.

Table 13.2 Prevalence of mental handicap at different ages

	Mental handicap	
Age	Severe (IQ 0–50)	Overall (IQ 0–70)
	per thousand	
7 years	2·4	7–19
		(10)
11–18 years	3·8	22·2

The other excuse was that there was no clear definition of mental handicap and therefore no clear accountability. The definition of subnormality in England is:

> *Subnormality.* A state of arrested or incomplete development of mind not amounting to severe subnormality which includes subnormality of intelligence and is of a nature or degree which requires or is susceptible to medical treatment or other special care or training of the patient.

There is no equivalent definition in Scotland which tends to use the American Association of Mental Deficiency definition (Grossman 1973):

> Mental retardation is lack of developmental and intellectual growth occurring at birth or shortly thereafter, adversely affecting a person's ability to adapt to his environment.

This definition places proper emphasis on adapting or coping ability. There is no doubt that the principal problem of the mentally handicapped is adapting to environments. Some, such as Bijou (1966), suggest that there should be no definition, as intelligence cannot be observed; but for everyday purposes it serves us well to have a definition of mental handicap or at least a model of mental handicap; and the model that this chapter recommends is one that stems from the American Association's emphasis on adaptation and coping. It is a 'rehabilitation' or more strictly speaking, 'habilitation' model. It leads to intervention. It identifies ways of helping the individual not just individuals that need help. The habilitation model, unlike legal or IQ-based definitions, is not used to determine who will and who will not get services but which services are most appropriate for the individual and for how long and what the immediate objectives should be, that is to determine the desired person's environment fit and then supply the means to accomplish it. This habilitation model is based on five points:

(1) the recognition of the humanitarian and legal principle of normalization;
(2) the recognition that low intelligence is a necessary but insufficient criterion of mental handicap;
(3) the acceptance that aetiological systems of classification are largely irrelevant and classifications should be based on observable behaviours;
(4) the emphasis on the importance of social criteria of functioning and performance (coping and adaptive behaviour) in evaluation and classification;
(5) recognition of the effects of the expectation of others on influencing behaviour of mental retardates.

What this seemingly pompous catalogue means is that modern approaches to, and appraisals of, the mentally handicapped, rather than being based on an IQ test such as the Standard Binet, are based on schedules such as the Adaptive Behaviour Scale (Nihira *et al* 1974) and the Borders Schedule (Paton 1981), which readily identify deficits and excesses and proper targets for individual mentally handicapped persons. This habilitation model of mental handicap is necessarily more complicated than one simply of low intelligence with a cut-off for mental retardation at IQ less than 70. Not all people with IQ less than 70 cannot cope and many above IQ 70 cannot cope. Similarly, this habilitation model moves us away from preoccupation with weird syndromes. It doesn't really matter much to the mentally handicapped person's future, living and work setting whether he has Hallerman–Strief syndrome or not. The fifth point reminds us that the mentally handicapped are largely the way they are because we choose them to be that way. For instance, when we speak we speak to their parents or benefactors, and seldom to them. We do not encourage the mentally handicapped person to ask for clarification. We do not show sufficient patience because of their dysarthric blurred speech and eventually, because of repeated lack of success, they give up.

A Multitude of Problems

The Range of Problems

The mentally handicapped present many health problems which prevent a purely social view of mental retardation. They seldom have no additional handicaps (only 5 per cent are free of some superadded problem). In institutions 29 per cent have seizures and of these 12 per cent have daily seizures; 14 per cent have additional visual, motor and hearing deficits. Forty two per cent have communication deficits. Multiple handicap means that a multiplicity of agencies are involved, in caring, treating and in funding. Sixteen per cent of persons in institutions are non-ambulant and 25 per cent are doubly incontinent.

Many of the mentally handicapped have additional behaviour problems. In institutions 16 per cent have severe and 16 per cent moderate behaviour problems. In the community, it is estimated that 12 per cent have behaviour disturbances (DHSS 1972; Ballinger and Reid 1977). Of this catalogue of problems, three types of problems—psychiatric disorders, brain damage and disorders of communication—are particularly important to the psychiatrist concerned with rehabilitation.

Presentations of Functional and Organic Brain Disorder

Most behaviour problems of the mentally retarded are maladaptive actions or conduct disorders. Primrose (1971) found 60 per cent of admissions to a mental deficiency institution were for antisocial reasons and 8 per cent for psychiatric reasons. Reid (1976) found that the frequency of psychosis among in-patients was 1·2 per cent for affective and 3 per cent for schizophrenic psychoses.

If we raised the threshold of mental handicap by five IQ points we would increase the prevalence rate twofold and a different book would have to be written. It is thus important that psychiatrists do not use too loosely the terms 'mental subnormality', 'psychosis', 'neurosis', etc. These are inferred hypothetical constructs. There is a case in theory for abandoning diagnostic labels altogether and substituting comprehensive formulations of the predicament of each patient. Yet in practice clustering of clinical signs does occur. Reid *et al* (1978) in a cluster analysis of the behaviour problems of profoundly retarded people found 'ragbag' clusters for which 'porridge' labels were necessary—a 'manneristic-autistic' group, an 'overactive' group, a 'multiple-problem' group (e.g. noisiness, regurgitation) and a 'wilful-conduct' group.

Apart from a few such studies, most of the literature on psychiatric aspects of mental handicap consists of accounts according to existing diagnostic categories. In the case of the severely and profoundly handicapped these are of little use. The more severely handicapped the less the clinical features of mental disorder approximate to the clusters found in adult psychiatry. MacGillivray (1957) used the term 'larval psychosis' for the states of excitement and apathy which some severely and profoundly handicapped persons displayed. As Hucker *et al* (1979) have succinctly put it: 'The presence of mental handicap modifies the clinical picture and causes delay and difficulty in diagnosis; regression to a childlike state of dependence and hysterical features are common. Behaviour change is more important than symptomatic complaint as an indication of psychiatric disorder and psychotic illness should always be considered as a possible cause of acute behaviour disturbance. Whilst the classical features of affective psychosis can be found in the severely handicapped a confident diagnosis of schizophrenia is usually impossible in those of IQ less than 50'. The presence of brain damage and co-existing epilepsy and hyperkinesis complicates the presentation of psychiatric illness. In the subnormal, temporal lobe attacks, however, particularly those with complex aura are relatively rare.

Exceptions to the general rule that seizures tend to become less frequent with age are early childhood autism and Down's Syndrome. Hyperactivity, aggression and apathy are more common in mentally retarded patients with seizures than those without. It is not only the severely handicapped who can be overactive. Between IQs 50 and 70 various estimates suggest that 3 to 6 per cent have epilepsy, and its sequelae of over-, or under-activity and irritability. The sleep electroencephalogram is of value in sorting out the possible causes of dullness in subnormal epileptics especially when there is episodic apathy. Lennox (1942) estimated that drugs are responsible for only 5 per cent of the deterioration in over 1000 patients with epilepsy. The trend away from polypharmacy, conscientious review of detailed epileptic status with construction of retrospective (over several years) bar graphs, and the routine blood-level monitoring of anti-convulsants, of folic acid, and calcium have led to better control and fewer side-effects.

Hyperkinesis has to be distinguished from 'overactivity'. The former is a continuous irritating overactivity which is constantly present no matter who is there. The latter is situationally determined. Both tend to decrease as the frontal cortex matures. Amphetamine is useful in pure childhood hyperkinesis where the EEG is normal.

There is no evidence that perceptual deficits or chromosomal anomalies play any part in the aetiology of psychosis. There is some evidence that brain disorder associated with Klinefelter's and XYY karyotype causes impulsiveness. The incidence of XXY and XYY syndromes is high in special hospitals. XXY and XYY electroencephalograms have less occipital activity and more slow waves—like children's EEG's. Behaviour stereotypes must be accepted with caution. A large number are undetected in the community. Certain genetically determined disorders are associated with maladaptive behaviours. Familial hyperuricemia (Lesch–Nyhan disease), recessive sex-linked progressive ocular-cerebral degeneration (Norrie's disease) and de Lange dwarf syndrome are all associated with self-mutilation and aggressive outbursts.

Fraser (1980) has pointed out that the literature has little useful to say about the retarded person's neuroses or the effects of life events on them. Yet situational distress and depression are prevalent. It does seem that the mentally handicapped make the 'functional shift' from 'neurotic' to 'endogenous' depression with more facility.

Corbett (1979) has similarly commented on the inadequacy of our ways of describing personality disorder in the retarded.

Little fundamental research had been done by psychiatrists into the reproductive biology of mental handicap—masturbation, sexual aspirations of phantasies and needs of groups of mentally handicapped folk. Mildly mentally handicapped people are vulnerable to charges, often unsubstantiated, of sexual misconduct, and in Scotland are unlikely to have had any sex education information or coping skills. There are films and programmes available, for example the Elementary Adult Sex Education Curriculum (EASE).

Corbett (1979) has also commented that there are few adequate trials of drugs used with the handicapped, and that the patients on trials are often heterogeneous, their characteristics ill-described and the rating scales invalid. Avoidance of medication until the behaviour is thoroughly de-scribed, withdrawal of multiple drug prescribing, blood level monitoring of neuroleptics and antidepressants and cognizance of drug interaction leads to better control and fewer side-effects. Given precise diagnoses, medication is as effective as for those of normal intellect; neuroleptics for schizophrenia, antidepressants for unipolar depression and lithium for bipolar affective illness. The treatment team also needs a greater *rapprochement* between radical behaviourism and medicine. Life-endangering self-mutilation needs more effective weapons than DRO (differential reinforcement of other behaviour) or Time Out; and more humane ones than Aversion. We also need more trials of the service relevance of what seems a major behavioural technical advance—the utilization of errorless learning with the severely and profoundly handicapped. We need urgently to clarify professional dynamics.

Psychiatry is a multi-professional business, mental handicap even more so. In general psychiatry a multi-professional team is often an option—desirable, but still an option; in mental handicap teamwork is essential but needs clear thinking about legal responsibility, managerial accountability, and terms of reference. The legal aspect will now be considered; the other aspects later in this chapter.

It was axiomatic in the Mental Health Acts of England and Scotland that everything possible should be done to encourage informal treatment and rehabilitation. However, the Acts do not take account of the fact that mentally handicapped people, unlike mentally ill people, who form another major category in the Acts cannot often give informed consent to admission. In new guidelines to the Scottish Mental Health Act 1960 emphasis has been placed on responsible medical officers and nurses ensuring that mentally handicapped people understand the Act. This is however easier said than done. Particularly droll in the past has been the unsupervised handing out of legal documents to detained mentally handicapped patients informing them of their rights. Positive guardianship, i.e. benefactors with a duty to ensure the handicapped person gets his statutory benefits and citizens' rights might redress the balance. The duty placed on the Mental Welfare Commission and on the Health Boards and Responsible Medical Officers to discharge informal patients 'should they cease to suffer from mental disorder in the form of mental deficiency' and the requirement that the mental deficiency must be 'susceptible to medical treatment', is obviously not in tune with modern concepts of mental handicap. The Mental Welfare Commission, a purely Scots derivative of the Board of Control, is rightly regarded by legal circles throughout the world as a valuable concept. However, its reluctance to give advice and its low profile in its protection of mentally disordered people have made it the subject in recent years of some criticism. Relocating the retarded in the community has fewer legal safeguards than in the days of active formal guardianship.

Talking to the Mentally Handicapped

The mentally handicapped suffer from a range of communication problems. The development of language is in slow motion compared with the normal. At three years the sufferer may only be linking two words together; normal children are linking two words together at eighteen months. The mentally handicapped also have the problem of linking words with ideas. This difficulty seems to be especially correlated with low intelligence. It is as if the retarded do not know what words they ought to know. The words they pick up tend to be nouns rather than verbs or relational terms. The problems are not only of vocabulary and grammar but also of interactional aspects of language. The mentally handicapped get very little chance to learn in infancy what are called 'illocutionary acts'—asking questions, requiring, ordering. Retarded people have little ability to ask people to repeat what they have said, to say that they have not understood them. They are often dysarthric or fuzzy in their speech; they have trouble with their articulation and with their prosody. There is a higher incidence of stuttering in the mentally handicapped, particularly in Down's Anomaly (who do not have larger tongues but are adenoidal and have open mouths). The mentally handicapped have a much higher incidence of deafness, which presents as high-frequency deafness and is often not immediately noticed. The retarded also have problems of non-verbal signalling. Leuder (1980) showed that Down's Anomalies emotional relationships were expressed mainly in non-verbal communication detectable in body head orientation, arm position and body mobility. The manner in which retarded people chose to affect their audiences depended on their social relationship to the audience, particularly on the distribution of power and the relationship of reciprocity and negotiability. Covert communication, in which the subject attempts to affect his audience by strategic means (altered eye contact, closed seating position, gesture and posture), and aggression are both functional ways of relating when the distribution of power is unequal and not negotiable, for example between a patient and his therapist.

The training of the psychiatrist ought to make him more sensitive to this form of language. Therapist-sensitivity should consist of both a self-awareness and awareness of the patient. Rehabilitation counsellors, doctors and therapists ought to have a greater sensitivity to the verbal aspects of their own and their patient's communication processes. Certain gross non-verbal behaviours are directly tuned to the relationship, and through an understanding and recognition of these non-verbal behaviours, professionals can become aware of their own attitudes towards their clients and of their clients' attitudes towards them. A negative climate exists where there is a high eye blink rate, little eye contact, increased movements in the lower body, reduced hand movements, and negative head nods; and where the client's body leans away from the therapist and has greater orientation away from him. A positive climate exists where there are smiles, high eye contact, positive head nods, hand gestures, forward body lean, and direct orientation. To facilitate the interview when a negative climate is detected, the therapist focuses on his own non-verbal behaviour in order to determine the cause of the patient's alienation. The therapist can discuss it with the patient and manipulate his own eye contact and body orientation in a direct attempt to improve the relationship.

There are ground rules for communicating with the retarded. Each utterance should be addressed to the retarded person, using his name. Clear, even exaggerated, facial and arm gestures should amplify speech. The therapist should ensure that the retarded person is looking. If he is not looking he is almost certainly not listening. The grammar used should be simple enough for the handicapped person to understand. Passive, passive negative, and embedded sentences should be avoided. The professional should give the handicapped person time to process, understand and respond. This may need great patience. Consistent labels are necessary. The onus is on the therapist to ensure that the listener can decode grammar. The mentally handicapped person may not signal if he is puzzled. The professional should give the mentally handicapped person a chance to make proper replies and not only ask questions in a form which require 'Yes/No' answers or simple nouns. He thus encourages useful 'verbing'. A rehabilitation programme for the retarded person should include experience of dialogue in small groups—on a wide range of topics to encourage 'interaction management'. The programme should have access to a speech therapist who can advise on the need for more specialized help such as Bliss[1] (McNaughton 1975) or Makaton[2] (Cornforth et al 1974) for the severely handicapped or dysarthric. The past decade has witnessed a breakthrough in remediation, so it is now technically possible to improve the communication skills of almost any person (Schiefelbusch 1979).

Deficits, Obstacles and Setbacks

The mentally handicapped have multiple learning problems—not only in accomplishing the three R's; they are clumsy in intellectual, motor and other higher cerebral functions. It is comparatively easy to programme a mentally handicapped person on how to use a frying pan, but more difficult to programme him for the setbacks, reversals and exigencies which happen when the doorbell rings, the chip pan goes on fire, he scalds himself and the fire brigade arrives.

The therapist should know that some of the programmes developed for the mentally handicapped do not teach functions but simply teach the mentally handicapped to work the programmes. It is necessary to fit programmes to each person's needs, existing knowledge and motivations. In the past it has been fashionable to develop standard programmes for the mentally handicapped which were not tailored to their individual needs. In other words programmes must start from where the handicapped

1 A Graphic Symbolic System of Visual Aids.
2 A Manual Sign Language.

individual is. Where he is—his deficits, his excesses, and his skills—can be pinpointed using the Adaptive Behaviour Scale or the Borders Schedule.

For each person there must be a programme and precise teaching objectives. This programme should be an individual plan for his life helping him learn to live by learning to play, to work and to cope from nursery school training until further education college and beyond.

The rehabilitation of the mentally handicapped involves knowing their threshold for fatigue. They are often easily fatigued, in the initial period of going out to work particularly so. If feasible, it may be wise to start with a four-day week. Like the physically handicapped they will also be too tired for leisure. Often we have too high expectations of the mildly mentally handicapped, and too low expectations of the severely and profoundly handicapped. Under-stimulation is as great a problem as over-stimulation.

The Order of Priorities in a Mental Handicap Service

Prevention, Identification, Early Intervention

If the handicapped person is to lead a life which contributes something there needs to be a Mental Handicap Service which accepts that its priorities are to promote: *prevention* of primary and secondary mental handicap; *early identification*; *early intervention programmes*, which start as soon as the mentally handicapped person is identified, and which are known to be useful and are continuously evaluated for the individual; *domiciliary support* in childhood and in adult life; *specialized facilities* for the blind, deaf, and the aged mentally handicapped; and *a very much improved quality* of life for those who must be in hospital. These facilities also require additional specialized staff and more use of ordinary un-specialized professionals. It is part of the principle of normalization that nothing should prevent the mentally handicapped person from being looked after by ordinary professionals in an ordinary setting. Conversely, nothing should prevent the mentally handicapped person from having access to specialized staff.

Prevention of mental handicap is beyond the scope of this chapter, but unless we take a very narrow view of the psychiatry of mental handicap, we ought to take account of the next step after prevention, early identification, and what ought to follow immediately, early intervention. A psychiatrist may well be involved as soon as mental handicap is identified by helping the parents through the periods of shock, disbelief, anger, adaptation and reorientation, and by recognizing their chronic sorrow, the existential acceptance of an unpleasant reality. Early identification also means that the psychiatrist (although it is not primarily his business) must be capable of syndrome recognition and know the likely prognosis and complications for each syndrome; for example he should monitor each Down's Anomaly for hypothyroidism which is seventeen times as common in Down's as in the average population, be sceptical about the mongol stereotype of biddability, and should anticipate dementia in unusual presentations in mongols in their thirties. Similarly he should know that the enthusiastic furthering of Down's Baby Programmes and Portage schemes[3] (Shearer and Shearer 1972), providing family advice in the first year, reduces the severity of mental handicap. He should understand the dynamics of the mental handicap team and its relationship with other agencies, and also participate in the Joint Care Group which can best decide properly the criteria for admission to the various living settings available in an area. He should be aware of the advantages and disadvantages of labelling a person as 'retarded' and be able to maintain an objectivity about jargon, fashion and fad in mental handicap (for example the vilification of *all* institutions); and be adaptable in considering non-handicapped peers first as resources and substitute families for fostering.

The Path to Independent Living

The need for hospital care for mentally handicapped children has been decreasing rapidly in the past decade. Rehabilitation of handicapped people starts with their having experience of living in families. If the institutional problems of helplessness, over-compliance and childishness can be short-circuited or wholly avoided, then rehabilitation is made much simpler. Nevertheless the hospital is likely to remain for the foreseeable future a necessary component in mental handicap although, as mentioned earlier, in Nebraska 'core units' surrounded by clusters of independent or semi-independent alternative living units (ALUs) have replaced the hospital concept. However, the psychiatrically ill, mentally handicapped person cannot in Britain be readily fitted into units for the psychiatrically ill, and intensive treatment units in mental handicap hospitals are necessary. The mental handicap hospital should at present function as a resource centre offering a range of medical, nursing care, relief, respite, assessment, treatment and training facilities. Particularly, the temptation to switch mentally handicapped people from unit to unit for convenience sake must be resisted. Friendship ties in the profoundly handicapped are often not obvious until a lifelong friend is peremptorily transferred or his soul mate dies suddenly.

In a comprehensive service for the handicapped the pathway to independent living is clear: from the institution, via workshop dormitories in rural areas, on-site residence (working and living in the same setting), to the local authority hostel, where there is high autonomy for residents, a high staff ratio and highly trained staff; on to sheltered housing, which until recently was a facility available only for the elderly, but now such special housing (e.g Ark Special Housing Association) is being used for the

---

3 A kit consisting of developmental programmes and targets.

mentally handicapped. Group homes for mentally handicapped people (living autonomously) are more a problem of fitting personalities together than of finding people of sufficient intelligence, but it is unlikely that present institutions will be able to provide many of the ability and adaptive potential to fill more group homes following the great push in the past five years to get people to independent living. A specialist community nurse or specialist social worker supervises these homes. Cardiff University Social Services (CUSS), helped by funds from the Manpower Services Commission (MSC), have experimented successfully with students and retarded teenagers sharing a house.

The Path to Employment

The track to competitive employment starts with inactivity and leads via prevocational training and vocational training to 'outreach' employment facilities and, for a few, open employment.

On leaving school at the statutory leaving age some young mildly mentally handicapped people who have been in Special Schools go directly into open employment. In many cases, like their contemporaries, they start by spending some time on the *Youth Opportunities Programme* (YOP), the Manpower Services Commission's special provision for the employment of unemployed young people between the ages of 16 and 19 years. There are four main elements in the programme: work experience on employers' premises, project based work experience, community service programmes and training workshops. The Youth Opportunities Programme also includes work introduction courses and short training courses in basic employment skills. Any young person can spend up to one year on the YOP and can transfer from one element to another. Handicapped young people can spend up to two years on the YOP if necessary.

The Employment Rehabilitation Centres located in many of the large centres of population provide employment assessment. Many of them offer the *Young Persons Work Preparation Course* (YPWPC), a course designed for school leavers with special needs. The aims of this course are: (1) work preparation; (2) employment assessment; and (3) an educational input by trained teachers.

Some Colleges of Further Education now offer *Link Courses* to Special School pupils. This usually means attendance at college one day per week during the last year of schooling. Such courses are designed to give the young people the opportunity to move from the sheltered atmosphere of their schools to the larger, more adult Colleges of Further Education and to develop increased social competence and better knowledge of themselves and the world around them. In some of these courses the youngsters are given the chance to do some practical work in college departments and this provides a measure of vocational assessment.

A small number of Colleges of Further Education also offer one- or two-year full time courses for mentally handicapped school leavers, and in some cases for such young people who have left school for some time and have been in Adult Training Centres. The courses available (called Extension Courses) cater for mildly mentally handicapped and low-ability school leavers. The aim of these courses is again to increase social competence and in general to prepare the students for adult life including work, if they are capable of it and can be placed in employment.

Many of the mentally handicapped school leavers have reasonable potential but they are less mature and experienced than their peers and often require initially extra instruction and supervision. Facilities like the Extension Courses and the YPWPC and at a later stage the YOP afford such young people time in which to mature and develop basic skills.

Some of these youngsters eventually prove capable of a good standard of work and develop a high degree of independence but their tempo of work is too slow for open industry. Such young people, provided they are registered as disabled (Section 2), can be considered for employment in *Sheltered Workshops* or *Sheltered Industrial Groups*. *Sheltered Industrial Groups* (SIG) can be set up in the public sector, for example Local Authority Parks and Gardens or in industry. A SIG involves two organizations, the 'firm' with whom the employees work and the 'sponsor' who is responsible for paying their wages and bearing the cost of administration. The 'firm' pays for the work done and the MSC contributes a capitation grant. Employees should have a capacity of at least one-third of the work done by an ordinary worker if in industrial work and 60 per cent if in outdoor work. They receive the rate for the job. The National Society for the Mentally Handicapped provide 'start off' cash to firms to take on retarded young people through the Pathway scheme.

For the severely mentally handicapped there are hospital industrial therapy units, adult training centre units incorporating special care units, and employment rehabilitation centres which may be residential and often have special youth and handicap sub-sections. Open employment which the severely mentally handicapped can cope with includes janitorial work, hotel and kitchen work, horticultural and park work, and assembly and reclamation work. Severely mentally handicapped people working under supervision in 'enclaves' or 'work stations' can achieve the productivity of youngsters of normal intelligence.

The Mechanics of Rehabilitation—A Multi-Professional Business

Work with the handicapped requires different professionals working together in a range of relationships, so the psychiatrist must be very clear about his skills, his authority, his accountability and what other professionals can do to help. Some wariness about the use of teams is justified and particularly about imprecise 'team' rhetoric, and about individuals who are inordinately afraid to take independent, decisive actions. The multidisciplinary team is neither good nor bad. It is simply unavoidable in the field of mental handicap. The word 'team' is often used in a sloppy way when what is meant is simply a network of professionals whose paths occasionally converge. Full teamwork is rarely required. The idea that all members of teams are always equal is also misleading and the word 'teamwork' has become an unreflective orthodoxy which is sometimes used fraudulently. Strictly speaking, a *team* is a small, clearly bounded group unchanging in identity over a long period of time in face-to-face work; the members are often together, share values and have the same outlook. It has a definite institutional base. There is always an issue of leadership. A *network*, by comparison, consists of interaction between a range of professionals, who may not know each other personally and do not have to consider each other's acceptability. No permanent or definite face-to-face group activity exists. Individuals may come and go according to duty systems, shifts, rotas, etc. (Hey 1979). It is in a network that doctors usually meet other professions in the field of mental handicap. Teams are sometimes necessary, for example, in psychodynamically orientated adolescent treatment units, but when the group is multi-professional the network is the usual *modus operandi*.

Mental handicap in the 1960s was a most unpromising field, but the breakthrough in psychology and linguistics and mental handicap in the last decade has meant that it is now theoretically possible to deliver some help to every child regardless of his intellectual functioning. In order to deliver such programmes as Bliss Symbols and Makaton Signalling, a new relationship has had to develop between teachers, therapists and doctors. A therapist or psychologist, not the doctor, will commonly be the leader of the programme (Wirz 1981).

Changes in society have meant that previous medical practice in this field had to change. Institutions had become too isolated, too expensive, and were wasteful of Health Service resources; doctors' legal status in such places sadly needed clarification.

Let us take an example of such a change. The traditional institution looked after (say) 20 profoundly handicapped children in its children's ward. Three qualified nurses were involved. Another 60 profoundly handicapped children had been identified in that district. Traditionally the contact point occurred only when the family became exhausted, the child grossly behaviourally disturbed; the family doctor then sought admission, which might or might not be possible depending on bed availability. The nurses had vast experience in child development, in toilet and feeding training, in coping with the behaviour problems and sleep reversal, but were probably rather under-stimulated by having only 20 children to look after, these being the profoundly handicapped children for whom physio-therapy and prophylactic positioning was probably the most successful activity. *Low* turnover leads to low morale. A survey in the community showed that the 60 families felt content about the purely medical care they were receiving, but would dearly like the sort of advice that these nurses could give from their experience, and also would dearly like occasional respite to go on holiday, etc. In theory, there was therefore no absolute shortage of highly trained professionals, but there was a shortage of accessible down-to-earth immediate advice and help. The management model of this service was therefore changed minimally by one nurse metamorphosing into a community specialist nurse who could herself receive referrals from health visitors and educationalists and other doctors. Those referrals she brought back to the mental handicap team. She saw the families in flexible hours, advised, arranged relief, and trained parents to use the Portage Development kit (in the use of which she had also been trained). As much as possible she used the wider network of ordinary professionals, again working on the principle that wherever possible the mentally handicapped person should be looked after by ordinary professionals in ordinary settings in the community. The cost was allowing one nurse to become a car-user and sending her on two courses and a team meeting once a week in what had become a high turnover, interesting-to-work-in, special care nursery. This cost could be set against the referrals of each of these cases independently to these members.

All very democratic, yet the reader will still have a picture of a consultant as leading the team, as being a final arbiter in matters pertaining to his specialty, having trained to have profound knowledge and technical experience in his chosen speciality, equipped with a knowledge of allied disciplines so that he can assess the utility of other people's work. The Brunel Institute describes three relationships which the leader has with the team—a managerial relationship, a co-ordinating relationship, and a prescriptive relationship. A managerial relationship involves assigning, allocating, appraising performance, and developing. It implies authority to select staff, describe work, and initiate promotion. A co-ordinating relationship involves preparing and issuing detailed plans and programmes, attempting to overcome obstacles and setbacks and applying authority to gain information about progress, but does not imply authority to override sustained disagreements, appraise personal performance or set new directions. A prescribing relationship implies the right to set up a specific task to be carried out and the right to check its implementation but no other right to manage or direct.

The problem is that doctors are legally accountable for all three relationships and there is confusion in the Health Service in the field of rehabilitation (and particularly in the field of mental handicap) about team functioning of disciplines at management and administrative levels and team functioning at clinical levels. Fowlie (1979) has identified three distinct levels of multi-professional working: Level One—Corporate Management, at for instance Health Board level; Level Two—this occurs when several disciplines for example are participating in a Joint Care Team, or are gathered together to plan a new occupational therapy department; and

Level Three—the treatment of individual patients. Corporate management is an idea borrowed from industry; each manager is responsible for the others' managerial but not professional decisions. This idea has got confused with that of multi-professional teams. There is some evidence in the Health Service that corporate management can work at Level One, but there is little evidence of success below that level. The problem is that there is an assumption that the contribution in corporate management of each member is always equal and carries equal weight; in reality each member does not have equal accountability. Such formulae become nonsense when individuals with vastly different qualifications have equal authority. (Let us not get the notion that this is a sociological plot. The Brunel Institute is very clear about the distinctions between trainees, practitioners, consultants, and principals). As regards Level Two—multi-professional planning and watch-dog groups—there seem to be no ground rules as regards representation, balance or accountability, except the general obligation of each member not to impede; but one prima donna from another profession can stop everything! There are three social systems working against teamwork at Level Two, authority systems, career systems, and political or power-game systems.

One profession simply does not understand the authority system or legal structure of another profession. It is important to find out about this. How senior is an officer in charge of a hostel or a district social work adviser? It is also important to find out about other professionals' legal basis. As regards Level Three—the doctor's treatment of his patient—every statute is clear: the other professions are consulted or invited by the doctor to participate. Clinical leadership can be delegated but authority cannot.

Effective (re)habilitation requires good multi-professional practice particularly in the field of mental handicap. The contemporary psychiatrist must have a proper frame of reference about his accountability in a team or network, and be aware that multi-professional approaches all the time must compete with the loyalty demanded by the careers structure of the traditional department. To paraphrase Whyte (1955): 'The upward path to the rainbow of achievement leads smack through the conference room. There, multi-professional groups of senior people meet offering lip service to multi-professional consensus, but have reached seniority themselves by a very different ethic.'

Acknowledgements

My thanks to Miss Sue Brogan for her information on employment opportunities.

References

Ballinger, B and Reid, A (1977). Psychiatric disorder in an Adult Training Centre and a Hospital for the Mentally Retarded. *Psychological Medicine* **7**, 525–8

Bijou, S (1966). A Functional Analysis of Retarded Development. In *International Review of Research in Mental Retardation* (ed. N Ellis), vol. 1. Academic Press, New York

Butler, E and Bjaanes, A (1978). Observational Studies of Behaviour in Community Settings. In *Observing Behaviour* (ed. G Sackett), vol. 1. Ohio Park Press, Baltimore

Corbett, J A (1979). Psychiatric Morbidity and Mental Retardation. In *Psychiatric Illness and Mental Handicap* (eds F James and R Snaith). Royal College of Psychiatrists, Gaskell

Cornforth, A, Johnson, K and Walker, M (1974). Teaching sign language to deaf mentally handicapped adults. *Apex* **2**, 23–4

DHSS (1972). *The Census of Residential Accommodation 1970.* DHSS, London

Fowlie, H (1979). Paper delivered at Seminar on Mental Handicap, Eastern District Hospital, Glasgow, 19 November 1979

Fraser, W (1980). A Chair at St George's. *Journal of Mental Subnormality* **26**, 3–8

Grossman, H (1973). *A Manual on Terminology and Classification in Mental Retardation*, American Association of Mental Deficiency, Washington DC

Hey, A (1979). Organizing Teams—Alternative Patterns. In *Teamwork* (eds M Marshall, M Preston-Shoot and E Wincott) BASW Publications, Birmingham

Hucker, S, Day, K, George, S and Roth, M (1979). Psychosis in Mentally Handicapped Adults. In *Psychiatric Illness and Mental Handicap* (eds F James and R Snaith). Royal College of Psychiatrists, Gaskell

Lennox, W G (1942). Brain injury, drugs and environment as causes of mental deficiency in epilepsy. *American Journal of Psychiatry* **99**, 174–80

Leuder, I (1980). Some Aspects of Communication in Down's Syndrome. In *Language: Social and Psychological Perspectives* (ed. H Giles). Pergamon, Oxford

Lyle, J G (1960). The effect of a motivation environment upon the verbal development of imbecile children. III The Brooklands Residential Family Unit. *Journal of Mental Deficiency Research* **4**, 14–23

MacGillivray, R (1957). The larval psychoses of idiocy. *American Journal of Mental Deficiency* **60**, 570–5

McNaughton, S (1975). *Teaching Guidelines. Bliss Symbols.* Farleys, Fareham, Mass.

Nihira, K, Fisw, R, Shellhaas, M and Leland, H (1974). *Adaptive Behaviour Scale.* American Association of Mental Deficiency 1974 Review, Washington DC

Nirje, B (1968). *The outlines of the new Swedish mental retardation law.* Swedish National Association of Retarded Children, Stockholm

Paton, K (1981). The Borders Schedule. In *The Care and Training of the Mentally Handicapped* (eds C Hallas, W Fraser and R MacGillivray). Wrights, Bristol (6th edn)

Primrose, D (1971). A survey of 502 consecutive admissions to a Subnormality Hospital. *British Journal of Mental Subnormality* **32**, 25–8

Reid, A (1976). Psychiatric disturbances in the mentally handicapped. *Proceedings of the Royal Society of Medicine* **69**, 509–12

Reid, A H, Ballinger, B R and Heather, B B (1978). Behavioural syndromes identified by cluster analysis in a sample of 100 severely and profoundly retarded adults. *Psychological Medicine* **8**, 399–412

Schiefelbusch, R (1979). Paper presented at Fifth IASSMD Conference, Jerusalem

Shearer, M and Shearer, D (1972). *The Portage Programme.* Council for Exceptional Children, Neston, Virginia

Whyte, W (1955). *Money and Motivation. An Analysis of Incentives in Industry.* Harper and Row, London

Wirz, S (1981). The Pragmatics of Language—the Mentally Handicapped. In *Communicating with Normal and Retarded Children* (eds W Fraser and R Grieve). Wrights, Bristol

Index